Peaceful Parent, HAPPY KIDS

*How to Stop Yelling
and Start Connecting*

DR. LAURA MARKHAM

A Perigee Book

A PERIGEE BOOK
Published by the Penguin Group
Penguin Group (USA) Inc.
375 Hudson Street, New York, New York 10014, USA
Penguin Group (Canada), 90 Eglinton Avenue East, Suite 700, Toronto, Ontario M4P 2Y3, Canada
(a division of Pearson Penguin Canada Inc.) • Penguin Books Ltd., 80 Strand, London WC2R 0RL,
England • Penguin Ireland, 25 St. Stephen's Green, Dublin 2, Ireland (a division of Penguin
Books Ltd.) • Penguin Group (Australia), 707 Collins Street, Melbourne, Victoria 3008, Australia
(a division of Pearson Australia Group Pty Ltd.) • Penguin Books India Pvt. Ltd., 11 Community
Centre, Panchsheel Park, New Delhi—110 017, India • Penguin Group (NZ), 67 Apollo Drive,
Rosedale, Auckland 0632, New Zealand (a division of Pearson New Zealand Ltd.) • Penguin Books,
Rosebank Office Park, 181 Jan Smuts Avenue, Parktown North 2193, South Africa • Penguin China,
B7 Jaiming Center, 27 East Third Ring Road North, Chaoyang District, Beijing 100020, China

Penguin Books Ltd., Registered Offices: 80 Strand, London WC2R 0RL, England

While the author has made every effort to provide accurate telephone numbers, Internet addresses,
and other contact information at the time of publication, neither the publisher nor the author
assumes any responsibility for errors, or for changes that occur after publication. Further,
the publisher does not have any control over and does not assume any responsibility
for author or third-party websites or their content.

First edition: December 2012

Library of Congress Cataloging-in-Publication Data

Markham, Laura.
Peaceful parent, happy kids : how to stop yelling and start connecting / Laura Markham.
        p.   cm.
Includes bibliographical references and index.
ISBN 978-0-399-16028-8
1. Child rearing.   2. Parent and child.   I. Title.
        HQ769.M2857   2013
        649'.1—dc23   2012031273

PRINTED IN THE UNITED STATES OF AMERICA

20   19   18   17   16   15   14   13   12

Most Perigee books are available at special quantity discounts for bulk purchases for
sales promotions, premiums, fund-raising, or educational use. Special books, or book excerpts,
can also be created to fit specific needs. For details, write: Special Markets, Penguin Group (USA) Inc.,
375 Hudson Street, New York, New York 10014.

Peaceful Parent, Happy Kids

"Dr. Laura Markham offers us suggestions that help us create strong relationships with our children. If we all followed Dr. Laura's original and authentic advice, we would indeed change the world."

—Peggy O'Mara, founder of Mothering.com

"*Peaceful Parent, Happy Kids* can change your parenting life. Dr. Laura Markham shares an invaluable set of insights that are new to the world of parenting. She will show you how to deliver your love and guidance in a truly nurturing way, and how to avoid parental burnout in the process."

—Patty Wipfler, founder of HandinHandParenting.org

"Dr. Laura teaches by example, holding parents with compassion as she gives them priceless, easy-to-use strategies to create a secure, healthy attachment with their child."

—Lysa Parker and Barbara Nicholson, founders of Attachment Parenting International and authors of *Attached at the Heart*

"Dr. Laura Markham's guidance on fostering connection and coaching instead of controlling are important ideas, and they can make a huge difference in your life as a parent. Her explanation of why parents need to regulate ourselves first—before we can help regulate our children—is a revolutionary idea. Read it and you'll see why she calls her work 'Aha! Parenting.'"

—Lawrence J. Cohen, PhD, author of *Playful Parenting*

"Dr. Laura Markham's work is practical, easy to apply, and transformative. Get a cup of coffee, find a comfy chair, and be prepared to get great advice from a wise, new friend and fellow parent."

—Jacqueline Green, host of *The Great Parenting Show*

"A much-needed resource . . . encouragement and actionable, doable advice for parents to strengthen their connection with their children and take care of themselves. Clearly helps parents see how what they are doing today impacts and influences what happens tomorrow, yet the tone is gentle and nonjudgmental. Such a user-friendly format for (often) weary parents."

—Lisa Sunbury, RegardingBaby.org

continued . . .

"Dr. Laura Markham's compassion, wisdom, common sense, love, and understanding radiate in each carefully chosen word, example, and suggestion throughout this well-written, easy-to-read, delicious book. From her chapter on effectively managing anger, 'Listen to your anger, rather than act on it,' to my favorite quote, 'Your child is acting like a child because he is one,' you'll know you've found your parenting bible. Thank you, Dr. Laura."   —Rev. Susan Nason, parent educator and consultant

"My entire family dynamic has positively changed, and I attribute it mostly to Dr. Laura Markham and AhaParenting.com. I suspect you will not think it corny when I say you are changing the world."
     —Jennifer Andersen, OurMuddyBoots.com

"I've searched high and low for parenting guidance that is sensible, simple, effective, and adaptable. That does not heap guilt upon me. That strikes a chord so it's easy to remember when I need it most. I have found it in Dr. Laura Markham. My relationship with my four-year-old has improved a thousandfold since trying your methods. The way you teach this simple message of love has made it revolutionary for me."
     —Daniela, mother of girls, ages two and four

"Following your advice has meant our son rarely has tantrums anymore. Dr. Laura's advice really works and makes being a parent (and a child, I'd say) much better. I don't pretend I am perfect all the time, but she helps me learn and do better by my son."
     —Beatrice, mother of a two-year-old boy

"You have enabled me to *change* myself, something I never thought I could do. Your writing taught me to really reflect on who I was first, which was key to my ability to reflect on myself as a parent."
     —Kimberley Yvette Price, TheSingleCrunch.com

"Dr. Laura, I tell everyone I know and even strangers about your peaceful form of parenting. Instead of creating blow-up moments, you are creating connections, loving times, and sharing real emotions with our children. Thank you, Dr. Laura Markham, for bringing so much knowledge and love to parenting.   —Carrie B., mother of two boys under age four

For Daniel, Eli, and Alice,
Who taught me to love.

And for parents everywhere,
Whose love is shaping the next generation,
and transforming humanity:
Our future rests on your shoulders.

One generation full of deeply loving parents would change the brain of the next generation, and with that, the world.

—CHARLES RAISON

CONTENTS

PART THREE: COACHING, NOT CONTROLLING

FOREWORD

My next-door neighbors taught me a great lesson one morning as I watched David teach his seven-year-old son, Kelly, how to push the gas-powered lawn mower around the yard. As he was showing him how to turn the mower around at the end of the lawn, his wife, Jan, called to him to ask a question. When David turned to answer the question, Kelly pushed the lawn mower right through the flower bed at the edge of the lawn—leaving a two-foot-wide path leveled to the ground!

As soon as David saw what had happened, he began to lose control. He had put a lot of time and effort into making those flower beds the envy of the neighborhood. The moment his voice climbed higher in a semi-rage toward poor Kelly, Jan quickly ran over to him, put her hand on his shoulder, and said, "David, please remember . . . we're raising children, not flowers!"

I've devoted myself for more than forty years to inspiring

and empowering hundreds of thousands of people who want to achieve their professional and personal goals. And for most people, one of their most challenging goals is to raise a thoughtful, productive, and compassionate child—and to enjoy an authentic, intimate, joyful relationship with that child right through the teen and young adult years. And, as I'm sure you know, it is not an easy job.

Every day in my workshops I see adults struggling to heal and overcome the limiting effects of their childhood wounds. Did these people have bad parents? No. Like most of us, their parents were good people who were limited by their own upbringings, who often forgot they were raising children, not flowers—or who simply never learned how to be good parents.

The parents I teach and coach often strain to break these cycles, to create a fresh start with their children, but the best of intentions are not always enough to heal old scars. We want to be inspired and peaceful parents, but the hopped-up culture and our stressful times make it, well, just plain hard. We're sometimes so bogged down by our own emotions and pressures that the slightest mishap by one of our kids will send us over the edge. And we can recite, as we go over that edge, the litany of what we needed to do to be better parents: be more patient, be less stressed, stop yelling, be more encouraging and supportive. Yet all of us find achieving these goals much harder than it sounds.

The parents who succeed seem to have a secret. They're more peaceful, calmer, but they also stay more connected—to their kids and to their own inner wisdom. They aren't just more patient—they seem more present and joyful with their children. This, of course, produces better-behaved kids—so there's less need to work at being patient through clenched teeth. When their kid accidentally mows down the flowers, they already remember that what's most important is how they're raising their children, not how beautiful or impressive their flower garden is.

Peaceful Parent, Happy Kids is a book that lets us inside this secret of successful parenting. Dip into any one of the thorough, practical, inspirational chapters, and Dr. Laura Markham shows us how to replenish our spirits so we can give our kids the best of ourselves, not what's left of ourselves. Chapters like "Peaceful Parents Raise Happy Kids" remind us of this profound but often neglected truth.

The parents I know don't have much time to read. The beauty of this book is that Dr. Laura includes Action Guides. Each of these nuggets of wisdom is short enough to read at one sitting, whether before bed, waiting in the car, or while you're trying to calm yourself down before re-engaging with your kid. Step-by-step blueprints like "How to Keep Your Cool When Your Kid Melts Down" and "Use Connection to Make Bedtime Easier" are simple enough to absorb and implement in the heat of battle.

The battle, of course, is never actually between a parent and child. That is just the after-manifestation of a battle that is waged inside the parent. Giving our children the best of ourselves requires that we do some inner work, resolving the conflicts, which is never an easy challenge. But what better motivation to engage in that work than our love for our children? Dr. Laura offers us parents a repertoire of strategies to heal our own wounds and deepen the inner connection with our own true selves and thereby make it easier to create our longed-for deeper connection to our children. It really is true, as she reminds us, that it's never too late to have a happy childhood.

Having Dr. Laura Markham on your bedside table is like having an angel on your shoulder, whispering useful secrets in your ear. These are the secrets every mother and father needs to know to become a more peaceful and effective parent—and as a result, a happier person.

—Jack Canfield
  Coauthor, *Chicken Soup for the Parent's Soul*
  and *Chicken Soup for the Mother's Soul*

Secrets of Peaceful Parents

Parenting is one of the toughest things we do. The pressures of everyday life leave many parents feeling guilty, plagued by a sense that we could do a better job if only we had a little more time, were a little less tired, or simply knew where to begin. Human beings weren't designed to handle the amount of stress our modern life loads on us, which makes it difficult to hear our natural parenting instincts. It's almost as if we're forced to parent in our spare time, after meeting the demands of work, commuting and household responsibilities. Even worse, our culture erodes our relationship with our children and woos them away from us at too early an age.

But there are parents who raise wonderful children, without a lot of drama. They seem at peace with themselves as parents. Their children seem to be thriving. What are their secrets? What exactly makes their children grow into terrific teens and adults? What if you could find out what they do, and put it into practice with your own children?

You can. These parents have a secret. In fact, they have a whole secret life, inside their heads. They talk to their children differently. They talk to *themselves* differently. They're approaching the whole experience of parenting from a new perspective. You might say they've had some big Aha! Moments that have shifted the way they raise their children. This shift changes the way we perceive and respond to our children on every level, but we can condense it to Three Big Ideas. Big ideas, but simple and replicable—for every parent.

THREE BIG IDEAS

1. Regulating Yourself

Most parents think that if our child would just "behave," we could maintain our composure as parents. The truth is that managing our own emotions and actions is what allows us to feel peaceful as parents. Ultimately we can't control our children or the hand life deals them—but we can always control our own actions. Parenting isn't about what our child does, but about how we respond. In fact, most of what we call parenting doesn't take place between a parent and child but within the parent. When a storm brews, a parent's response will either calm it or incite a full-scale tsunami. Staying calm enough to respond constructively to all that childish behavior—and the stormy emotions behind it—requires that we grow, too. If we can use those times when our buttons get pushed to reflect, not just react, we can notice when we lose equilibrium and steer ourselves back on track. This inner growth is the hardest work there is, but it's what enables you to become a more peaceful parent, one day at a time.

The Aha! Moment here is that an adult's peaceful presence has a more powerful influence on a child than yelling ever could. Your own emotional regulation—a fancy way of saying your ability to stay calm—allows you to treat the people in your life, including the little people, calmly, respectfully, and responsibly. That's what produces children who are emotionally regulated, respectful and responsible. Part 1 of this book will give you the tools to manage your emotions, even on those days when your child pushes all your buttons.

2. Fostering Connection

Children thrive when they feel connected and understood. Parenting effectively depends above all on your connection to your child. Period. Otherwise we have little influence ("My kid won't listen!") and parenting becomes an exhausting, thankless task. Children need to feel deeply connected to their parents or they don't feel entirely safe, and their brains don't work well to regulate their emotions and follow parental guidance. So focusing first on connection produces children who are not only happier, but easier. Ready for the Aha! Moment? This loving connection that makes our hearts melt is what puts the joy back in child-raising. In Part 2 of this book, you'll see how to strengthen and sweeten your connection with your child.

3. Coaching, Not Controlling

Small humans rebel against force and control, just as big humans do. Luckily, they're always open to our influence, as long as they respect us and feel connected to us. What raises great kids is coaching them—to handle their emotions, manage their behavior, and develop mastery—rather than controlling for immediate compliance. Thoughtful parents know that what they do today either helps or hinders the person their child is becoming. They "emotion-coach" so that their child develops the emotional intelligence essential to managing feelings and making wise choices. They use empathic limits rather than punishment—even just time-outs and consequences—to coach their child's development of self-discipline, rather than simply forcing their child into obedience. They're guided by core values so they don't compromise on respectful relating or family time, but they also don't sweat the small stuff. That makes for more peaceful parents and happier children. The Aha! Moment here is that the coaching approach that works best in the long-term to raise happy, responsible adults is actually more effective than traditional parenting in producing self-disciplined, cooperative kids in the medium term. Part 3 of this book will show you why—and how you can raise that child.

What's Different About This Book

Most parenting books focus on changing the child's behavior. And yes, this book will help you support your child to become his or her very best self. But we'll be approaching this from the perspective of our Three Big Ideas—Regulating Yourself; Fostering Connection; and Coaching, Not Controlling. You'll find that each of these Three Big Ideas is a constant thread throughout this book, as well as being the focus of Parts 1, 2, and 3, respectively. Because you'll have to manage your own triggers and emotions to effectively coach and connect with your child, you'll find consistent reminders to Regulate Yourself so you can return to a state of equilibrium before intervening with your child. Because Connection is at the very heart of peaceful parenting, you'll find an emphasis throughout this book on staying fiercely connected to your child, whether you're trying to get her out of the house in the morning or keeping him from hitting his brother.

The third, and longest, section of this book—Coaching, Not Controlling—does focus on your child. But instead of tips to control or manipulate his behavior with punishment and bribes, you'll find step-by-step blueprints on how to coach your child to support both his short-term and long-term development into a more confident, resilient, self-disciplined, emotionally intelligent person. We focus on your daily interactions with your child, which fall into three basic categories, each of which is explored in its own chapter. Here's a preview:

- **Emotion coaching.** Young children's brains are still growing, like their bodies, so their rational brain centers haven't yet learned to moderate their strong feelings. Whether we're aware of it or not, we give our child constant messages about feelings—implying that they're either dangerous or simply part of being human. I'll give you hands-on tools to coach your child so that she can better manage her emotions, and thus her behavior.

- **Loving guidance.** Children rely on us to guide them in this big and confusing world. Unfortunately, our own childhood experiences and cultural messages tell parents to guide with punishment, force, and control. Instead of threatening (*"One, two, three . . ."*), or manipulating, we'll get to the root of your child's behavior—the feelings underneath it. I'll help you address those feelings and nurture your child's emotional intelligence, so she can learn to manage her own emotions, and therefore her behavior, which is what creates self-discipline.

If you're looking for a more positive approach to discipline—that helps kids *want* to behave—this chapter is for you.

- **Supporting mastery.** Children are naturally curious, but too often we undermine their desire to learn. Building on the foundation of connection, emotion coaching, and positive guidance provided in this book, the last chapter gives you tools to protect your child's natural curiosity and support his emerging passions while encouraging the confidence and resilience he needs to succeed in life.

As we consider each of these topics, we'll apply our Three Big Ideas to transform every interaction with your child. In each chapter, I'll suggest specific, nuts-and-bolts ways to put these ideas into real-life practice as your child moves through each developmental stage. Reading through the developmental stages will crystallize for you why the way you soothe your infant and handle your toddler's tantrum helps develop her ability to tolerate frustration at four, get along with her sibling at six, or stand up to the mean girls at eight. In fact, while this book ends at age nine, you'll understand how to avoid raising a child who slams out of the house when she's twelve or experiments with drugs at fifteen. Each chapter finishes with how-to Action Guides—concrete game plans that help you solve the everyday challenges of raising children. I hope you'll experiment, play, and adapt them to your family.

In each chapter, you'll also see how to use these same Three Big Ideas to help you find more peace, confidence, and joy as a parent. It's hard work. But you'll be rewarded. As you yell less and connect more, your child will become more cooperative on a daily basis. But even more important, you'll see him thrive, growing into a happy, confident, self-disciplined person. The good news is that this is the easier way to parent. Yelling, threatening, and punishing can ruin anyone's day. Peaceful parents find it much easier to be calm and patient. Why? Because this kind of parenting creates a better parent-child relationship, which produces better-behaved children—and parents who enjoy their child more. Peaceful parents have actually found a way to put the joy back into parenting.

You Can Be a More Peaceful Parent

Providing a loving, compassionate, scream-free, judgment-free household has not just been a gift to my children, but a gift I have given to myself. I have grown by leaps and bounds not just as a parent, but as a person as well. I am so grateful for Dr. Laura Markham, who has been a shining light in my life.

—Jennifer, mother of four kids, ages fifteen, twelve, nine, and six

This book has grown out of my work with thousands of parents through the Aha! Parenting website and in private coaching. I'm trained as a clinical psychologist, specializing in child development and parenting. I spend my days thinking about what helps children thrive, and I work with parents to help them raise happy, emotionally healthy, self-disciplined kids.

The more parents I meet, the more convinced I am that all parents are doing their best for their kids. But most parents haven't been given the information they need—to help their child grow into a wonderful human being. In fact, parents hear a lot of counterproductive, even destructive advice that ends up making parenting a struggle:

> "How will she learn to self-soothe if you don't let her cry?"
> "Praise him and tell him what a good boy he is as often as
>   you can!"

"Oh, she's upset ... quick, distract her!"

"The best way to stop a tantrum in the supermarket? Tell
    him you're going home and just walk away. Believe me,
    he'll follow!"

"She's just manipulating you."

As I'll explain, many of today's common child-raising practices
create unnecessary struggle and tension between parents and children. We're told to control our child's behavior, but how? Force
works only while kids are small, and when we don't respond to the
needs and emotions driving that behavior, the problems worsen.
Meanwhile, we're unwittingly sabotaging the healthy emotional
development we all want for our children. Worse yet, this can erode
our empathy for our child, because instead of following our
instincts—which, naturally, tell us to respond to the needs of our
little one—we harden our hearts. Over and over, I hear from parents
who wish they had understood the ideas in this book when their
child was born. *Peaceful Parent, Happy Kids* is designed to help you
create an exceptional relationship with your child—and, in the process, to raise a happy, self-disciplined, emotionally healthy human
being.

The Embrace of Great Love

Whether you're looking for scientific research to guide your parenting decisions, wondering how to handle a specific challenge, or ready
to tear your hair out, you've come to the right place. No one is completely peaceful all the time, or we'd all be enlightened. Every time
you choose to treat yourself and your child with more compassion,
you take a step toward inner peace and more happiness.

As you make your way through this book, please remember to

give yourself credit for every bit of progress in the right direction. All change comes one step at a time. Life is simply the slow accumulation of moments, and each moment gives us a new chance to change directions. Even if we change our reaction to only a few things that happen today, we'll find ourselves heading in a new direction. Before we know it, we're in a whole new landscape.

We all want to raise children with whom we stay close, children who adore us, children who carry on our legacy of love when we're gone. We all want our grown children to flourish with the roots and wings we gave them, to look back on childhoods brimming with the love and laughter of parents who made them feel so good about themselves that anything seemed possible. Every day of your kids' childhood, you're creating that future.

There are no perfect parents, and no perfect children. But there are many families who live in the embrace of great love. This book is dedicated to you creating one of those families.

PART ONE

REGULATING YOURSELF

One of the pieces you provided that seemed to have been missing before was that I needed to help myself, and give forgiveness and patience to myself, as much as I was trying to do with my daughter. And I needed to learn, really internalize, that her acting up was not a reflection on me or my parenting (at least in most cases!) but rather on how she was feeling and what her needs were at that moment.

—Alene, mother of two kids under age four

1

Peaceful Parents Raise Happy Kids

There's an old saying: Raising children is the toughest work there is. But why is it so difficult? When I ask an audience this question, parents usually propose two reasons. First, because the stakes are so high. And second, because there are no clear answers about how to do it right.

One answer is right, and one is not so right. The stakes are certainly high. But we actually do know a great deal about how to raise a happy, responsible, considerate, emotionally healthy, self-disciplined child. There is a great deal of valuable research on this most important topic, and parents will be delighted to learn how sensible it is. Over and over, studies show that parents who respond with warm, respectful attunement to the unique needs of their individual child, setting limits supportively and coaching their child's emotions constructively, raise terrific kids. Sensible, but hard. As every parent knows, the hard part is managing our own emotional triggers so that we can make this a reality even some of the time.

Regardless of your child's unique challenges, if you want to parent well, you have to work on yourself, too. A child doesn't cause the anger or anxiety that hooks us into power struggles; that comes from our own fear and doubt. Our own childhood experiences, our own early traumas—major and minor—are part of who we are. What's more, they're the part of us that takes charge whenever we're upset; so when you're angry or frightened, you know that's almost always an early bad experience driving your reactions. Children have a way of triggering those unhappy feelings from our own childhoods, so the only way we can be peaceful parents is to mindfully prevent old feelings from causing new problems.

In fact, the things we most want for our children depend on our own inner work. We all want to raise children who are happy people, loved by others and lucky in love. If we can reflect on our own early childhood relationships and learn to nurture ourselves, we can offer our child—*you can offer your child*—the secure connection that will provide a foundation for loving relationships for the rest of her life. We can't control what happens to her. But we can make it likely that she'll surround herself with people who treat her well and help her find deep meaning in her life.

We also want to raise children who can manage their behavior, both because they're easier to live with and because that's our job as parents. We know how to raise those children, too. When we regulate our own emotions, our children learn to regulate their emotions. That allows them to regulate their behavior, presuming they're connected enough to us to want to.

Finally, we want our children to be successful. Not necessarily in the sense of earning the rewards offered by our society for achieving, but in the sense of discovering, honing, and sharing their unique gifts throughout their lives. We know how to help children do that, too. Much of it has to do with managing our own anxieties, which leaves our child free to discover for himself and build confidence and resilience.

Some children are born with more difficult temperaments, and for those children our inner work as parents is even more important. But regardless of what your child brings into the world, the way you respond to her will shape her ability to make the most of her life. Your child will delight and exasperate you, thrill and annoy you. By accident, really, your child will ask you to grow, too. If you can notice when you're triggered and restore yourself to equilibrium before you take action, if you can soothe your own anxiety, if you can reflect on your own experience and make peace with it, you can raise happy, emotionally healthy children who are successful in every sense. You can become a peaceful parent, raising happy kids.

Your Number One Responsibility as a Parent

Mindfulness: Allowing an emotion to take hold and pass without acting on it.
    —Benedict Carey[1]

Mindfulness: Not hitting someone in the mouth.
    —Eleven-year-old, quoted by Sharon Salzberg[2]

Your child is fairly certain to act like a child, which means someone who is still learning, has different priorities than you do, and can't always manage her feelings or actions. Her childish behavior is guaranteed, at times, to push your buttons. The problem is when we begin acting like a child, too. Someone has to act like a grown-up, if we want our child to learn how! If, instead, we can stay mindful— meaning we notice our emotions and let them pass without acting on them—we model emotional regulation, and our children learn from watching us.

There's a reason the airlines tell us to put on our own oxygen masks first. Kids can't reach those masks or be relied on to use them properly. If we lose function, our kids can't save us, or themselves. So even if we would sacrifice ourselves to save our kids, it's our responsibility to put on our own masks first.

Kids can't manage their own rage by themselves, either. They can't find their way through the tangle of jealousy that pushes them to whack their little sister. They need our help to handle the fear that we don't love them because they somehow just aren't quite good enough. They know that if they were good enough, they wouldn't want to hit their sister, or sneak that piece of candy, or throw themselves down on the floor and scream. But they can't help themselves, however hard they try not to. (Sort of like when we eat that extra piece of cake.)

So just as with the oxygen mask, it's your job to help your child with his emotions, which is what helps him with his behavior. Unfortunately, when you're stressed out, exhausted, and running on empty, you can't be there constructively for your child any more than if you black out on the plane.

That's why your first responsibility in parenting is being mindful of your own inner state. Mindfulness is the opposite of "losing" your temper. Don't get me wrong—mindfulness doesn't mean you don't feel anger. Being mindful means that you pay attention to what you're feeling, *but don't act on it*. Anger is part of all relationships. Acting on it mindlessly, with words or actions, is what compromises our parenting.

Emotions are useful, like indicator lights on a dashboard. If you saw a blinking red light in your car, you wouldn't cover it up or tear out the wiring that caused it, right? You would listen to the information and act on it, for instance, by taking your car in for an oil change. The challenge with human emotions is that so often we're confused about what to do when we feel them. We're hardwired to respond to all "negative" emotion (those blinking red lights in your psyche that light up throughout your day) in one of three ways: fight, flight, or freeze.

Those strategies work well in most emergencies. But parenting—despite our fears—is not usually an emergency. Usually, in parenting and in life, the best response to upsetting emotions is to reflect, not react. In other words, don't take action while you're triggered.

You can count on finding yourself hijacked by fight-or-flight hormones at times, but if you can train yourself to notice when you start to lose it, you have the choice to return yourself back to a state of equilibrium. That peaceful place inside ensures that our actions are wise and loving.

But what happens when we just can't get there? When something our child is doing is driving us crazy, and all our efforts to calm down aren't working?

Breaking the Cycle: Healing Your Own Wounds

In the absence of reflection, history often repeats itself . . . Research has clearly demonstrated that our children's attachment to us will be influenced by what happened to us when we were young if we do not come to process and understand those experiences.
    —Dan Siegel[3]

The famed psychologist D. W. Winnicott made many wise observations about parents and children. My favorite is that children don't need perfection from their parents. All we need to do is to avoid harming them, and to offer them the "ordinary devotion" that has always been required of parents.

Unfortunately, this is not as easy as it sounds. First, there is nothing ordinary about devotion. Devotion, as parents know, is walking the floor at 2:00 a.m. holding a screaming baby with an ear infection. Devotion is forcing yourself into the kitchen to make your kid's dinner after a long day, when all you really want is to curl up on the couch and zone out. Devotion is taking off your jacket on a cold night to tuck it around a sleeping child in the backseat of the car. This ordinary devotion is the same intense love that has caused parents throughout human history to hurl themselves between their child and danger, from flying glass to enemy soldiers.

But even if we express our devotion in our willingness to put our children first, it is still not easy to be a "good enough" parent. Even a devoted mother or father often inadvertently hurts or scars a child. This includes parents who adore their children, who would be completely heroic and self-sacrificing if the situation called for it. Why the gap between our intentions and our actions? The reason is that while we would never consciously hurt our child, so much of parenting, like every relationship, happens outside our conscious awareness.

The truth is that virtually all of us were wounded as children, and if we don't heal those wounds, they prevent us from parenting our child as we truly want to. If there's an area where you were scarred as a child, you can count on that area causing you grief as a parent—and wounding your child in turn.

We can all think of examples: the father who unwittingly repeats his father's judgmental parenting with his own son. The mother who can't set limits on her children's behavior because she can't bear their anger at her, and ends up raising self-centered, anxious kids. The parents who work overly long hours at their jobs because they doubt their own ability to be interested in (translate: to love) their infants. For all of us, the task is to consciously examine our own scars—some modest, some more painful—so that we don't inflict new ones on our children.

The wonderful news is that being parents gives us a map for where those scars are, and a chance to dig deep and heal ourselves. Our children have an uncanny ability to show us our wounded places, to draw out our fears and angers. Better than the best Zen master or therapist, our children give us the perfect opportunity to grow and heal. Most parents say that loving their children has transformed them: made them more patient, more compassionate, more selfless. We'll always experience heightened sensitivity around the issues that shaped our early psyches, but as we heal the lingering hurts, our behavior is no longer driven by them, and we find that these scars inform us, motivate us, make us better parents.

So, how can you heal your own childhood issues, and become the parent you want for your children?

- **Parent consciously.** If we pay attention, we'll notice when our child pushes our buttons. Not that kids don't act like kids—they always do. That's age appropriate. But what bothers some parents would be greeted by others with a calm, warm, humorous attitude that helps kids *want* to behave. Whenever we get "triggered," we've stumbled on something that needs healing. Seriously. Any time your child pushes your buttons, he's showing you an unresolved issue from your own childhood.

- **Break the cycle. Use your inner pause button.** You don't have to repeat history with your kids. Even if you're already well down the wrong path, *stop*. Take a deep breath and hit the pause button. Remind yourself of what is about to happen unless you choose another course. Close your mouth, even in midsentence. Don't be embarrassed; you're modeling good anger management. Save your embarrassment for when you have a tantrum.

- **Understand how emotions work.** Anger is a message that something isn't working in our lives. The problem is that it's also a biological state that doesn't help us find the best solutions. When we're in the grip of the chemical reactions that make us "angry," we do and say things we would never choose to do otherwise. When your body and emotions are in fight-or-flight mode, your child always looks like the enemy. Take a breath and wait until you calm down before you make any decisions or take any actions.

- **Hit the reset button on your own "story."** If you had a painful childhood, you can't change that. But what you *can* change is what you're taking with you from that childhood: your "story." You do that by reflecting on it, feeling the painful feelings, but also considering new angles. If your father abandoned the family and you concluded that you weren't good enough, it's time to set the record straight and understand, from your adult vantage point, that you were more than enough and that his leaving had nothing to do with you. If your mother hit you and you concluded that you were a bad kid, a more accurate understanding would be that your mother was frightened and would have hit even the most angelic child in the world. You were just like any child: reaching out for love and attention in the only ways you knew. Coming to terms with your story and rewriting it can be a painful process, but it's liberating. It's also the only path to being the peaceful parent you want to be to your child.

- **De-stress.** We all have a harder time being the parent we want to be when we're stressed out. Develop a repertoire of habits that help you de-stress: regular exercise, yoga, a hot bath, meditation. Can't find the time? Involve the whole family. Put on music and dance together, go for a walk, put everyone to bed with books early on Friday night for a quiet, relaxing evening and catching up on your sleep. Prioritize slowing down and you'll find ways to do it.

- **Get support in working through old issues.** Every parent needs support and a chance to talk about the hard work she's doing. Sometimes we can do that informally with friends or relatives. Sometimes a more formal "listening partnership" with another parent, as advocated by Patty Wipfler of Hand in Hand Parenting, can be a lifesaver. You might want to be part of a parenting support group or community. If you feel stuck, find a counselor to help you move forward more happily in your life. There's no shame in asking for help; the shame would be in reneging on your responsibility as a parent by damaging your child physically or psychologically. If you think you need help, please don't wait. Reach out now.

No parent is perfect, because humans are by definition imperfect. No matter how much we work on ourselves, we will not always impact our children positively. But every time you pay attention, hit your inner pause button, and manage your stress, you're becoming more peaceful. And that gives your child a greater shot at happiness.

Winnicott was right. Our children don't need perfection from us. What they need is a parent who embraces growth, makes amends, and opens her heart when it wants to harden.

How to Manage Your Anger

This approach is so powerful and has been life-changing for me. The best part about it is that you don't have to be perfect. You have to be real,

honest, and able to say you were wrong. Instead of creating blow-up
moments in your day you are creating connections, loving times, and
sharing your real emotions with your children. These real moments teach
our children how to be the best they can be, not perfect, just real.

—Carrie, mother of two boys under age four

As long as you're human, you'll still sometimes find yourself in
fight-or-flight mode, and your child will start to look like the enemy.
When you're swept with anger, you're physically ready to fight.
Hormones and neurotransmitters are flooding your body. They
cause your muscles to tense, your pulse to race, your breathing to
quicken. It's impossible to stay calm at those points, but we all know
that clobbering our kids—while it may bring instant relief—isn't
really what we want to do.

So commit now to no hitting, no swearing, no calling your child
names, and no threats. What about screaming? Never at your children; that's a tantrum. If you really need to scream, go into your car
with the windows rolled up and scream where no one can hear, and
don't use words, because those make you angrier.

Your children get angry, too, so it's a double gift to them when
you commit to constructive anger management. You not only don't
hurt them, you offer them a role model. Your children will certainly
see you angry from time to time, and how you handle those situations will teach them a lot. Will you teach them that might makes
right? That parents have tantrums, too? Or that anger is part of
being human, and that learning to manage anger responsibly is part
of growing up? Here's how:

- **Take five.** Recognize that an angry state is not the best place
  from which to intervene in any situation. Instead, give yourself
  a time-out and come back when you're able to be calm. If your
  child is old enough to be left for a moment, you can go into the

bathroom, splash water on your face, and do some deep breathing. Just say, as calmly as you can, *"I am too mad right now to talk about this. I am going to take a time-out and calm down."* Exiting does not let your child win. It impresses upon him just how serious the infraction is, and it models self-control. If your child is young enough to feel abandoned when you leave, just use the kitchen sink instead. Then, sit on the couch for a few minutes. Whether you're in your child's vicinity or behind a closed door, use this time to calm yourself, not to work yourself into a further frenzy about how right you are. Breathe deeply and silently, and say a little mantra that restores your calm. Your child will be watching. Don't worry that you need to teach her a lesson about what she did wrong. She's getting one of the most important lessons she'll ever learn: how to responsibly regulate big emotions.

• **Help your body discharge anger.** When you feel this angry, you need a way to calm down. Stop, breathe, remind yourself it isn't an emergency. Shake the tension out of your hands. Take ten deep breaths. If you need to make a noise, hum. You might try to find a way to laugh, which discharges the tension and shifts the mood. Even forcing yourself to smile sends a message to your nervous system that there's no emergency and begins calming you down. Tap the acupressure point on the side of either hand (where you would karate chop) while you breathe and express your intention to calm down. If you feel you need to physically discharge your rage, put on some music and dance.

• **Change your thoughts so you can change your feelings.** If you're thinking your child is a spoiled brat who will grow up to be a thug, you can't calm down. The truth is, your child is a very young person who is in pain and is showing you that by his behavior. Remind yourself, *"He's acting like a child because he IS a child. . . . My child needs my love most when he least 'deserves' it. . . . He's asking for my help with his legitimate needs and feelings."*

- **Listen to your anger, rather than acting on it.** Anger, like other feelings, is as much a given as our arms and legs. What we're responsible for is what we choose to do with it. Anger often has a valuable lesson for us, but acting while we're angry, except in rare situations requiring self-defense, is hardly ever constructive, because we make choices we would never make from a rational state. The constructive way to handle anger is to limit our expression of it, and when we calm down, to use it diagnostically: what is so wrong in our life that we feel furious, and what do we need to do to change the situation? Sometimes the answer is clearly related to our parenting: We need to change our approach before things get out of hand, or start putting the children to bed half an hour earlier, or do some repair work on our relationship with our nine-year-old so that she stops treating us rudely. Sometimes we're surprised to find that our anger is actually at our spouse who is not acting as a full partner in parenting, or even at our boss. Sometimes anger is a reminder that we need more sleep or a chance to vent regularly to a friend who will accept the full range of our feelings. And sometimes the answer is that we're carrying around anger we don't understand that spills out onto our kids, and we need to seek help though therapy or a parents' support group.

- **Remember that "expressing" your anger to another person can reinforce and escalate it.** Despite the popular idea that we need to "express" our anger so that it doesn't eat away at us, research shows that expressing anger while we are angry actually makes us more angry. This in turn makes the other person hurt, afraid, or angry, and causes a rift in the relationship. Rehashing the situation in our mind always proves to us that we're right and the other person is wrong, which again makes us more angry as we stew. What works is to calm down, and then find a constructive way to address whatever is making us angry so that the situation is resolved, and our anger stops being triggered.

- **Wait before disciplining.** Nothing says you have to issue edicts on the fly. They will never be what's best for your child's long-term development, or even what's best to prevent a repeat of the problem. Say as little as possible until you calm down, just something like: *"I need to calm down before I can talk about this."* If you take a ten-minute time-out and still don't feel calm enough to relate constructively, you can say, *"I want to think about what happened, and we'll talk about it later."*

- **Avoid physical force, no matter what.** Spanking may make you feel better temporarily because it discharges your rage, but it does lasting harm to your child and ultimately sabotages the positive things you do as a parent. Spanking, and even slapping, has a way of escalating into harmful and sometimes even deadly violence. Do whatever you need to do to control yourself, including leaving the room. If you can't control yourself and end up resorting to physical force, apologize to your child, tell him hitting is never okay, and get yourself some help.

- **Avoid threats.** Threats made while you're angry will always be unreasonable. Since threats are effective only if you're willing to follow through on them, they undermine your authority and make it less likely that your child will follow the rules next time.

- **Monitor your tone and word choice.** Research shows that the more calmly we speak, the more calm we feel, and the more calmly others respond to us. Similarly, use of swear words or other highly charged words makes us and our listener more upset, and the situation escalates. We have the power to calm or upset ourselves and the person we are speaking with by our own tone of voice and choice of words. (Remember, you're the role model.)

- **Consider that you're part of the problem.** If you're open to emotional growth, your child will always show you where you need to work on yourself. If you're not, you'll find yourself caught in the same vortex with your child over and over. Your child may be acting in ways that aggravate you, but you are not a helpless victim. Take responsibility to manage your own emotions first. Your child may not become a little angel over-night, but his acting out will diminish dramatically once you learn to stay calm.

- **Still angry? Look for the underlying feelings.** Don't get attached to your anger. Once you've listened to it and made appropriate changes, let go of it. If that isn't working, remember that anger is always a defense. It shields us from feeling vulnerable. To dissolve anger, look at the hurt or fear under it. If your daughter's tantrums scare you, or you're upset at your son for hitting his little sister because you were once the little sister who got hit, reflect on those feelings and heal them. Once you're willing to feel the underlying feelings, you don't need the defense of anger, and it will dissipate.

- **Choose your battles.** Every negative interaction with your child uses up valuable relationship capital. Focus on what matters, such as the way your child treats other humans. In the larger scheme of things, her jacket on the floor may drive you crazy, but it probably isn't worth putting your relationship bank account in the red.

- **If you frequently struggle with your anger, seek counseling.** Don't be embarrassed to ask for help. You're taking responsibility as a parent to avoid hurting your child physically or psychologically.

How to Stop Yelling at Your Child

I love all your advice. But I find it only works when I can stay calm, which is really hard. I'm a yeller. My mother was a yeller. I come from a long line of yellers. How do I break that cycle?
   —Cynthia, mother of three kids under age six

Most parents yell. We don't even notice ourselves doing it half the time. Our voice just gets louder and louder. Or we do know we're doing it, but at that moment, it seems completely justified. After all, did you *see* what that kid *did*?!

But we all know that our kids respond better if we don't yell. Yelling escalates a difficult situation, turning it from a squall into a storm. And really, how can you expect your child to learn to control his own emotions if you don't control yours?

If, instead, we can stay calm, it settles everyone else down. We model emotional regulation. We're able to intervene more effectively to solve the problem. Our child learns how to move herself from upset to calm. Our relationship with our child strengthens. He cooperates more. She starts to control her own emotions more.

And if we're honest, we know it's our own stuff that's making us yell. Some parents (truly!) would look at the same behavior and be able to stay empathic or joke about it. Because no matter how bad your child's behavior, it's a cry for help. Sometimes the behavior requires a firm limit, but it never requires us to be mean. And you can't help your child while you're shouting.

It isn't easy to stop yelling. You can desperately want to, and still find yourself screaming. If you were yelled at, it takes tremendous work not to yell. But if you know that you want to stop yelling, I assure you that it's completely possible—no matter how ingrained it is. It's not rocket science. It takes about three months. Like learning the piano, you start playing scales today, you practice daily, and soon you can pick out simple tunes. In a year you can play a sonata. I've seen hundreds of parents do it.

Will it be hard to stop yelling? Yes. It doesn't happen as if by magic. It takes constant, daily effort. No one can do it for you. Not yelling may seem like a miracle, but this is something you can do. If you keep working at it, someday you'll suddenly realize that you can't remember the last time you yelled. Want to get started?

- **Commit yourself.** Research shows that when we consciously, verbally "commit" ourselves to a course of action, we're likely to achieve it, especially if we work at it daily. By contrast, simply "wishing" something would be different, or even "regretting" things we've done, doesn't usually change a thing. So write down your intention ("I will speak respectfully to my child") and post it in a place where you'll see it frequently.

Picture how lovely it will be in your home when you don't yell. Imagine yourself responding calmly—maybe even empathically, or with a sense of humor!—to the things you yell about today. Keep revisiting that image. You're programming your subconscious.

- **Make the commitment to your family.** There is a catch, though. You have to commit yourself to someone else. Specifically, you have to commit to your child that you intend to stop yelling, because your child is really the only person who will be there to keep you honest. A bit scary? Yes. But you're role modeling, and if you want a child who doesn't yell at you, this is the way to get there. So explain to your kids that you've decided to stop yelling. Make a "Respectful Voice" sticker chart to reward yourself. At the end of every day, your child (!) decides whether you merit a sticker. This is what keeps you accountable.

(Are you against sticker charts for kids? So am I, because they teach the wrong lessons, which we'll talk about in the discipline chapter. But since parents have all the power in the family, this is a way to empower the child to hold the parent accountable. I'm not worried about teaching the parent the wrong lesson. Just don't give in to the temptation to impose a sticker chart on your child for respectful voice at the same time. He's got less self-control than you do while he's angry, and he'll learn best from your modeling.)

- **Stop, drop, and breathe** every time you notice yourself raising your voice, or about to raise your voice. How?

- **Stop talking** as soon as you notice yourself losing your temper. Close your mouth. Can't stop making noise? Hum, if you must. But close your mouth.

- **Drop it.** Really. Let it go for the moment. It's not an emergency. (If it is, get everyone out of danger and then come back to this process.) Just step away from the situation.

- **Breathe deeply ten times.** Shake out your hands. This shifts you out of your "reptile brain"—the fight, flight, or freeze response—and into conscious presence. Now you have a choice about how to act.

- **Remind yourself: You're the grown-up** and your child is learning from everything you do, right now. Look at your child and say, *"I'm working hard to stay calm. I don't want to yell. Let me calm down, and then we'll try a do-over, okay?"*

- **Do whatever works for you to calm your body's fight-or-flight response**—more deep breaths, say a mantra, splash cold water on your face, look at your Respectful Voice sticker chart, remind yourself that your child is acting like a child because he *is* a child. Remind yourself that there's no emergency.

- **Try a do-over.** When you're out of fight-or-flight, you'll know because your child will no longer look like the enemy but like your own beloved baby, the one you've promised to cherish, love, and guide positively so she grows into a loving, wonderful person. **Now, start the interaction over.**

Hard, right? *Very* hard when you're swept with neurochemicals that tell you to attack. But simple. You just delay the interaction until you're calm.

- **Wondering how your child will learn if you don't raise your voice?** When kids are scared, they go into fight-or-flight. The learning centers of the brain shut down. Your child *can't* learn when you yell. It's always more effective to intervene calmly and compassionately. Besides, when you yell, you lose credibility with your child. Kids become less open to your influence.

- **Wondering if maybe you're letting your kid off too easy?** He's hurting, and his "misbehavior" is an SOS that he needs your help. He's acting out because he has big feelings he can't yet understand and articulate verbally. Of course you set limits and redirect behavior. But your guidance *never* needs to be mean or scary. You want your child to follow your guidance because he loves you and would never want to disappoint you, not because you scare him.

- **Wondering if you're being inauthentic?** Your child saw that you were very upset. She also saw that you were responsible about managing your own emotions. Being authentic about the truth of your experience never requires you to "dump" them on someone else, unfiltered. As the Dalai Lama says, "Be kind whenever possible. It is always possible." Besides, they're *your* feelings, and only part of the emotion is coming from this current interaction with your child. Most of it comes from your own past, and the way you're seeing this situation.

- **And what if you find yourself yelling, despite your best efforts?** You will in the beginning—more than once. But it isn't a mistake if you learn from it. Use each time you miss the mark as an opportunity to change something—about your

A THREE-MINUTE PROCESS TO SHIFT YOURSELF FROM UPSET TO PEACE

Dr. Laura . . . You say that the way to avoid yelling is to wait until I'm calm and then try a do-over with my son. But when I get mad, I don't calm down so quickly. It could take an hour of trying to distract myself. Meanwhile, my son still did something wrong and I need to set him straight.

—Jen, mother of one

The "stop, drop, and breathe" process assumes that you can calm yourself quickly enough to try a do-over of whatever pushed your buttons. But when your body goes into fight-or-flight, you're pumped full of neurochemicals telling you to attack. Your child looks like the enemy, and you feel an urgent need to "set him straight."

But it doesn't take the body an hour to calm down, unless you encountered a tiger. Seriously. Whatever your child did, it really was not an emergency. If it's taking more than a few minutes to calm down, it's because you haven't told your body it was a false alarm. Your body is still in fight-or-flight. And your mind is still on the warpath, so it takes an hour to "distract" it.

Whatever your child has just done, you will react more constructively from a place of calm. Here's a three-minute Aha! Moment to shift you into a new way of looking at things and calm your fight-or-flight reaction.

Minute One: What's the Thought That's Upsetting You?
- Say it silently to yourself. It might be something like *"He's disrespecting my authority. . . . I have to nip this in the bud"* or *"He's just manipulating me!"*

- Consider that this thought that's driving your upset almost certainly comes from fear. That means it isn't as true as the interpretation of the situation that comes from love.

Minute Two: Realize There Is Always Another Side to Every Story

- Consider that your parents no doubt had this thought about you once or twice, and you came out okay. Your child will, too.
- Consider the situation from your child's perspective. For instance, *"He's showing me how upset he is. . . . He's allowed to have his feelings."*
- Consider how your upsetting thought makes you treat your child. If you let go of that thought, how would you respond to your child?

Minute Three: Help Your Body Release the Feelings

- Tap the acupuncture point on the edge of your hand (the karate chop point) while you breathe deeply.
- Say to yourself while tapping: *"Although I'm upset, I'm safe. I can calm myself and heal this situation."*
- If you find yourself yawning, that's great—your body is releasing. The more you practice this, the more quickly your body will calm.

Now, return to your child, and start over from a place of love. Sound hard? It is, because when we're angry we're swamped with attack hormones. But when we open our perspective a bit, we get to the root of the attitude that triggers the yelling, and we change it. Every thought comes from fear or from love. Choose love.

routine, or your attitude, or your self-care—so you can do better next time. Support yourself so you can change.

Notice you can still guide your child—just respectfully. If you do this every time you find yourself yelling, or about to yell, you'll soon develop enough mindfulness to stop yourself before you begin yelling.

When Your Child Melts Down: How to Keep Your Cool

When my kids are having meltdowns, I find myself just wanting to get as far away as possible, and it's really hard to empathize with them.
    —Laura, mother of two

Children get upset often, because of their inexperience and cognitive immaturity. It's our ability to stay calm when they're upset that helps them develop the neural pathways to calm themselves. But most of us find it tough to stay empathic when our child starts to lose it. Something in us wants to scream *"No!"*

- *No, I don't have time for this right now!*
- *No, you're embarrassing me; people are looking!*
- *No, what am I doing wrong that she's having a tantrum again?*
- *No, why is she doing this to me?!*
- *No, why can't you just suck it up the way I do?*

Bingo. Most of us learned as children that our feelings were unacceptable, even dangerous. So when our child has a meltdown, the little one inside us gets triggered. Danger signs flash. As always when danger looms, we feel a sense of panic. We just want to get away (that's flight) or we feel a sudden rage—we want to *make* him shut up (that's fight) or we go numb (that's freeze).

Holding him with empathy, allowing him to let all those feelings out? Accepting his outburst even when it's directed at us, without taking it personally? That's a stretch for most parents. All of our good intentions fly out the window.

And yet every child has numerous experiences of fear, anger, frustration, and sadness. They need to express those experiences and have us listen. Over time, this teaches them to befriend their emotions so they can manage them. In fact, we're the role model. Our child learns how to regulate her emotions and behavior from watching us regulate *our* emotions and behavior.

So what can we do to address our own deep-rooted reaction to our child's upset, so we can be there for our kids?

- **Acknowledge your own feelings.** Our panic in the face of our child's raw emotions is an issue from our own childhood. The only way to uproot it is to see how it served us when we were little. Say to your rising panic: *"Thanks for keeping me safe when I was little. I'm grown now. These feelings are okay."*

- **Remind yourself that it isn't an emergency.** *"It's natural that I feel this way when my child is upset. But whatever happens, I can handle it."* This isn't a threat; it's your beloved child, who needs your loving help right now. If your mind persists in setting off alarms, tell it you'll deal with those concerns later, not now.

- **Remind yourself that expressing feelings is a good thing.** Your child will feel these feelings, no matter what. The only question is whether you make it okay for him to express them, or whether you teach him they're dangerous. Once he feels his emotions, they'll evaporate. (If you're wondering, it's the emotions he represses that pop out without warning and make him act out.) Even if you can't say a wholehearted *yes!* when your child starts to melt down, try to move from your automatic *no!* to a warmhearted *okay*, just the way you do at other times when your child needs you.

- **Take the pressure off.** You don't have to fix your child or the situation. All you have to do is stay present. Your child doesn't even need the red cup, or whatever he's crying for; he needs your loving acceptance of him, complete with all his tangled-up feelings. His disappointment, rage, grief? They're all okay, and they will all pass without you doing a thing except loving him.

- **Take a deep breath and choose love.** Every choice we make, at its core, is a move toward either love or fear. Let your caring for your child give you the courage to choose love. Not just love for your child, but love for the child you once were, and the parent you are now. Just keep breathing and saying to yourself, *"I choose love."* Too corny? Research shows this works. But you can easily find another effective mantra: *"This, too, shall pass.... I came out okay and she will, too.... I can handle this...."* Whatever works for you.

- **Tolerate the emotion without taking action.** You can act later, if you want. Or even in a few minutes, once you calm down. For now, let yourself feel it. Breathe your way through it. Name the emotion if that helps. Okay, anger. But what's under the anger? Hurt? Fear? Disappointment? Notice how it feels in your body.

- **Keep it simple.** Your child needs you to witness her outpouring of emotion and let her know that she is still lovable, despite all these yucky feelings. Explanations, negotiations, remorse, recriminations, advice, analysis of why she's so upset, or attempts to "comfort" her (*"There, there, you don't have to cry, that's enough."*) will all shut down this natural emotive process. Don't force her to express herself in words; she's doesn't have access to the rational brain when she's so upset. Of course, you want to "teach"—but that needs to wait. Your child can't learn until she's calm. You don't have to say much. Your calm, loving tone is what matters. Maybe:
  - *You are safe. I am right here.*
  - *I hear you. Everybody needs to cry sometimes.*
  - *You're telling me to go away, so I will move back a little bit, but I won't leave you alone with these scary feelings.*
  - *When you're ready, I'm right here to hug you.*

- **Find a way to process your own feelings.** Nothing triggers primal emotions like parenting. You also need to vent, which means feeling those emotions and breathing your way through them without taking action. Some of us can do this by journaling, or by crying, but you may need to find someone to simply listen to you. Someone who will resist giving you advice. Someone who won't be shocked when you admit that you wanted to slam your kid against the wall or leave him there in the grocery store, because they know everyone has felt this way, and you wouldn't actually do it. Someone who won't get triggered and go into a panic about whether it's okay for you, or your child, to feel such things. Someone who will let you cry, who will be there for you just as you're there for your child.

This is hard work for parents, but a great gift to our children. The good news is that once we say *yes* to children's full range of feelings, they learn to manage them in healthy ways. In fact, you'll see positive results immediately after every "tantrum" that you meet with love, because your child will feel so much better after emptying that full backpack of feelings. That's unconditional love in action.

You *Can* Nurture Yourself While Raising Your Child

The turning point for me was when Dr. Markham talked about parenting with your own cup full. If we enter the day empty, we have nothing to give to our children. Finding ways to refresh my energy is vital, so I get up at 6:00 a.m. every morning and go for a walk by myself. It helps me energize and focus so I'm ready to meet the day and the needs of my children. Having playdates with friends is also vital, so I've joined some groups in my church to ensure we all get the "friend time" we need.

—Amanda, mother of a four-year-old and a one-year-old

The number one resolution of parents everywhere? Be more patient. But having to summon up your patience is a signal that your cup is already dangerously empty. Willpower takes us only so far. The real job is keeping your cup full so you have plenty of joy and presence to share with your child. Kids love our joyful presence and become happier and more cooperative.

If you're finding yourself frequently resentful, depleted, or exhausted; if your mind chatter often includes negative thoughts about your child, or if you're yelling at your child on a regular basis, you may be suffering from what I call SAP disorder—Sacrificing yourself on the Altar of Parenthood. That's when we forget to give ourselves the attention we need. It isn't good for us to feel deprived. It kills our natural joy. And it isn't good for our kids, who end up with a resentful, negative, impatient parent. (Guess whether that makes them behave better.)

Ultimately, you're the one responsible for how you spend the short life you've been given. On your deathbed, there won't be anyone else to blame if you've been unhappy. The secret work of adulthood is that we are all still growing up, and parenting forces us to learn to parent ourselves as well as our child. If you're old enough to have a child yourself, your parents are off the hook. It's your responsibility now. You deserve all the tenderness you would shower on a newborn baby. Giving that love to ourselves transforms our parenting—and our lives.

Does that mean you should tell your kid he can forget about getting his needs met, that it's about time your needs came first? No, of course not. Parenting is about nurturing your child, which means noticing what she needs and trying to make sure she gets it. You are, after all, the grown-up. But we can be peaceful parents only to the degree that we "parent" ourselves.

It's partly a matter of changing what you do: nurturing yourself in small ways throughout your day. And it's partly a matter of changing your attitude: finding peace inside yourself. The solution is to tend to ourselves as well as we can each moment of the day, just as we do our child. To honor both our needs and theirs. The bad news is, this takes work. But that work—the internal work of embracing ourselves with compassion—is what transforms us. Here's how:

- **Make it a habit to tune in to yourself as often as possible throughout your day.** Just take a deep breath and let it flood your body with well-being. Breathe in calm, breathe out stress. Simply being present with yourself is an essential form of "attention" that we all need.

WHEN YOU'RE FEELING OVERWHELMED

- **Focus on what matters.** Are your kids fed? Have you hugged them and told them how much you adore them? Kids sense when we're stressed and disconnected, and act out, so often a hug reels them back to their best selves, too.
- **Find support.** Parenting is the toughest work humans do. We all need more support. As essayist Anne Lamott says, "Take yourself through the day as you would your favorite mental patient relative: with great humor and lots of small treats." I don't mean more cookies. How about a sweet kiss from your spouse (even if the marriage doesn't feel perfect right now). A hug from your child (even if he's not perfect, either!). Finding someone you can vent to about how hard it is (who won't try to fix you or your child).
- **Support yourself.** Talk to yourself like someone you love. Post uplifting messages around the house to boost your mood. Leave the dishes in the sink and have a long soak in the tub. Give yourself permission to really notice the sunset. Before you sleep, find three things to appreciate about yourself. Get enough sleep.
- **When you lose it, use it.** Okay, you blew it. So use this opportunity to demonstrate a life lesson on how a mature person apologizes, reconnects, and repairs. Every crisis is an opportunity to get closer if you're willing to see things from both sides, with an open heart.
- **Take a do-over.** When you find yourself starting to raise your voice, stop, breathe, and say, "*So sorry, that's my crankiness talking. . . . Let's try a do-over. . . . Here's what I meant to say. . . .*" You're taking responsibility for your own

irritability, so your kids don't feel like bad people. And you're modeling so they can course-correct, too.

- **Appreciate your child.** Even if he drives you crazy, there's something about him you love. When you notice, it's like telling him, *"More of this, please."* He'll blossom accordingly.

- **Never walk away emotionally.** Your child depends on you to hold the vision of her at her best. If she senses you're giving up on her, she'll give up on herself. Has she strayed? Go get her. But don't join her on the low road. Embrace her with your love and she'll rejoin you on the high road.

- **Just keep choosing love.** If you pay attention, you'll notice that life holds constant choices. Should you be harsh with your child because you're frightened that if you aren't, he won't learn? Should you point out to your spouse that you were right? Should you let yourself stop cleaning and take a bubble bath? At the core, every choice is between love and fear. Choose love as often as you can. Every day you get fresh chances to interact with your child in a way that heals both of you. Your life is the sum of your choices. You'll make bad ones, sure. But every choice turns your ratio around.

Of course, if you're having a hard day *every* day, that's a sign that you need to change something in your life. You deserve to feel good. And your child deserves the best of you, not what's left of you.

- **Every time you notice you're getting resentful or irritable, stop.** Ask yourself, *"What do I need right now to stay in balance?"* Then, give it to yourself—whether your child is there or not. (Five minutes to sit on the back steps and listen to the birds? A glass of water? Five minutes of dancing to great music?) If you can't do it right now, make a date with yourself for later. (A bath after the kids go to bed? A glass of wine with your spouse? More sleep tonight?)

- **Notice the challenging times of day and find ways to nurture yourself through them.** It's your life, and you're in charge, whether it feels that way or not. Letting yourself feel victimized doesn't help your kids. Does bedtime drive you crazy? Make a plan to make it better, whether that's sharing more responsibility with your spouse, starting earlier, posting a schedule, getting more sleep yourself, or enjoying a cup of tea while you read to your child.

- **Soak in the beauty and joy of every moment you can.** Stop rushing and revel in your child's laughter, the sweet smell of his hair, her joy in mastering something new. "Smelling the roses" replenishes your spirit. It makes life worth living. The fullness of your presence is what inspires your children to connect and cooperate. And it cures SAP disorder.

Ten Rules to Raise Terrific Kids

In just a month I have seen a big change in my daughter. When I can keep from getting upset, and instead turn things into a game or joke, while still enforcing the rules, she doesn't tantrum. She listens when I say no *better and is just happier and sweeter. It really is all about me acting better, so she does, too!*

—Brianna, mother of a two-year-old

Parents often ask me what rules are important to raise great kids. It seems to me that the most important rules to raise terrific children are for us, not our children. We begin with taking responsibility for ourselves and end with connection as the ultimate rule. Everything in between is about coaching for the long term.

1. **The most important parenting skill: Manage yourself.** Take care of yourself so you aren't venting on your child. Intervene before your own feelings get out of hand. Keep your cup full. The more you care for yourself with compassion, the more love and compassion you'll have for your child. Remember that your child will do every single thing you do, whether that's yelling or making self-disparaging remarks about your body.

2. **The most important parenting commitment: Be your child's advocate and don't give up on him.** You don't yell at a flower that isn't thriving; you water it. Appreciate who your child is and respond to what she needs, not what you think she should need. Every child deserves at least one person who is 110 percent on their side. That doesn't mean your child is always right. It means your child is always worth the extra effort; that every bit of love you put into your child makes a positive difference.

3. **The most important parenting secret: Discipline, despite all the books written on it, doesn't work.** Punishment

always worsens your child's behavior. Avoiding it is the most important thing you can do to raise children who are responsible and considerate. Instead of punishment, guide kindly and set limits on behavior but always empathize with feelings, including the feelings your child has about the limits you set. Both empathy and guidance/limits are essential; neither by itself is successful.

4. **What kids need that no one tells you: a safe place to express feelings while you "listen."** If you want to raise a child who can manage his behavior, he first has to manage the emotions that drive that behavior. And if you want a child who can manage his emotions, he first needs to know he has a safe place (your arms) to cry and rage where he won't be shushed. Laughter releases the same tensions as tears, so playing with children is also a terrific way to support them in expressing their fears and frustrations. Kids who get help with their big emotions when they're little learn to manage their own feelings (and therefore behavior) at an early age.

5. **What your child wishes you understood: She's just a kid, trying as hard as she can.** Expect age-appropriate behavior, not perfection, and keep your priorities straight. Your child is taking shape before your very eyes—she's still developing, and she'll grow out of most of her inappropriate behavior. Her messy room matters much less than how she treats her little brother.

6. **The most useful mantra: Don't take it personally.** Whatever your child does, it will be a lot easier for you to respond peacefully if you notice when you start getting triggered. This isn't about you; it's about your child, who's an immature

human doing his best to learn and grow, with your support. Cultivate a sense of humor. This will also help you avoid power struggles. No one wins a power struggle. Don't insist on being right; help them save face. When your buttons get pushed, use it as an opportunity to excavate that button so it isn't controlling you.

7. **What you need to remember when times get hard: All misbehavior comes from basic needs that aren't met.** Meet their needs for sleep, nutrition, chill-out time, cuddling, connection, fun, mastery, and safety. Let kids know in advance the behavior you expect. Give them "scaffolding"—teaching, little by little—so they can manage what's expected of them. Children *want* to be successful. (If they don't, that's a relationship problem, not a behavior problem.)

8. **The best parenting expert? Your child.** Let him show you what he needs, from infancy on. Listen with your heart. Be willing to change and grow—and learn to enjoy the process.

9. **The only constant? Change.** What worked yesterday will not work tomorrow, so your parenting approach needs to evolve as your kids do. Each of us seems to get the perfect child to learn whatever we need to know.

10. **What matters most: Stay connected and never withdraw your love, even for a moment.** The deepest reason kids cooperate is that they love you and want to please you. Above all, safeguard your relationship with your child. That's your only leverage to have any influence on your child. It's what your child needs most. And that closeness is what makes all the sacrifices of parenting worth it.

PART TWO

FOSTERING CONNECTION

It's the moments where I stop, check out of my own headspace, and reconnect with the fact that I love my children and am ready to be there for them in this moment that are the game-changers. My children feel the love, they feel validated, and they feel heard. When I barrel on with my own mind full of "busy adult stuff," I make life so much harder for myself and my children. That disconnect makes us all suffer.

—Amber, mother of two

2

The Essential Ingredient
for Peaceful Parents,
Happy Kids

The security of knowing that someone is on his side, watching out for him, is what allows a child to risk bumps, scrapes, and disappointment—in other words, to learn, grow, and develop resilience. When children feel securely connected to us, they learn to love themselves and to love others. The old saying that we give our kids roots so they can later grow wings is as true as ever, and as ever it requires a secure bond for those roots to really sink in. What's more, a good connection with your child is the secret to being a happy parent. That's why Fostering Connection is one of the Three Big Ideas at the heart of this book.

As we'll see, our other two Big Ideas are also contained within Fostering Connection. Coaching, Not Controlling just isn't possible if your kids don't feel like you're on their side in a very deep, unspoken way. And as for Regulating Yourself, your own emotional wholeness will determine how deeply you can connect with your child.

Why Connection Is the Secret to Happy Parenting

Parents sometimes approach connecting with their child as a duty. After all, we have a long list of obligations, and what we really want is an hour to ourselves without anyone tugging on us. But the truth is, that rewarding bond is our payoff for all the hard work. The moments that make our hearts melt make all the very real sacrifices worthwhile. And our children need to know that we take joy in them or they don't see themselves as worth loving. In fact, your ability to enjoy your child may be the most important factor in his development. That's what prompts you to do—automatically—all the things that help him thrive, from cooing during infancy to rough-housing at age three and chatting at age five.

That deep connection is also what makes peaceful parenting possible. Children freely, even enthusiastically, cooperate when they believe that we're on their side. When they don't have that belief deep in their bones, our standards of behavior seem unfair, contradicting what they perceive as their own best interests, whether that's taking the biggest piece of cake or lying to us.

No amount of "parenting skills" can make up for an eroded parent-child bond. It's like riding a bike up a very steep hill. By contrast, parenting with a good relationship is like coasting downhill—you still have to pay attention and stay on the road, and twists and turns certainly arise, but the momentum is with you.

A close bond gives us access to our natural parenting know-how and lets us see things from our child's point of view, which makes us better parents. And it makes children more open to our influence, even as they move out into the larger world of friends, school, and the rest of their lives. Study after study shows that the best protection for teens from the excesses of the culture and the peer group is a close relationship with parents. You're building that connection from babyhood on.

Let's look at how Connection unfolds during childhood.

Connection as Your Child Grows

BABIES (0–13 MONTHS): WIRING THE BRAIN

What's as important as food for your baby to develop optimally? *Connection.* Humans are born ready to love and be loved. All emotional development—including our ability to regulate our emotions, control our tempers, delay gratification, and form healthy romantic relationships—is built on the nurturing we receive as infants. In fact, our brains take shape in direct response to our interactions with our parents.

Newborn brains come into the world with a lot of developing to do. That's how humans retain the flexibility to adapt to the conditions of different environments. So your interactions with your infant over his first year will determine a great deal about how his brain and nervous system are wired for the rest of his life. Your baby learns to regulate himself physiologically, and therefore psychologically, from his contact with you. Your loving touch regulates his stress and growth hormones. His heart rate synchronizes with yours. As Sue Gerhardt describes in *Why Love Matters: How Affection Shapes a Baby's Brain,* the baby is "establishing . . . the normal range of arousal" so he "coordinates his system with those of the people around him. Babies of depressed mothers adjust to low stimulation and get used to a lack of positive feelings. Babies of agitated mothers may stay over-aroused and have a sense that feelings just explode out of you."[1]

Here's how this works during the normal back-and-forth that

parents automatically engage in with babies. Your baby gazes at you. You smile and coo. She smiles back and kicks her feet in excitement. You coo and smile with more excitement to match her exuberance, and the two of you "dance" together emotionally, feeling increasingly loving and delighted. After a while, your baby has had enough excitement. She needs to calm herself, to return to a lower level of arousal. She looks away. Some parents would get in her face to coax more smiles, but you're tuned in. You realize your baby needs a break. You speak more soothingly. She glances back at you: Is it safe to engage? Yes, it is. You are smiling gently, having ratcheted down your energy level. She snuggles down, content. You picked up her cue. She learns that she can make her needs known, and you will respond by helping her. It's a delicious, safe universe. There's excitement and there's soothing. With your help, she can handle whatever comes.

What happened? Your little one just learned an important lesson in self-regulation from her interaction with you. She can get happy, worked up, even overexcited. When she starts to feel dysregulated, carried away, she can send out an SOS. You will help her calm herself. Life is safe. Or, more precisely, you are keeping her safe. You help her regulate her feeling state, whether those feelings are good or bad. Her attachment to you will keep her safe. She can trust in the universe.

During the first year of your child's life, this interaction will be repeated many times. We can accurately say that your child is learning a lesson about trust, which is physiologically etched into your child's brain. During this interaction and all the ones that follow, neurobiologist Allan Schore says, "The mother is downloading emotion programs into the infant's right brain. The child is using the output of the mother's right hemisphere as a template for the imprinting, the hardwiring, of circuits in his own right hemisphere."[2] You're even determining the size of his hippocampi[3] (more development confers better learning, stress management, and mental health), anterior cingulate (emotional regulation), and amygdala (emotional reactivity). This early brain wiring influences happiness levels and mood later in life, because better wiring means a better ability to connect with others, regulate positive or negative emotions, and soothe ourselves.

Prioritizing your connection with your baby makes caring for her easier, because it makes for a contented baby who grows into a secure, happy, cooperative child. Soothing is essential to all infants, whose brains develop the capacity to regulate negative emotion directly from the experience of being soothed. Most, although not all, infants insist on being held and carried much of the time, which helps them regulate themselves physiologically. Newborn sleep patterns sync to their mother's, so infants who sleep near Mom are better able to regulate their arousal levels and respiration, which reduces the risk of sudden infant death syndrome (SIDS). Connecting with your infant also helps you understand her unique cues and needs, which builds your confidence as a parent. Once the baby learns that her caretakers are reliably nurturing and protective, she builds on this internal security as she proceeds to the next developmental tasks of exploration, mastery of the environment, and forming relationships with others.

You may think of what's now called *attachment parenting* as a new trend, often credited to Dr. Bill Sears. But there's nothing new about it; we've been doing it for as long as humans have existed. Dr. Sears himself says, "Attachment parenting is not a new style of parenting. . . . In fact, it's the way that parents for centuries have taken care of babies, until childcare advisors came on the scene and led parents to follow books instead of their babies." Attachment parenting is now supported by an impressive body of academic theory and research, but the basic idea is simple and intuitively obvious. Human babies are born helpless compared to other mammals.

They need parents to keep them close until they're able to survive on their own.

Unfortunately, a myth has developed in our society that attachment parenting requires parents to live by self-sacrificing rules. It's just not so. You don't have to wear your baby constantly or co-sleep to create a secure attachment bond. The only core guideline—again, it's common sense—is that healthy attachment requires being in tune with and responsive to the cues of your unique infant. And what parent doesn't want, in her heart, to do exactly that?

So let's redefine attachment parenting. It's simply responding to your baby's emotional as well as physical needs, which in infancy usually include staying in close physical proximity to the parent. As with everything in parenting, our ability to do this depends on our own emotional growth. In fact, the research on this is eye-opening. We can predict during pregnancy—before the child is even born!—whether a child will be securely attached to a parent. How? Simply by interviewing the parent. If we were securely attached to our own parents, our baby will almost certainly be securely attached to us. If, on the other hand, our parents didn't reliably meet our needs and we became preoccupied with or avoidant of our own desire for connection, we'll be uncomfortable connecting intimately with our baby. Luckily, this correlation doesn't rely only on what happened to you, but on how you've come to terms with it. When you reflect on your childhood, surface the emotions, and edit your life story from a compassionate adult perspective, you actually grow your orbitofrontal cortex—and in the process you become able to parent your baby responsively to create a secure attachment. In fact, how we as parents have come to peace with our own attachment histories is a more reliable predictor of secure attachment than any other factor, including specific parenting practices such as co-sleeping or even how much time we spend with our child. The happy news is that as you come to terms with your own childhood story, you subtly change your emotional availability to your child, and your child blossoms accordingly, whether she's an infant or a nine-year-old.

Are you worrying about whether your child had enough attunement as a baby? Setting up optimal architecture in the first three years as your little one builds his brain is obviously preferable to remodeling later. But the latest research shows that the brain does keep growing and changing throughout life. When you soothe your four- or six-year-old, his brain is still learning from you how to soothe itself. He may need to do a bit more crying to heal his experience of having felt separated or afraid, but he's young enough to be open to that healing. Your patience with his emotional meltdowns is the key to his overcoming any earlier hurts. It just becomes even more important to remember that his challenging behaviors are a red flag that he needs your emotional help. The understanding you give your child is always healing.

And no parent is always in sync with her baby. As researcher Edward Tronick says, "Only maybe twenty, thirty percent of the time is the interaction 'perfectly' in sync. The rest of the time, you're in sync, you're out of sync, you're getting back into sync. This not being in sync frees up parents from that constant burden of being perfect—because you can't be perfect. No matter how hard you try, you can't be. When you reconnect, one of the things that can happen—not always, but some of the time—is that you create something new. You figure out a new way to do something together that you have never done before. If you create something new, you grow. And babies are about growing."[4]

TODDLERS (13–36 MONTHS): BUILDING SECURE ATTACHMENT

Let's watch what happens to the parent-child connection when our baby hits the "terrible twos." As a toddler, he's now capable of

ASSESSING ATTACHMENT

The "Strange Situation" orchestrates a brief but stressful separation and reunion in a situation that is strange to the child. Using the child's response to the situation, researchers classify fifteen-month-olds as:

- **Secure:** These toddlers protest the parent's departure and are easily comforted by the parent when he or she returns. Referred to as *securely attached*, they may be stressed by the separation but trust that the parent, upon his or her return, will offer comfort and security. They turn out to have better relationships with the parent to whom they're securely attached, but that's not all. As they develop, these children are ranked as better adjusted in virtually every way, including interpersonally and academically.

- **Resistant/ambivalent/preoccupied:** These toddlers protest the parent's departure but reject comfort from the parent upon his or her return. They've apparently learned that their parent is not always dependable in meeting their needs and find it hard to take comfort from the parent. In fact, they seem angry, as if the parent is withholding what they need. As they mature, these children stay focused on seeking the reassurance of relationships, but because of their fierce neediness they tend to create unfulfilling involvements. Their preoccupation with the search for love may keep them from appropriately attending to other age-appropriate developmental tasks, such as learning and experimenting with independence. These children often become over-involved with peers in an attempt to fill unmet attachment needs.

- **Avoidant:** These toddlers may not protest the parent's departure, and they do not seek comfort upon the parent's return. They don't express age-appropriate comfort needs, apparently because they assume those needs will not be met in the relationship. Although they appear more independent in this laboratory situation, they are no more independent at home or in school, and in fact are rated by daycare teachers as more whiny and demanding than other children the same age. In fact, when their physiology is monitored during the Strange Situation, it turns out that these toddlers have soaring heart rates and cortisol levels, indicating that while they have learned to mask it, they are actually very upset when the parent leaves the room. As they grow older, these lonely children find their emotional needs overwhelming and frightening and thus repress them. Unless they have the opportunity to experience therapy or another transformational love relationship, they may not develop much capacity for intimacy. While they may succeed in academics or sports, their lack of social skills often limits their happiness and even their career success.

regulating his physiology but still relies heavily on you to help him regulate himself emotionally. His emotional controls in the frontal cortex are still under construction. Ironically, while the job of the toddler is asserting himself as an active explorer of his world, he can start developing those wings only if he's securely attached in his relationship with us.

We now have more than forty years of research, including longitudinal studies, tracking the effect of secure attachment. As securely attached babies get older, they form better relationships with others, have higher self-esteem, are more flexible and resilient under stress, and perform better in every aspect of life, from schoolwork to peer interactions.

Extraordinary as it may seem, fifteen-month-old toddlers have already developed interpretations about how relationships work and strategies to get their interpersonal needs met. Unless something changes, they will use these strategies for the rest of their lives.

Let's assume our hypothetical fifteen-month-old has developed a secure attachment. She's learned she can count on her parents to respond to her cues. Now that she can toddle, she's ready to explore the world. Does she still need her parents? Desperately. As Gordon Neufeld and Gabor Mate, authors of *Hold On to Your Kids*, say, her parents are her North Star, the point around which she orbits.

Just try taking her to the playground and sitting near her sandbox on a park bench. While she's playing, she'll regularly look up at you for reassurance. Then move to the next park bench over. You're no farther from her than you were before. You watch for her to look up, so you can immediately call her name. She sees you right away, waving to her as usual. But does she go on playing? No. She frowns. She may even cry. She almost certainly calls for you or toddles over. She "refuels"—gets a hug—and only then goes back to the sandbox. What happened? Her North Star moved. She had to reorient herself.

How Does Daycare Affect Your Toddler?
What happens at home will always be much more important than what happens in daycare, because your child's attachment to you is so dominant in his psyche. Nonetheless, if your little one is in daycare more than twenty hours a week, those hours will certainly have an impact on your child's development. Some of this impact is positive, because the child learns peer skills and gets ample opportunity

for exploration. But babies are designed to be in close contact with a primary adult. Parents are more attuned to their child, usually have fewer children to tend to, and simply care more, so they're better at meeting babies' needs. Unfortunately, the United States does not ensure paid family leave, so approximately half of all babies in this country spend most of their waking hours during their first two years away from their parents. This is the critical developmental period during which the emotion centers of the brain develop.

What does this mean in practice? When you smile at a two-month-old, it takes her some time to smile back at you. That dance is part of what develops the neurons in the orbitofrontal cortex, the brain center for emotional intelligence. But when a daycare worker smiles at a baby, she can't wait around for the baby to smile back—she has two or three other babies to tend to. Over and over throughout her day, the baby may miss the attunement she needs. By contrast, a baby in one-to-one care with a responsive caregiver may have her needs met almost as well as by a parent.

By the toddler years, a child whose needs have been responsively met will be better prepared for group care. Parents should know, however, that two-year-olds who spend the most time in childcare tend to have the most behavior problems.[5] This is understandable, since toddlers who are under stress—and separation from the parent is a stressor for a young child—tend to act out more. Luckily, the same studies find that high-quality parental care protects children from the negative effects of daycare.[6] In other words, your child may act out more because of the time apart, but if you handle his behavior with understanding, your relationship, and his psyche, will remain intact. Happily, kids in daycare are as compliant as other kids by age three. This may be the perfect age to begin "school," since kids are more able to express their needs verbally and can wait to have them met. Research psychologists are still conducting the longitudinal studies that will give us the information we need about

IF YOUR SITUATION REQUIRES DAYCARE

- Choose warm, nurturing, flexible care with a high staff-to-child ratio.
- Put daycare off for as long as you can.
- Keep the hours as reduced as you can.
- Consider postponing another child until your first is a pre-schooler, so you can increase the bonding time with both. The toddler years are even more trying than usual for kids in daycare, and it's tough for even the most dedicated parent to stay patient with a toddler when you're sleepless and distracted with a newborn.
- Consider eliminating TV time. This eliminates a possible cause of aggression (which is more likely when kids are in daycare) and also shifts your child's focus back to you as the leader from whom he takes his cues.
- When you're home, engage warmly with your child in all the ways described in this book to strengthen your bond. If your child is a difficult toddler, remember that part of it is the daily separation, and step up your connection with lots of physical play. The best protection you can give your child is always a happy, peaceful relationship with you.

the effects of daycare, but we do know that the quality of the care matters tremendously. And since so much of the brain development that determines mood, anxiety, and depression tendencies in later life occurs during the first year, in some measure the results are already known. It's only common sense to try to give infants the attuned connections they need during that first, critical year.

PRESCHOOLERS (3–5 YEARS): DEVELOPING INDEPENDENCE

You're still the center of your preschooler's existence, the North Star (or attachment leader) around which he orients himself. He knows, at a primal level, that if he were to be separated from you, he would be unprotected and face terrible risks, possibly including death. He may negotiate with you like an attorney in training, and he's increasingly able to do without you while at school or with friends, but Mother Nature has made him dependent for a reason. That reason is not just his need for protection; his dependence on you also makes him open to your guidance. He may not always seem to "listen" to you, but you're still his most trusted source for information about the world, and even about himself.

Many parents who easily comforted their toddler's separation anxiety begin to get frustrated or worried when she has a hard time separating from them to start preschool. "What's wrong with my child?" they may wonder. "Why isn't she more independent?"

To answer that question, we need to consider what independence really means. When we think of an independent child, we usually think of a kid who separates easily as a toddler, who can take off on sleepovers without looking back by age five, heads off for a month to sleepaway camp at age nine. That's an independent kid, right?

Actually, no. It turns out that these scenarios may not have much to do with independence. They're about separation from the parent, which isn't necessarily the same thing as independence. Children are biologically designed to orient around a North Star or attachment leader, so when they're away from us they're depending on someone, whether that's a best friend or a teacher. That dependence is usually a good thing in relation to the teacher, because the child is more willing to accept her influence and direction. But orienting around a peer is a risk factor for children.

What's more, the fact that a child can easily separate from his parents isn't necessarily a good thing. We wouldn't expect a four-month-old to be independent; that would be an indicator of abnormal development. And remember our fifteen-month-old who doesn't look up when Mom leaves him in the Strange Situation? Is he actually more independent? No. The young toddlers who didn't seem to notice the parent leaving the room were *not* the children who grew up to be independent. They were the avoidant children who had given up on having their needs met, so they disguised their anxiety, even though their hearts were racing. These kids might head off to camp without a backward glance, but that easy separation from the parent might actually be a sign of a frayed attachment that will handicap them in their ability to form relationships with others.

Children need an attachment figure to feel grounded. That's hardwired for survival; the parent provides the secure base for the child to feel safe enough to explore the world. When we "push" children into emotional independence, research shows, they become more needy. Sometimes they get overinvolved with their peer group and fixate on other children as attachment objects.

We can think of emerging independence as the child trusting his secure attachment to a parent enough that he can engage with the world and successfully perform his age-appropriate developmental tasks. That means playing with other children without hitting them, or interacting appropriately with a teacher, or participating on a sports team without tantrums, or taking responsibility for homework. In the beginning, these tasks usually involve the parents, but over time, the child begins to interact with the world on his own. That's emerging independence.

So instead of thinking about independence as having to do with our child's separation from us, let's view independence as our child's ability to feel confident and competent interacting with the world and managing his life, as we gradually reduce our role from direct intervention to sideline availability to telephone backup to moral support.

What makes a child independent? Roots and wings. Independence is rooted in secure attachment—knowing that Mom and Dad are there when needed. Once children know we're available if they want us, they can focus on their appropriate developmental tasks, which include becoming more independent in handling their responsibilities. If they don't know if they can rely on Mom and Dad, children become preoccupied with trying to win attention and approval, and it gets in the way of mastering age-appropriate developmental tasks. If this affirmation isn't forthcoming from parents, kids become preoccupied with getting it from peers, often with ugly results.

The wings? Feeling powerful! When we allow children's natural assertiveness to blossom by giving them control over the aspects of their life where that's appropriate, we're also encouraging their developing independence. As we've seen, this starts early. As little ones pass the one-year mark, they become more assertive. They need the experience of power in the most positive sense—that they can act on the world and get the desired result. They also need to know that we're still available as backup. That developing sense of feeling capable in the context of our guidance is what helps children develop confidence, which is the beginning of independence.

ELEMENTARY SCHOOLERS (6–9 YEARS): FOUNDATION FOR THE TEEN YEARS

How did this happen? Your preschooler has somehow become a full-fledged elementary school student. It's so much easier—they have so much more self-control. They're more cooperative and affectionate.

But this is where things get complicated. You're just living your life, trying to hold a busy household together and get dinner on the table, while your child is shaping into the person he or she will become. During the school years, most parents are so exhausted and overwhelmed by life that we're relieved to have our child increasingly focused on the peer group.

But if you spend weekdays apart and cram weekends with sports, screen time, and sleepovers, it's easy for your worlds to become increasingly distant. Now he's so self-sufficient, so peer-oriented, and so preoccupied with his various screens that it's possible to go a whole weekend and barely see your eight-year-old. You may not be able to see it yet, but your influence is already starting to wane, as your child begins to shape his behavior outside the home to the norms of schoolmates and media images.

Kids naturally turn to the peer group for companionship and to media for clues about social "norms." The danger is when they don't feel firmly anchored to their parents as their North Star and begin to orient around their peer group or media values. If we don't cement a close connection before our children hit middle school, they turn elsewhere for bonding and guidance. Sadly, by the time we realize we're losing our child to the peer group, it's hard to get their attention.

Your goal during the elementary years is to build a strong relationship with your child, which will provide a counterbalance to peer culture and a solid foundation to get you through the teen years. How?

- **Develop family rituals that foster connection.** Family meetings. Sunday morning brunches. Saturday lunch dates with Dad on the way to weekly grocery shopping. Apple-picking trips every September, or making costumes together before

Halloween. Whatever works for your family, turn these connection opportunities into routines, so that everyone looks forward to them and they happen reliably.

- **Resist the impulse to say yes to one more playdate so you can get more done.** Instead, spend some downtime just hanging out with your child. Now is when you lay the foundation for a great relationship later.

- **Take your cues about independence from your child.** Maturity doesn't come in a straight line; small regressions are normal. Remember that after periods of independence that require "grown-up" behavior, such as sleepovers, your kid's "baby self" will come out for extra attention from you. Instead of shaming her into "acting her age," meet those needs by reconnecting with her on a visceral level.

It may seem like you just finished potty training, but the tween years are right around the corner. This is your last, best chance. Take advantage of these sweet, reasonable, elementary years while you're still the center of your child's life.

Connection Basics

The single most valuable concept I have taken away from your daily emails and website is simply remembering that all any one of us ever really needs is love. It seems so simple but can be so hard in the heat of the moment. Since becoming familiar with your work, I have started repeating back to my son what it is that he is saying or wanting. Whether I am willing to meet his desire or not, I know I am meeting a critical need to

feel heard and validated. For him, sometimes knowing that I hear is enough . . . and as it turns out, connecting with me was really all he needed.
    —Ashley, pregnant and mother of a two-year-old

In my clinical practice, I often see families reach crisis points as their children reach specific ages. This happens first around thirteen months, when babies become toddlers and begin having tantrums. At this point, some parents look for positive strategies that allow them to keep their toddler safe and offer guidance, while convincing him that they're on his side. Those families are on the road to a win/win relationship; as long as they keep listening, resist punishing, and attend to any rifts, they'll stay close to their child for life.

What about the families that begin punishing their toddler? They're pushing their little one away each time and lessening their influence with their child without even knowing it. As long as we can scare her and drag her into time-out, our child may obey our directives. But her willingness to listen to us diminishes with every punishment, and by the time she's five or six and too big to physically control, her attitude will be rebellious. This will continue to escalate into the teenage years, when kids slam out of the house to look for love in all the wrong places, unwittingly rejecting the safety net of the family.

If you've been punishing your child, you may think this scenario is alarmist. After all, your child loves you. Most of the time, he even does what you tell him. And you're right, to some degree. Children are designed to love their parents—even, sadly, when those parents harm them. But their chances of survival increase if they don't obey the directives of adults who aren't on their side, and if you punish, your child has ample evidence that you aren't always on his side. So punishment diminishes your influence and erodes your closeness with your child, which becomes more apparent as your child gets older and less dependent on you.

Is it too late? Never. You can always strengthen a frayed bond with your child. But it does take work, fierce intention, and a whole lot of love. This chapter will show you how.

HOW TO CONNECT MORE DEEPLY WITH YOUR CHILD

Every day I do the ten minutes of child-directed play, and when my husband is home he does, too, so some days she gets twenty minutes of undivided attention. This has been the key for us. Immediately after our playtime my daughter is more cooperative, willing to listen, and less upset. The more often I connect with her on her terms, the more I see my happy, cooperative, confident, respectful, and loving daughter. She even shares her toys with her brother after we play with her. For us it worked like a light switch; the trick is keeping up the playtime and working on our emotional regulation when things aren't easy. Connection, connection, connection. It's worth it!

—Teresa, mother of a three-year-old and a baby

Assume that you'll need to put in a significant amount of time creating a good relationship with your child. Quality time is a myth, because there's no switch to turn on closeness. Imagine that you work all the time and have set aside an evening with your husband, whom you've barely seen in the past six months. Does he immediately start baring his soul? Not likely. In relationships, without quantity, there's no quality. You can't expect a good relationship with your daughter if you spend all your time at work and she spends all her time with friends, screens, or the sitter. So as hard as it is with the pressures of jobs and daily life, if we want a better relationship with our children, we have to free up the time—daily—to make closeness happen.

We earn our children's trust with our daily behavior: following through on the promise we make to play a game with him, picking him up on time, understanding even when he isn't at his best. You don't have to do anything special to build a relationship with your child. The good—and bad—news is that every interaction creates the relationship. Grocery shopping, carpooling, and bath time matter at least as much as that big birthday party you've planned for him. He doesn't want to share his toy, or go to bed, or do his homework? How you handle each challenge as he grows is one brick in the foundation of your relationship and his psyche. Because so much of our time with our children is about managing the tasks of daily life, it's important to be sure that your routines are filled with fun, giggling, and warmth, rather than just moving your child through the schedule. Play is one of the most reliable ways to smooth the tensions and build trust with your child.

Unfortunately, life, with its infinite distractions and constant separations, has a way of eroding connection. Jobs, school, technology, exhaustion, and the responsibility to keep our children on busy schedules conspire to keep us from deeply connecting. Daycare is a separation, but so, to a child, is bedtime. In fact, to a young child, any time your attention is focused elsewhere is a separation. That's why they act up as soon as we get on the phone or start cooking dinner. Even when you take your child on errands, she may well experience your focus on the list and the store clerks as a separation, and act out, demanding your attention.

That's why all parents need to repeatedly reconnect with their children, just to repair the daily erosion created by life's normal separations and distractions. Effective parenting is almost impossible until the positive connection with your child has been re-established, so think of this as preventive maintenance, before there's a problem. Parents naturally provide an anchor, or compass, for children to attach to and stay oriented around. When they're apart from us they need a substitute, so they orient themselves around teachers, coaches, electronics, or peers. When you re-collect your child physically into your orbit, re-collect him emotionally as well.

Be prepared for your child's dependency needs to make an appearance when your child is reunited with you, in the form of what Anthony E. Wolfe, author of *Get Out of My Life, but First Can You Drive Me and Cheryl to the Mall?*, calls the "babyself." What's a babyself? Your child has been happily playing at childcare, but as soon as you show up, he has a meltdown. That's because he's been repressing his dependency needs so that he can function independently in a demanding environment. Your safe presence signals to him that he can relax and let down his guard. So his grown-up self (what we call his executive functioning) takes a much-needed break, and the babyself takes charge, whining, helpless, and acting out. This is not the time for guidance; he can't act his age right now. Scoop him up, give him that snuggle he needs, and get him out of there. Some little ones need to cry for a few minutes in your arms before they're ready for the car seat; preschoolers may revert to baby talk. Accept all this as proof of the age-appropriate solace your child finds in your company. Some parents object to this as "encouraging dependency." I see it as allowing the dependency that is there anyway, which will otherwise go undercover. Don't worry; your child won't be dependent forever. In fact, kids who get their dependency needs met make a healthy transition to independence faster. Kids who get their dependency needs squashed turn to the peer group to meet them or find little addictions like electronics to keep those needs at bay.

HOW DO YOU KNOW WHEN YOUR RELATIONSHIP WITH YOUR CHILD NEEDS WORK?

The biggest challenge to my patience has always been when my daughter seems to be willfully refusing to cooperate. Inspired by your newsletter,

I decided to do an experiment. When she became defiant I simply went over to her and gave her a big hug and told her how much I love her, then repeated the request in a soft voice. The effect that doing this had on my blood pressure was impressive, but the effect it had on her behavior was beyond belief. She went from defiant to eager to please in a single hug.

—Kristin, mother of a three-year-old

The most obvious sign that your relationship with your child needs some repair work is defiance. Children will always have priorities that differ from ours, but they want to feel good about their relationship with us, so they actually want to cooperate. When they don't, it's usually a signal of disconnection. So defiance isn't a discipline problem, it's a relationship problem.

Because young children are so forgiving and seek their parents' approval and closeness at least some of the time, most parents say they have a good relationship with their children. We certainly know we love *them*, even if we lose our temper. But by the time they're in sixth grade, fewer than half of kids in the United States describe their communication with their parents as positive.

If you feel you aren't getting through to your child; if your child doesn't listen or follow your requests or seems hardened to your anger; if you regularly yell, give "consequences," or put your child in time-out, then your relationship with your child needs work. But even if your child simply seems difficult, she may be giving you the message that she needs something from you that she isn't getting.

That doesn't mean you've somehow botched your parenting. Many children are more challenging to connect with because they're colicky, or strong-willed, or born with a specific challenge, such as a genetic predisposition to anxiety or depression. Other children encounter risk factors such as divorce, illness, separation, a mother's postpartum depression, or a sibling born while they're still babies themselves. The norm today of small children spending a lot of time with nonparents simply doesn't work for all children. Many parents follow outdated parenting advice in their desire to do their best for their child. And our culture doesn't teach parents how to emotion-coach, so sometimes an emotional backpack overflowing with frustration or anxiety keeps a child from feeling close. Finally, it's just in the nature of human relationships that we encounter conflict with our child. In all of these cases, a child may feel disconnected and act defiant. That's always a signal that we need to do some repair work on the relationship.

It takes patience, the ability to regulate our own emotions, luck, and hard emotional work to repair a frayed relationship. The good news is that it's never too late to heal your bond with your child. Since separations and conflicts happen daily, little repairs need to be a daily ritual. Larger repairs take more concerted time and attention, and sometimes the help of a therapist, but are always possible. No one can take your place in your child's heart; you will always be her parent. She may seem to have hardened her heart to you, but your sweet little girl is in there, waiting to be reconnected with you.

CONNECTING WITH A DIFFICULT CHILD

What if you have a child who doesn't seem to be motivated by connection? Kids on the autism spectrum, or those who have sensory processing issues, are good examples. These kids *do* want to connect; you just have to be creative to find the ways of connecting that work best. If your child fits this description, I urge you not to give up on seeking connection. Pay close attention to the way your child responds and adjust your attempts accordingly.

What about kids who are simply challenging? Who seem to be trying to drive you away by shrieking and sticking their fingers up your nose and spitting on you? Believe it or not, those kids want to be close, too. In fact, the way to ease their problematic behavior is actually to connect more, not less. Let's consider how this works.

When Jonathan was about thirteen months old, he began to whine constantly. He woke up crying and fussed all day long. Determined and not easily distracted, he screamed if his mother changed his diaper or his father picked him up to move him away from the television screen. He refused the sling, but insisted on being picked up and held on his mother's hip much of the time. There, he would pull her hair, put his fingers in her nose, or scream in her ear. When his mother, Brooke, tried to get anything done around the house, Jonathan tore the books off the shelf and threw them around, or emptied every cabinet he could reach. He would look right at her and hit the dog, or pull his diaper off and pee on the floor. Brooke felt she must be doing something terribly wrong as a mother.

Brooke began by taking care of herself—always our first parenting responsibility. She started taking Jonathan out of the house every morning so she could meet up with other parents and children. When his whining diminished, she realized he must have been bored at home with her all day. She also worked on her own tendency to get into power struggles with her toddler, by reflecting on how her parents had forced her to acquiesce to their wishes even on things that in retrospect seemed trivial. She decided to give her strong-willed son more control over his own life and began offering him choices: "Red cup or blue cup?" To reduce her irritation, she babyproofed the house more thoroughly so that she could simply shrug when he "got into things" at home, telling herself that he was stretching his IQ and fostering independence with every exploration. All of these changes helped make things easier, but Jonathan was still often challenging.

Brooke decided to try creating more connection. She consciously looked Jonathan warmly in the eye as often as possible and began offering frequent unsolicited snuggles, rather than picking him up only when he whined. Brooke worked to create a safe, fun connection by initiating roughhousing sessions with Jonathan, during which they rolled around on the rug wrestling and laughing. His giggling during these play sessions allowed his age-appropriate toddler anxieties to surface and evaporate, so that he became a bit more flexible. Brooke, in turn, began to approach Jonathan's body with more respect, letting him wash his own face and changing his diaper standing up while he played. As Jonathan became more affectionate, Brooke realized that his aggressive physical behavior toward her was actually a clumsy attempt at connection. She began to respond playfully, for instance, *"Are you trying to put your fingers in my nose again?! No way! Okay, let's play Nose Fingers. See if you can get close.... I got away.... Okay, my turn.... Can I get my fingers close to your nose?... Oh, you are so quick!"* When he wanted to spit on her, she took him outside for a spitting contest with her, again transforming his aggression into connection. Finally, when she did need to set a limit and Jonathan was inconsolable, Brooke reminded herself that he just needed a chance to cry and held him sympathetically, rather than becoming exasperated. Sometimes he would arch out of her arms, but within a few minutes he would climb into her lap and cling to her while he sobbed. Within a month of her new approach, Brooke reported that Jonathan had transformed. "He's still stubborn, but he seems so much happier now, and life is so much easier." Brooke is learning how to cope with the unique needs of her challenging, strong-willed child.

Is it always this easy? No. Children can be difficult in so many ways. But deepening our connection with our child will always help, no matter how challenging the child or the situation.

Action Guides

YOUR CHILD'S EMOTIONAL BANK ACCOUNT

It's part of our job description to set limits with our children, deny their unreasonable requests, and correct their behavior. Sometimes we're skillful enough that our child doesn't even perceive those interactions as negative—but that's rare. More often, their perception is that we're denying them something they want, but they give us the benefit of the doubt because all the other loving, affirming interactions create a positive balance in our relationship account.

But try as we might, all of us sometimes have less than optimal interactions with our children, and our relationship balance dips into the red. That's when children develop attitude, whether they're two or ten. So if you notice some friction with your child, it's time to check your account balance. Do this even if you think your child is just going through a difficult stage. You might be surprised by how much easier that stage is once your child feels more connected to you.

- **Challenges signal that your relationship account is in the red.** How many loving connections have you had with your child in the past two days?

- **What can you do to refill your relationship account with your child?** Think of two things you can do today. For instance: *"Sit with her after school while she has her snack and does homework, so I can hear more about her day. . . . Start bedtime earlier so I can spend ten minutes after lights out just connecting."*

- **Consider what contributed to your being overdrawn.** What can you do in the future to make sure you keep your account with your child in the green? Write down five things. For instance, your list might look like this: *"Figure out ways to have more fun together as we go through the afternoon and evening routine so it isn't always about nagging. . . . Turn off my phone in the evening so I can be more available to help her through the bedtime routine without yelling. . . . Be sure to spend time every evening after bedtime story just snuggling for five or ten minutes. . . . Go to bed earlier so I'm more rested and patient in the morning and don't snap at her. . . . Go out for brunch together once a month on Sundays."*

WHAT'S SO SPECIAL ABOUT SPECIAL TIME?

Here are the changes in our children, just from starting Special Time:
* *They're noticeably less needy and more independent throughout the day.*
* *There's a lot less sibling rivalry.*
* *The "need" for screen time has decreased by about 50 percent.*
* *They now leave me alone to complete chores because they know that they'll get my time when I'm finished.*
—Christine, mother of two, ages six and eight

Parents who implement Special Time with their child always tell me they see significant changes in their child's behavior. Why? Because Special Time:

- Gives the child the essential—but unfortunately so often elusive—experience of the parent's full, attentive, loving attention, without which he can't thrive.

- Reconnects us with our child after the separations and conflicts of everyday life, so she's happier and more cooperative.
- Gives children a regular, safe opportunity to "unpack" all those sad, scared feelings they've been stuffing in their (figurative) emotional backpacks, which will otherwise spill out as contrary behavior.
- Deepens our empathy for our child so we can stay more compassionate and see things from his point of view.
- Builds a foundation of trust and partnership between parent and child, which is a precondition for him to trust us with his big feelings when he's upset (as opposed to lashing out).
- Convinces the child on a primal level that she really matters to the parent. (Of course you know she does, but sometimes she has doubts.)

Every child benefits from Special Time to reconnect with each parent often, if possible every day. Think of it as preventive maintenance to keep things on track in your family. And if you're having issues with your child, adding Special Time is the first thing to change. How do you do it?

1. **Announce that you want to have Special Time** with each child for fifteen minutes, as many days in the week as you can. Call it by the most special name there is, your child's name—for example, "Lauren Time."

2. **Choose a time when any other children are being looked after by someone else** (unless they are old enough to stay reliably occupied with something even while they sense their sibling getting something they'd like to have for themselves).

3. **Set a timer for fifteen minutes, with your child.** Turn off all phones so you can't hear incoming calls.

4. **Say, "Today you get to decide** what we will do with our 'Jonah Time.' Tomorrow I get to decide. We'll alternate. So now I am all yours for fifteen minutes. What would you like to do?"

5. **Give your child 100 percent of your attention** with no agenda and no distractions. Just follow his lead. If he wants to play with his blocks, don't rush in to tell him how to build the tower. Instead, enjoy watching your child explore, play, create. Occasionally say what you see: *"You are making that tower even taller. . . . You are standing on your tiptoes to get that block up there."* If she wants you to pull her in a circle on her skates until she falls down over and over, consider it your workout for the day and make it fun. Resist the urge to judge or evaluate your child. Don't suggest your own ideas unless she asks. Refrain from checking your cell phone. Just show up and give your child the tremendous gift of being seen and acknowledged.

6. **If she wants to do something that she isn't usually allowed to do,** consider whether there's a way to do it safely since you're there to help her. Maybe you always tell her that it's too dangerous to jump off the dresser onto the bed, but for Special Time you can push the bed next to the dresser and stay with her as she jumps to be sure she's safe. Maybe he has always wanted to play with his dad's shaving cream but you weren't about to let him waste a can of it, or to clean it up. For Special Time, you might decide to gift him with his own can of cheap shaving cream and let him play with it

in the tub, and then the two of you can clean it up together. If you can't grant her desire (go to Hawaii), find a way to approximate it (make grass skirts and play hula dancing together).

Why bother? Your child learns that you really do care about his desires, even if you can't always give him what he wants (so he's less likely to feel like he never gets his way, and more likely to cooperate in general). And since these desires will no longer be forbidden fruit after your child has a chance to indulge her curiosity and experience them, she's less likely to try them behind your back.

7. **When it's your turn to decide what to do,** initiate games to build emotional intelligence and bonding. Quiet talking and cuddling is okay once in a while, but your goal is to help your child release pent-up anxiety—another word for *fear*—and the most direct path is laughter. That usually means rough-housing in a way that gets your child giggling. I know, it sounds like a lot of energy for a tired parent. But it's only for fifteen minutes, and you'll find it energizes you, too. Do any game that gets your child laughing, which usually means engaging him in what scares or upsets him—but just enough to let him master it. Check "Playing with Your Child: Games for Emotional Intelligence" in Chapter 3 for ideas. You might also tackle a specific issue that your child is struggling to master, by, for instance, playing school. Let him be the teacher and assign you tons of homework and embarrass you when you don't know the answer. Or play basketball and let her dominate the court. In all these games, the parent bumbles ineffectually, blusters and hams it up, but just can't catch the strong, fast, smart child who always bests us. The goal

is giggling, which releases the same anxieties that are off-loaded with tears, so whatever gets your child giggling, do more of it.

8. **End Special Time when the timer buzzes.** Special Time needs boundaries around it to signal that the rules aren't the same as in regular life. When the timer goes off, give your child a big hug and tell him how much you loved this time together, and that you will have Special Time again very soon. If your child has a meltdown, handle it with the same compassionate empathy with which you would greet any other meltdown. (*"It's so hard to stop Special Time, I know."*) But don't think of that as extending Special Time, just as you would not "give in" to anything else that your child has a tantrum about.

9. **Be aware that often your child's emotions will bubble up during Special Time,** especially at the end. That doesn't mean she's a bottomless pit. It means she feels safer with you after this time together, so all those feelings she's been lugging around are now coming up to be processed. Or it means that letting go of you brings up all those feelings of how hard it is to share you. Often kids use the end of Special Time to express their upsets, so it's good to schedule a little cushion at the end in case your child has a meltdown, especially when you're just starting out, or when your child has been having a hard time. When the meltdown begins, just empathize, and give yourself a pat on the back for being the kind of parent your child trusts enough to express all these big feelings. (See "Emotion-Coaching Your Child Through a Meltdown" in Chapter 3.)

What's so special about Special Time? It transforms your relationship with your child. And since that relationship is what makes good parenting possible, you can't get more special than that.

DAILY HABITS TO STRENGTHEN AND SWEETEN YOUR RELATIONSHIP WITH YOUR CHILD

Parents are only human. There are days when all we can do is meet our children's most basic needs: Feed them, bathe them, keep an encouraging tone, hug them, and get them to sleep at a reasonable hour so we can do it all over again tomorrow. Given that parenting is the toughest job on earth—and most of us do it in our spare time, after we work at another job all day—the only way to keep a strong bond with our children is to build in daily habits of connection. What kinds of habits?

- **Develop small rituals that reconnect you with your child throughout your day, especially around separations.** For instance, plan on a five-minute snuggle with each child first thing every morning to reconnect and ease the transition into the day, before requiring your child to move into "executive functioning." (Many parents use TV for this transition, which further disconnects them and leads to a child who dawdles— and a frustrated parent.)

- **Give your child a short emotional refueling before you move into a situation that she'll perceive as a disconnection—** bedtime, daycare, even shopping or making dinner.

- **Twelve hugs a day.** Bonding is primal; for most children it's dependent on feeling physically connected to you. As the family therapist Virginia Satir famously said, "We need four hugs a day for survival. We need eight hugs a day for maintenance. We need twelve hugs a day for growth." Hug your child first thing every morning, every time you say good-bye or hello, and as often as you can in between. Lie down for a chat and snuggle at bedtime every night with each child. This is as essential for your nine-year-old as for your toddler. If he won't submit to so many hugs, give daily shoulder or foot rubs.

- **Turn off technology when you interact with your child.** Really. Your child will remember for the rest of her life that she was important enough to her parents that they turned off their cell phones when they were with her.

- **Evenings are family time.** Stop working before dinner so you can devote your evening to your family. Turn off your cell phone and computer. Eat dinner together without interruptions from phones or TV. Let manners take a backseat to creating a warm tone that includes everyone.

- **Special Time.** Every day, ten to twenty minutes with each child, individually, and longer on weekends. Alternate doing what your child wants and doing what you want, and on your days to choose, resist the urge to structure the time with activities. Instead, roughhouse to help your child giggle out his anxieties and bond with you. (See "Playing with Your Child: Games for Emotional Intelligence" in Chapter 3.)

- **When you physically reconnect, consciously refocus your attention on your child.** Otherwise, it's natural to keep thinking about the meeting you just attended or what you need to pick up at the grocery store. Until you've re-established the connection, keep distractions to a minimum. If you turn off the radio when your child gets in the car, you're much more likely to make a connection and hear about what happened at soccer. When one of you arrives home, don't answer the phone during your greeting, even if it was a routine separation.

- **Attune to your child's mood.** Your moods are unlikely to be in sync after time apart. To reconnect, you will probably need to adjust your mood to match your child's.

- **Connect on their level.** Gordon Neufeld and Gabor Mate, authors of the book *Hold On to Your Kids* and originators of the phrase "collecting your child," call this "getting in their face in a friendly way." Start with a hug hello, make eye contact, and then stay in their space physically until you've re-established a warm connection. This is easy with a two-year-old, but is your eight-year-old too distracted to connect? Playfully "worship" her foot with a massage and she'll most likely start downloading her day to you. You're starting a tradition that will keep her willing to talk right into the teen years.

- **Don't let little rifts build up.** Your relationship with your child should feel good. Children need to know deep in their bones that their parents adore them and take delight in their company. If that's not how you feel, get whatever support you need to work it through positively. Choosing to withdraw (except temporarily, strategically) when your child seems intent on driving you away is *always* a mistake. Every difficulty is an opportunity to get closer, as you extend understanding and your child feels truly seen, heard, and accepted.

- **Remember the 5-to-1 ratio.** Scientists have found a way to predict which couples will end up divorcing: those who don't ensure that they have at least five positive interactions for every negative one. Maintaining this 5-to-1 ratio is probably effective insurance in every relationship, including between parents and children. If you notice a strained interaction with your child, that's your reminder to find five opportunities to connect in the very near future.

USE CONNECTION TO GET YOUR CHILD OUT THE DOOR IN THE MORNING

My daughter has a really hard time with transitions, including waking up in the morning. She was waking up yelling and angry. I started snuggling with her for five minutes when she wakes up—and we have turned the morning routine around! She now loves the close time and is ready to get up, happy, and cooperative when the five minutes are up.
   —Kym, mother of a five-year-old

If you're having a hard time getting your child out of the house on time, here's the secret. Reframe your idea of the morning routine. What if your main job were to connect emotionally? That way, your child would have a genuinely "full cup." Not only would he be more ready to cooperate with you, he'd be more able to rise to the developmental challenges of his day. How?

- **Get everyone to bed as early as possible.** If you have to wake your children in the morning, they aren't getting enough sleep. Every hour of sleep less than they need sets them back a year in access to brain function, meaning they act a year younger.

- **Get yourself to bed earlier.** I'm sorry to be the bearer of bad tidings, but if you have to use an alarm, you aren't getting enough sleep, either. Your child depends on you to start your own day with a "full cup." There's no way to stay patient when you're exhausted.

- **Build in extra time.** Get up earlier than your kids so you're emotionally centered before you interact with them. Plan on routinely getting to work fifteen minutes earlier than you're due. Half the time, you won't make it, but you also won't lose your temper at your kids because you won't actually be late. The other half of the time, you'll have a more relaxed start to your workday so you'll be more effective at work.

- **Prepare the night before.** Pack backpacks and briefcases, make lunches, lay out clothes, prepare the coffeepot, plan breakfast. Involve children the night before, too, so they choose their clothing and find that toy car.

- **Make sure you get five minutes of relaxed snuggle time with each child as they wake up.** I know, it sounds impossible. But if everything else is already done, you can relax for ten minutes. That time connecting with your child will transform your morning.

- **Use connection routines to make transitions easier.** Kids find transitions hard, and the morning is full of transitions. So if getting her out of bed is a challenge, end your morning snuggle by holding hands as you go downstairs together, and make that a meaningful connection time for your child, during which you both come up with something you're grateful for, or something you're looking forward to today. (Naturally, yours will relate to your child.)

- **Keep the routine as simple as possible.** There are no rules. Why can't she sleep in the T-shirt and leggings she'll wear to school? Why can't he eat a sandwich in the car instead of cereal at the table? Why can't you just put her hair in a ponytail or let her sleep with it in a braid to skip brushing it?

- **Realize that children need your help to move through the routine.** Empower your child by taking photos of him doing his morning tasks and making a chart with him that you can point to if he gets derailed. But if your goal is to give your child a good start to his day, then your job is helping him feel happy and connected as he moves through the routine. That might mean you bring his clothes downstairs with you and he gets dressed next to you while you're feeding the baby so you can acknowledge him: *"I notice you picked your blue shirt again. . . . You're working so hard on figuring out which shoe goes on which foot. . . . Today you're humming while you get dressed."* Remember, getting dressed is your priority, not his. Your presence is what motivates him.

- **Offer choices.** No one likes to be pushed around. Does he want to brush his teeth standing on the stool at the kitchen sink while you're getting the baby out of the high chair, or upstairs in the bathroom? Does she want to put her shoes on first, or her jacket on first? Cede control whenever you can.

- **Play it out.** Sometime on the weekend, grab a mom and baby stuffed animal. Have them act out the morning routine. Have the little one resist, whine, collapse. Have the mom "lose it" (but don't scare your child by overdoing it; have the mom be a funny, incompetent bumbler). Your child will be fascinated.

Then, hand your kid the mom and play out the scenario again, with you being the kid. Make it funny so you can both giggle and let off tension. Make sure to include scenarios in which the kid goes to school in his PJs, or the mom goes to work in her PJs, or the kid has to yell at the mom to hurry up and get ready, or the mom says, *"Who cares about that meeting? Let's tell the boss it's more important to find your toy car!"* Give him in fantasy what he can't have in reality. You may learn something about how to make things work better. Almost certainly, you'll see more understanding and cooperation from your child on Monday.

- **Ruthlessly prioritize.** If both parents are working full time while children are small, you'll have to let go of most other expectations during the week. That's the only way you can go to bed early enough to stay in a good mood in the morning. And your child depends on your good mood to regulate her own moods. Don't worry; these years don't last forever. You're laying a wonderful foundation for her to take more and more charge of her own morning routine.

Modern life puts pressures on kids and parents that undermine our relationships. But we need that connection to smooth the speed bumps of life. Our children need it, not only to cooperate but to thrive. Luckily, when we make connection our priority, everything else gets a little bit easier.

USE CONNECTION TO MAKE BEDTIME EASIER

Why is bedtime so hard for many families? Because the needs of parents and children clash. To parents, bedtime is the time they finally get to separate from their children and have a little time to themselves. To children, bedtime is the time they're forced to separate from their parents and lie in the dark by themselves. On top of that, children are exhausted and wound up, and parents are exhausted and fed up. No wonder it's the single most challenging time in most families.

But stressful, disconnected evenings punctuated by yelling and tears undermine your child's sense of security and ultimately make bedtime harder. We all want the last thing our child feels before falling asleep to be the safe warmth of our love, rather than angry threats. It's not easy to stay calm through all the bedtime testing, but it is possible. Here's how:

- Make a chart with pictures of your child doing each evening task, complete with times, so you can transform from traffic cop to partner, helping your child move happily through the routine.

- Divide parental time equally between children so that each one gets the connection she needs.

- Don't do anything else during the bedtime routine so that you can focus on moving it along rather than getting distracted by phone calls or emails.

- Remember that bedtime brings up all children's separation anxiety. Include a "separation" game like Hide-and-Seek or the Bye-Bye Game (discussed in Chapter 3) every evening to help your child giggle out some of that anxiety. But remember that kids also need a chance to calm down physically, so no rambunctious roughhousing in the hour before sleep.

- Banish electronic screens, which artificially depress the sleep hormone melatonin, for at least an hour before bedtime.

- Give each child ten minutes of private quality time after lights-out for a snuggle and check-in.

- Do whatever you need to do to stay calm. Losing your temper at bedtime will just trigger more separation anxiety and make things harder.

- If your child has problems falling asleep without being held, that's completely normal. Some children learn this skill on their own. Others need your help to learn it. The good news is that there are gentle methods that don't require you to leave your child alone to cry. Sleep issues are beyond the scope of this book, but there's lots of info on the Aha! Parenting website about them.

- Go to bed early enough yourself so that you aren't exhausted the next evening during the bedtime routine.

TEN WAYS TO BECOME A BRILLIANT LISTENER

The greatest compliment that was ever paid me was when someone asked what I thought, and attended to my answer.
    —Henry David Thoreau

The single most important skill for staying close to your child is listening. Not teaching, advising, or offering solutions. Not only does your child not want that from you, but it would get in the way of his coming up with his own solutions. What your child needs from you is deep listening. Sometimes you'll be listening to her words. Sometimes you'll be noticing that his actions are telling you something. Brilliant listeners hear beyond the words.

Becoming a brilliant listener is just a matter of developing the habit. But like all habits, it takes practice. How?

1. **Remember to close your mouth.** Is it a coincidence that the letters in the word *listen* can also be used to spell *silent*?

2. **When you begin any interaction with your child, pay attention.** Are you on autopilot, harried, reactive? If so, use your inner pause button. (Yes, you do have time for the pause button. It takes three seconds.) Stop. Breathe. Close the laptop. Look in your child's eyes. Now listen.

3. **Notice the little conversation openers** your child offers, and respond. It takes real self-discipline to tear yourself away from what you're doing to focus on a child's question, but it's an indication to him of whether he can count on you when he needs you. And much more important than any conversation you initiate, like when you try to get him to tell you what happened at school today.

4. **If you can't listen now, say so:** *"I hear you're angry about that. I want to focus on our discussion, and I can't while I'm trying to get everyone out the door to school. Can we make a date to talk about this after dinner tonight?"* Then, don't forget. Show up. That's how you earn your child's trust.

5. **Be fully present.** This is your time to listen to your child. That problem at the office can wait. Your child knows when you're really listening. She may not show it, but it erodes her sense of self-worth when you pretend to and don't.

6. **To open discussion, actively acknowledge and reflect his feelings,** without judgment or suggestion. *"You are so angry at your brother"* and *"You seem worried about the field trip today"* are conversation openers; *"You just have to make the effort to get along with your brother!"* and *"Don't be such a baby about the field trip; of course you're going!"* are conversation closers.

7. **Ask nonjudgmental questions that require real answers.** *"Who did you sit with at lunch today?"* or *"How was the spelling test?"* will get you a lot further than *"How was school today?"* Questions that begin with *"Why"* often make kids defensive; *"Why did you wear that?"* won't work nearly as well as *"What do you think most of the kids will be wearing on the field trip?"*

8. **Don't jump in with solutions and advice.** That means you'll have to manage your own anxiety about the issue. Your child needs a chance to vent, and he can't think well until he does. Then he needs a chance to figure out his own solutions, which is how he develops confidence and competence.

9. **Keep the conversation safe for everyone.** People can't listen when they're upset. If they don't feel safe, they generally withdraw or attack, and the thinking parts of the brain shut down. If you notice your child getting angry, scared, or hurt, back up and reconnect. Remind her—and yourself—how much you love her, and that you're committed to finding a solution that works for everyone.

10. **Keep the conversation safe for your child by managing your own emotions.** Don't take it personally. Breathe. Above

all, if you start feeling responsible (*"I could have prevented this!"*) or terrified (*"I can't believe this is happening to my child!"*), get a grip and put your feelings aside. This isn't about you right now, and your being upset won't help. In fact, no matter what your child is talking about, you can process it later. Remind yourself that what's most important here is helping your child work through these difficult feelings and, when he's ready, helping him come up with a plan of action that works for him.

BUT HOW DO I GET MY CHILD TO LISTEN TO ME?!

One of the most common questions I hear from parents is, "How can I get my kid to *listen* to me?" Children have a lot on their minds, from whom to sit with at lunch to soccer tryouts to the newest computer game. Parents can be dismally low on their list. Even toddlers have different priorities than we do, and they don't understand at all why it is so important to take their bath *right this minute!* Of course, the parents who ask me this aren't really talking about listening. They're wondering how to get their child to do what they say. The secret? Connection before correction. Here's how:

- **Don't start talking until you have your child's attention.** Get down on your child's level and touch him lightly. Look him in the eye. Wait until he looks up. Then start talking. If you can't do this for some reason—for example, if you're in the car—make sure you have his attention by asking, *"Can I tell you something?"*

- **Don't repeat yourself.** If you've asked once and not gotten a response, don't just repeat yourself. You don't have your child's attention. Go back to step one.

- **Use fewer words.** Most of us dilute our message and lose our child's attention by using too many words. Use as few words as possible when you give instructions.

- **See it from his point of view.** If you were busy with something you liked doing and your spouse ordered you to stop and do something else that was not a priority to you, how would you feel? Might you tune out your spouse? It will help immensely if you can acknowledge his view: *"I know it's hard to stop playing now, honey. But I need you to. . . ."*

- **Engage cooperation.** No one wants to listen to someone who's barking orders. Keep your tone warm and give choices. *"It's bath time. Do you want to go now or in five minutes? Okay, five minutes with no fuss? Let's shake on it."*

- **Soothe, don't inflame.** When we're emotional, kids get distracted by our emotion and lose sight of our message. If your priority is getting everyone in the car, don't waste time exploding about why they didn't listen to you and get ready when you first asked. That will just make everyone more upset, including you. Take a deep breath and help your child get ready. Once you're in the car, you can ask them to help you brainstorm ways to get out of the house on time.

- **Set up routines.** The more routines you have, the less you have to be a drill sergeant. If you take photos of your child doing her routine tasks and put them onto a small poster, she'll take responsibility for them over time. Your role will be limited to asking questions: *"What else do you have to do before you leave the house? Let's check the schedule."*

- **Model attentive listening.** If you stare at your phone while your child tells you about his day, you're role-modeling how communication is handled in your house. If you really want your child to listen to you, stop what you're doing and listen to him. It takes only a few minutes. Do this when he's a preschooler and he'll still be willing to talk to you when he's a teenager. You'll be so glad you did.

WHEN YOUR CHILD JUST SHUTS DOWN

I say, "I know something must've really made you mad at school today. I am here to help you but you may not smack your brother in the head. . . . You seem so mad. . . . Can you tell me what's going on?" She will yell, "Stop talking; I don't want to talk!"

—Chris, about her eight-year-old daughter

When our child yells at us, "Stop talking," it's usually because:

- **She's embarrassed to tell you about what happened.** Kids are often embarrassed to tell parents they've been bullied, for instance, because it makes them feel such shame; or:

- **She's worried about how you'll respond.** Will you agree with the teacher? Berate her for handling the incident badly? Call the other girl's mother and embarrass her? Act like she's an idiot who's not capable of solving her own problems? or:

- **The emotions feel so crummy to her that she doesn't want to feel them,** so she's trying to stuff them down and make them go away. If she tells you, she'll feel terrible again as they sweep over her.

Unfortunately, feelings that she can't express will still bother her, and she'll act them out—for instance, by smacking her brother. So how do we support our child to express the feelings that are making her act out? (After, of course, setting the clear limit that her brother is not for hitting.)

- **Don't make her talk.** Prying won't help her feel safe. She may or may not need to talk, but she does need to feel safe enough to express her feelings. Stay available and loving, and set appropriate limits as she expresses her anger, and sooner or later those feelings will bubble up.

- **Get her giggling.** If your child will let you start a pillow fight with her so that you both end up laughing a lot, it releases the same stress hormones as a big cry. Once she feels better, she'll be more likely to share what she was upset about. But she may not even need to talk about it. What she really needed was to melt those feelings that were stuck in her belly.

- **Use Special Time.** Often kids use this time to express their upsets, but they usually don't need to talk about what upset them—just to laugh, cry, or play the feelings out.

- **Earn her trust.** When she does share things with you, do you regulate your own emotions so you don't fly off the handle?

- **Find your compassion.** If we can get past our anger that she just smacked her brother and feel real compassion for the suffering she must be in, she'll sense that compassion in our tone. She may still try to resist feeling her emotions, but once she feels safe, they'll bubble up.

Why bother? You're helping your child develop emotional intelligence. You're supporting her in solving her problems. You're creating a stronger bond with her. And it sure would be nice if she stopped smacking her brother upside the head.

WHEN YOU AND YOUR CHILD ARE STUCK IN NEGATIVITY

My anger and exhaustion were as raw as my three-year-old's. . . . Finally it came to me from one of your newsletters. . . . I said, "It has been such a tough day and I think you need a hug." I picked him up and he clung to me like a monkey in that dark room and squeezed his body close to me so much that it took my breath away and all my anger just melted. Even though I had raised my voice and we both had said hurtful things to each other—in the end it is just about trust and love. I said, "I'm so sorry I yelled at you . . . It has been a tough night for you and for Mommy, and it is okay. . . . All of us can have tough days, and today was a tough day, wasn't it? Tomorrow we will have a better day, okay?" He nodded against me and I told him that I loved him, and we continued onto our evening song and connectedness rituals, like we had never had such a disastrous evening.

—Kristina, mother of two

We've all had those moments with our child. When we're stuck and we don't know what to do. When our own feelings are so raw, our frustration so intense, our cup so empty, we stop caring for the moment about what our child needs and just lash out.

Then we're overcome with remorse. But in that moment, with the tidal wave of our emotions washing over us, what can we possibly do to save the situation?

All we need to do is remember: Connect.

No matter how ugly your child is acting, what he or she wants more than anything in the world is to reconnect with you.

It may seem impossible, but if we feel the slightest glimmer of desire to turn things around, we can grab it. We don't even have to know how. We can just choose love. We can always find a way to reach out to our child and reconnect. We can always find a way to heal things, even when we're in a cycle of negativity that's gone too far.

So stop berating yourself for letting things get out of control. Hug your imperfect self. Reach out for your child.

In the end, it is always about love. Love never fails.

PART THREE

COACHING, NOT CONTROLLING

I've learned so much from your writing about how to interact positively with my son instead of having just "not yelling" as my only parenting tool. Now I can be firm without being angry and find humor in just about everything he does because I'm not tied up in a need to control his actions.

—Tricia, mother of a two-year-old

The transition from the baby to the toddler years at around thirteen months is famously difficult, as little ones become less distractible and harder to control. Parents who think of themselves as coaches have an easier time with this transition, and all the other transitions right into the teen years, than parents who think they need to control their child's behavior or feelings.

Most parents think it's our job to control our children, but when we try we're bound to fail. We find ourselves feeling powerless, casting about for a bigger stick or carrot to persuade our child. We respond to our child's behavior with force or threats to gain compliance ("Don't you speak to me that way, young lady!"), leaving her to figure out for herself how to learn self-management skills.

By contrast, when we think of ourselves as coaches, we know that all we have is influence—so we work hard to stay respected and connected, so our child wants to "follow" us. Like an athletic coach who helps kids develop strength and skills to play their best game, coaching parents help kids develop the mental and emotional muscle, and the life skills, to manage themselves and live their best life.

Besides connecting (which we focused on in Part 2 of this book), most interactions with our child fall into one of three categories: dealing with emotions, teaching appropriate behavior, and teaching skills. In the next three chapters, we'll explore how to approach each of these areas of life with your child from a coaching, rather than controlling, perspective. The result? A happy, self-motivated, responsible child with constructive life habits who wants to "do the right thing" and has the skills and resiliency to realize his dreams.

Consider the contrast in results between controlling and coaching:

In Response to Child's:	Parent Tries to Control	Parent Coaches
Inappropriate behavior	Works short-term when kids are young as long as parent is present.	Raises kids who *want* to "do right."
Anger	Forces kids to repress anger, which bursts out uncontrolled at other times.	Helps kids learn to manage anger.
Emotions	Child fends off emotion by becoming controlling, but lags in self-regulation.	Child develops self-regulation and resilience.
Developing values	Child is motivated to avoid punishment, not by concern for others.	Child "follows" parents' teachings.
Developing life skills, from brushing teeth to doing homework	Parent nags child, essentially taking responsibility.	Parent provides child with support to enjoy becoming responsible for himself.
Developing self-motivation	Child resents pressure from parents.	Child feels empowered and motivated.

3

Raising a Child Who Can Manage Himself: Emotion Coaching

If your emotional abilities aren't in hand, if you don't have self-awareness, if you are not able to manage your distressing emotions, if you can't have empathy and have effective relationships, then no matter how smart you are, you are not going to get very far.

—DANIEL GOLEMAN, *EMOTIONAL INTELLIGENCE*[1]

Whether we know it or not, we're constantly coaching our child on how to handle emotion. In fact, most of our interactions with our child are emotional exchanges of one sort or another. The way we as parents respond to our child's feelings shapes his relationship with emotions—his own and others'—for the rest of his life.

It's certainly more convenient to shush or threaten an upset child than to help her process her emotions. Luckily, children who know from experience that their emotions will be heard learn to modulate them. Because emotion coaching helps your child develop emotional self-control earlier than her peers, it actually makes for easier parenting.

But let's not forget our other two Big Ideas here—Regulating Yourself and Fostering Connection. When we coach our child through turbulence, it's an essential time to stay connected. In fact,

WHAT'S EQ?

Someone who has a high emotional intelligence quotient (EQ) is smart about emotions, just as someone with a high IQ is smart in her thinking. Scientists are finding that while genes influence IQ, the brain is like a muscle and can be shaped and strengthened, allowing us to stretch our innate IQ. Similarly, while some of us are born calmer, or with more impulse control, these tendencies can be shaped and strengthened to expand our EQ. The core components of high EQ are the following:

- **The ability to self-soothe.** The key to managing emotion is to allow, acknowledge, and tolerate our intense emotions so that they evaporate, without getting stuck in them or taking actions we'll later regret. Self-soothing is what enables us to manage our anxiety and upsets, which in turn allows us to work through emotionally charged issues in a constructive way.

- **Emotional self-awareness and acceptance.** If we don't understand the emotions washing over us, they scare us, and we can't tolerate them. We repress our hurt, fear, or disappointment. Those emotions, no longer regulated by our conscious mind, have a way of popping out unmodulated, as when a preschooler socks his sister or we (as adults) lose our tempers or eat a pint of ice cream. By contrast, children raised in a home in which there are limits on behavior but not on feelings grow up understanding that all emotions are acceptable, a part of being human. That understanding gives them more control over their emotions.

- **Impulse control.** Emotional intelligence liberates us from knee-jerk emotional reactions. A child (or adult) with high

EQ will act rather than react and problem-solve rather than blame. It doesn't mean you never get angry or anxious, only that you don't fly off the handle. As a result, our lives and relationships work better.

- **Empathy.** Empathy is the ability to see and feel something from the other's point of view. When you're adept at understanding the mental and emotional states of other people, you resolve differences constructively and connect deeply with others. Naturally, empathy makes us better communicators.

when kids are in the grip of strong emotions, it's a signal that they need to reconnect with us, as we'll see in this chapter. And since we inevitably get triggered by our child's upsets, our ability to calm ourselves determines whether we can coach our child. This chapter will give you specific strategies for that as well.

Why Emotion-Coach?

Most parents take their job as teachers very seriously. We teach our children colors. Brushing teeth. Right from wrong.

But sometimes we neglect two more important lessons all children need to know: how to manage their feelings (and therefore their behavior), and how to understand other people's feelings. These two skills form the core of what psychologists have come to call the EQ, or the *emotional intelligence quotient*. It's a core part of human development, and while it sounds complicated, it's important for parents to wrap their arms around it.

Why does emotional intelligence matter? We all know the

answer, with a moment's reflection. Emotions matter. You can't tackle a big project if you're overcome by anxiety. You can't work through a marital conflict without understanding your spouse's perspective. You can't handle conflict on the job or with a friend if you don't manage your anger. In other words, the ability of a human being to manage his emotions in a healthy way will determine the quality of his life—maybe even more fundamentally than his IQ. Even a child's academic success is determined as much by EQ as by IQ, because intellectual learning depends on managing anxiety and motivating ourselves. Best of all for parents, children with solid emotional intelligence can better manage their emotions and therefore their behavior, so they tend to be both self-disciplined and cooperative. Kids like it. Parents like it. Everybody wins.

How do children develop the foundational traits of emotional intelligence? They learn them! Not from TV, not from school, but from you. You're emotion-coaching every day. Specifically, you're helping your child become aware of her feelings and express them in age-appropriate ways, which is the beginning of self-regulation. Once she's out of the grip of those big emotions, she can shift gears to solve whatever problem triggered them. Let's look at some specific strategies so you can do an even better job of emotion-coaching your child throughout childhood. We'll start with how newborn infants lay the foundations for emotional intelligence in their very brain structure.

Emotional Intelligence as Your Child Grows

BABIES (0–13 MONTHS): A BEDROCK OF TRUST

The primary developmental task for an infant is learning to trust. It sets the stage for all that lies ahead. Albert Einstein said that the most important question for each of us to answer is *"Is this a friendly universe?"* Infancy is when we answer that question.

Almost a hundred years ago, psychologist Harry Stack Sullivan originated the idea that infants pick up anxiety (which is a form of fear, or lack of trust) from their parents. Research confirms that a parent's touch, voice, and movements can either soothe a child or stimulate anxiety. Babies' stress hormones shoot up in response to angry voices—including those on TV—even while they're asleep. Our calm voice, loving eye contact, and secure hold as we care for our baby gives her the message that the world is a safe place where she can relax and trust. Every parent who has ever bathed an infant knows what I mean.

Humans are adaptable precisely because they're unfinished; the baby responds to her environment by "building" a brain that will best help her to flourish in that environment. If she has optimal conditions—physical nourishment, warm arms to carry and soothe her, a responsive caregiver who engages with her—she'll build a brain that's geared for prompt self-soothing, happy moods, and intimate connection. If the environment doesn't offer her what she needs, or it seems dangerous—for instance, loud noises without accompanying reassurance—the brain she builds may be hyper-vigilant and distrustful, primed for fight-or-flight and competition for scarce resources.

That's why it's our job as parents to provide our little one with the reassurance, as constantly as possible, that he's safe. Let's consider the profound shaping of the brain when your baby is flooded with panic chemicals, such as adrenaline and cortisol, two of the fight-or-flight hormones. Whether he's feeling hunger, indigestion, or the terror of having been put down alone (where his stone-age instincts tell him that tigers might eat him), he panics. Luckily, your baby's crying makes you crazy, so of course you pick him up to soothe him. Every time he cries and you respond, you're helping his brain wire itself for self-soothing when he's a little older. What you see is that he calms down when you comfort him. What's happening biologically is that his body responds to feeling safe in your arms by sending out soothing biochemicals, which in turn create more neural pathways and receptors for these self-soothing hormones. Psychologically, he learns that his hunger and other feelings can be alleviated, that help is forthcoming, that someone is protecting him, helping him regulate himself. No need to panic. He can trust in this friendly universe to meet his needs. And he begins to develop a positive working model of human relationships, one that feels warm and safe and loving.

THE TRUTH ABOUT SELF-SOOTHING

What about the advice you've heard that a baby will learn to self-soothe if you just leave her to cry? It's scientifically unsound, and a misuse of the term *self-soothe*. It's well documented that sustained, uncomforted infant crying causes increased heart rate and blood pressure, reduced oxygen levels, and skyrocketing cortisol, adrenaline, and other stress hormones. Babies who are left to cry may eventually cry themselves to sleep, but that's exhaustion, not soothing. She's still swamped with stress hormones, which shape her brain to become more emotionally reactive. True, babies learn what to expect, so they'll stop pleading to be parented during the night, or even during the day, if no one responds to their cries. Babies in orphanages don't perpetually cry, but we wouldn't consider their adaptation healthy.

Obviously, the experience of babies who receive responsive care from their parents during the day but are left at night to cry alone can't be compared to the experience of babies in an orphanage. My point is that the lack of protest doesn't mean the baby doesn't need the parents, only that the child has learned that the parents won't respond. In fact, while babies who have been sleep trained may go quietly into their cribs on subsequent days, their stress hormones still shoot up, just as they did during the sleep training. In other words, the baby is in a state of stress but stays quiet because he's been taught that asking for help is futile.[2]

Unfortunately, given what we know about brain development, it's reasonable to conclude that a baby whose cries go unanswered on a regular basis—whether night or day—is building a slightly different kind of brain. The flood of cortisol associated with uncomforted infant crying puts the immune system, learning, and other nonessential functions on standby while it focuses on the crisis at hand, which prevents her brain from building as many neural connections for soothing.[3]

Leaving our baby to cry also changes us as parents. We have to turn off our natural empathy for our baby, the same empathy that is so essential to helping our child develop emotional intelligence. Our natural tendency to see things from her perspective diminishes a bit, so we're likely to find parenting harder. Leaving our child alone to cry can be the first step on a slippery slope of disconnection that erodes both our ability to be the responsive parent our child needs and our own satisfaction as a parent.

Of course, it would be inconvenient if you had to be present to help your child regulate his emotions and physiology every time he gets upset for the rest of his life. Luckily, nature has a better idea. Over time, as upsets swamp him, he becomes able to use those neural pathways he's building to soothe himself. The more oxytocin he releases in response to your loving attention, for instance, the more oxytocin receptors he makes, and the more easily he can calm himself and feel good. He's even beginning to create nerve connections that allow his prefrontal cortex (the beginnings of his thinking brain) to counteract alarms in his amygdala (part of the emotional brain). You're the facilitator for your baby to build a brain and nervous system that makes it easy for him to manage his anxiety for the rest of his life.

Anyone who's ever spent time with a newborn knows they can be difficult to soothe. Don't worry. Your baby's brain development doesn't require that you be perfect. Human parents never are. You only have to be good enough, so that most of the time you show up in a soothing way when your baby needs you. It means you hold him while he cries and offer him what we all need when we're in distress: a compassionate witness.

Even if your little one keeps crying while you hold her, she feels your arms around her. This is very different from the uncomforted crying that is so stressful to infants. She may be in pain or she may simply be overstimulated and need to release all those pent-up stresses of being newly alive in an overwhelming world. Either way, your presence is doing its job, giving her the safety to express her emotions—and to feel heard. This crying actually releases stress hormones. Think of it this way: She had a hard day, or (even months ago) a hard birth, and she wants to tell you about it. She may be crying, but it's a good, cleansing cry. She's releasing all the cortisol, adrenaline, and other pent-up stress hormones from her overstimulating experiences in this crazy new world. Because you're holding her, her body is responding to her crying by building neural pathways to deliver calming hormones. This is hard work for you, but the good news is that if you can just keep breathing to calm yourself, and keep providing a safe "holding environment" for her, she'll eventually build the neural connections to soothe herself.

"Good enough" really is good enough. No parent can ever pick up on all of her baby's cues. We're human, so we get distracted, worried, anxious, scared, depressed, sick—in short, we can't always show up as we'd like to for our children. Remember researcher Edward Tronick's finding that even the most attentive parents are only attuned to about 30 percent of their baby's cues?[4]

The good news is that when we miss a cue from our infant and a small miscommunication or rift happens between us, we can repair it. In fact, the experience of the parent not understanding, but then reconnecting, is a crucial lesson for the baby. How does this happen? Let's say, building on our example from Chapter 2, that we've been having a lovely time playing with our baby. We shake the rattle and he laughs uproariously. But after a while, his excitement overwhelms him. He feels himself spinning out of control, frightened. He needs to calm himself, to return to a lower level of arousal. He looks away. Some parents would notice right away and realize their baby needs a break. But not us. We're having such a good time. It's so exciting to see our little one so happy! And maybe there's more; maybe we're not feeling so great about our parenting right now because soothing the baby can be challenging, but look, we can make him laugh, and laugh more . . . so we miss his cue. He continues to look away, even though we get in his face and shake the rattle more insistently. He's overwhelmed. His face crumples. He begins to cry.

So we misattuned. Our intrusiveness actually drove our baby to tears. Is he damaged for life? Luckily, no. We may be slow, but we aren't hopeless. We take a deep breath and shift gears, from excitement to soothing. We pick our little guy up and begin to speak soothingly. He continues to cry, but less loudly, and his breathing slows. He's calming down. He's learned that the universe isn't perfect, and sometimes he has to raise his voice to be heard, but he has the power to repair a rift in your relationship. Because you responded quickly to his distress—which has been shown to be the most important attunement to how infants adjust[5]—he's learned that it's a safe universe and he can count on you to respond when he needs you. Quick repair after a rupture in empathy by the parent is part of how children build resilience, or the faith that things will work out if they just keep trying. In fact, every time we misattune, our little one gets a small chance to practice regulating himself without our help.[6] Sometimes he won't be able to, but often he will, and he'll learn how—just like taking those first steps. So while you don't want to intentionally create difficult experiences for your child—life will supply plenty without your assistance—your misattunements really are learning opportunities as long as they're followed by reconnection and outweighed by positive moments.

Soothing your baby not only helps her learn to self-soothe, it helps her become a more calm, friendly, happy person, not just as a child but throughout life. Many studies show that babies who receive above-average levels of affection, attention, and soothing from their parents grow into adults who are more relaxed, emotionally regulated, and happier. Not surprisingly, they're even able to better regulate their weight.[7]

This ability to self-soothe is the precondition for emotional intelligence. And he'll develop it as he learns to trust that you're there to help him whenever he needs you, that you can read his cues and help him regulate himself. That's the foundation of secure attachment. Based on his first year with you, he'll conclude that it's a friendly universe, and that he'll be okay in it.

Now let's look at how he solidifies those good feelings about himself as life gets more complicated.

TODDLERS (13–36 MONTHS): UNCONDITIONAL LOVE

If you've been soothing your baby when she cries, she'll become more and more able to handle stress without getting hijacked by panic. That's a good thing, because the toddler years are probably the most challenging in human development, for parent and child alike. If we can help our toddler develop a healthy relationship with her emotions, she'll have the foundation she needs for a high EQ throughout her life. The side benefit is that high-EQ toddlers are a lot easier for parents.

Why are the toddler years such a challenge emotionally? Because job one for the toddler is asserting himself. Your toddler needs to feel that he has an impact on the world and some control over his experience. This developing sense of power is a good thing. It's what allows him to eventually take responsibility for himself.

Unfortunately, the toddler's task of self-empowerment often conflicts with another crucial developmental task, which is loving himself. Why? Because many parents aren't prepared for their delightful baby to emerge as an opinionated person, ready to advocate for his desires. Of course they still love him. But suddenly, those formerly doting parents—the embodiment of the friendly universe—are giving a very different message:

NO!... Don't touch that!... Lie still while I change you!... Stop crying, it won't hurt!... Then I'll put you into that car seat!... Don't you say no to me!... Leave that alone!... You broke it!... Don't you hit me!... Bad boy!... You bit me, you little devil!

When she notices how perfectly that slice of bologna will fit into the CD player, Dad smacks her hand. When she begins to howl because her doting parents have been transformed into monsters, Mom warns Dad: "Ignore her. We can't reward a tantrum." She howls harder. Her understanding parents, the ones she counts on to help her navigate both her inner and outer worlds, have abandoned her.

These parents adore their child and are doing the best they

can to teach her responsible rules. But the assumption that we have to withdraw our love to get our toddler to do what we want is a dangerous one. When we repeatedly break our connection with our child, whether in the name of discipline or independence, it undermines the close relationship we've worked so hard to build.

The toddler can't be blamed for wondering if the universe is friendly only when he does what it wants. He may well conclude that being himself is not acceptable. He can't yet control most of his behavior, and he can't really distinguish between his emotions (his "self") and his behavior, so even if you're careful to say, *"It's bad to hit"* instead of *"You're a bad boy!"* the distinction is lost on him. He interprets our attempts at discipline as a message that if he wants to be loved by the masters of the universe (his parents), he needs to repress certain emotions and pretend to be good.

Unfortunately, that's a losing strategy. The overlay of shame that develops from feeling that we're bad can shadow us through life. Most adults stumble across this repressed shame occasionally and find it at least temporarily disabling. It doesn't help the toddler's behavior, either. Humans can act only as good as we feel, and a child who feels that she's secretly "bad" isn't likely to act "good." It's classic to see a toddler smacking the family dog over the head while intoning, *"No! Don't hit the doggie."*

And what about those tantrums, the hallmark of the toddler? Like the rest of us, toddlers build up stress hormones such as cortisol and adrenaline as they cope with the upsets of daily life. As we get older, we can discharge those biochemicals by thinking and talking, in addition to the moving, crying, yawning, and sweating that little ones do. While toddlers are becoming increasingly verbal, their frontal cortex can't yet override their emotional centers to process strong emotions verbally. Luckily, nature has designed babies and toddlers with a fail-safe to discharge the physiological residue of their fears and frustrations: tantrums. Toddlers don't enjoy tantrums; they would rather feel connected and cherished. But when their emotions are swamping them, their brain development isn't sufficient to maintain rational control. So their physiology helps them restore equilibrium by having a meltdown to release all those feelings and the accompanying biochemicals.

As with soothing an infant, parents who patiently sit with their tantrumming toddler are helping him learn to self-soothe and manage his emotions. But too many parents make an all-too-understandable mistake. They assume tantrums are within their toddler's control, that he's "throwing" a tantrum to manipulate them and get his way. Some may respond to tantrums by threatening abandonment—otherwise known as ignoring the child until he calms down—or punishing the child in some way. The research on this is clear as a bell. When young children feel abandoned, it triggers anxiety that may temporarily stop the tantrum, but it creates deep insecurity. You know you would never leave your child in the grocery store, but he doesn't. And when we respond to toddlers with a little smack, they will sometimes pull it together in the moment. But toddlers whose parents respond to their challenging behavior with physical discipline end up more aggressive, whiny, and defiant by the time they're preschoolers.[8] We can understand this if we remember that the toddler is not a lab rat who can be trained with physical pain or threat. Instead, he's a complicated human. Parental disapproval signals possible abandonment, which triggers primal panic. His reaction, of course, is to try to comply. He concludes that his self-assertion, impulse to explore, sadness, disappointment, and anger are all bad and dangerous, so he tries to repress them. But it's a losing battle, especially considering that his frontal cortex is still under construction. These "bad" feelings pop out anyway as he hits the dog, pulls his mother's hair, and throws his plate across the room. His inescapable conclusion? "My emotions are dangerous and drive me to do bad things. I'm a bad person who disappoints my parents."

Happily, there is a road map through toddlerhood that protects your child's self-esteem and helps him develop emotional intelligence. Remember that lucky baby who had begun to develop a working model of relationships as warm, safe, and loving? Who was sure he lived in a friendly universe? Now his parents are likely to accept the full range of his emotions while limiting his destructive behavior. When he's afraid or disappointed, they empathize. When he has a tantrum, they hold him or stay close, acknowledging his anger and welcoming the tears behind it. Rather than seeing tantrums as undesirable behavior, these wise parents understand that their little one is telling them about his experience. From their loving acceptance, he learns that even the most challenging feelings are bearable. They sweep over us, we tolerate them, they dissipate. These emotions are just part of the big world the toddler is learning so much about every day; there are even names for them: *"You are so mad!"* ... *"You're sad to say good-bye to Daddy, so you're crying."* ... *"You want me to put away my phone and look only at you. You must be feeling jealous. You want me all to yourself right now."*

Of course, letting your toddler *act* on all his feelings would be reneging on your responsibility to guide him. Allowing feelings does not necessarily mean allowing actions based on those feelings. From the empathic limits you set, he learns that while he can be enraged at his playmate for taking the dump truck, it's not permissible to clobber the other kid.

Giving him words to reflect on his own feelings and those of others is developing what we think of as our toddler's conscience. Inside his brain, his budding understanding of words is building connections in the orbitofrontal cortex, which in concert with other areas of the prefrontal cortex and the anterior cingulate manages his emotions and helps him respond appropriately to the emotions of others. The emotional right brain, which has reigned throughout infancy, is gaining an administrator to help it interface with the rest of the brain.[9] As Sue Gerhardt says, "Through the orbitofrontal cortex's connections to the more primitive brain systems, it can inhibit rage reactions, switch off fear, and generally apply brakes to feelings that arise in the subcortical areas. The ability to hold back and defer immediate impulses and desires is the basis for our willpower and self-control, as well as for our capacity for empathy."[10]

When we say toddlers need civilizing, what we mean is that they need our help to develop the inner ability to manage their strong emotions so they can follow essential rules and get along well with others. How we respond to their messy emotions and wild behavior determines whether they build that kind of brain. Punishment and disconnection create more upset and less self-regulation. By contrast, empathic guidance helps our toddler develop a brain that can regulate itself emotionally within a few short years. This increased ability to calm his own fear and rage reactions gives him more access to the natural empathy that's been there all along.

PRESCHOOLERS (3–5 YEARS): EMPATHY

The precursors to empathy are innate in mammals. You may have noticed that dogs are uncomfortable when someone in the family whimpers or cries, and often offer comfort by licking or snuggling. When a baby hears another baby cry, she frequently begins to cry herself. Neurologists postulate that "mirror" neurons fire in our brains when we see someone experiencing strong emotion, so that we feel a taste of that emotion ourselves.

Why, then, aren't all humans empathic? There are some genetic differences underlying our empathic tendencies, but humans are communal creatures, and all of us are born with the potential to develop empathy. So when people intentionally hurt each other, it's empathy run amok, and it begins in early childhood.

As we've discussed, babies and toddlers who've been soothed and emotionally "understood" have a strong foundation for emotional intelligence. Another word for this style of parenting is *empathic*; we try to understand what our child is feeling and respond to it with acceptance and comfort. The emotional intelligence our little one is developing is what allows her to develop her own natural empathy into high EQ.

Let's look at what happens when a child hasn't laid the foundations for emotional intelligence. Let's say she wasn't soothed as an infant but was often left to cry. As a result, she's reactive and prone to throw tantrums easily. Unfortunately, her parents, who are well meaning but ill-informed, tell her that they'll leave her in the shopping mall if she doesn't pull herself together, so her abandonment radar is always scanning for danger. Because her working model of relationships is one in which someone withholds what she needs, she's fiercely needy and emotionally demanding. By the time she was a toddler, her challenging personality got her into constant power struggles with her parents. She's concluded that she can't count on her parents to help her with her emotions, so she rigidly tries to keep her feelings at bay. Unfortunately, repression doesn't work except temporarily, so she's frequently swamped by her emotions. Her feelings of dependency scare her since she can't depend on her parents to meet them, so she flies into a rage when she can't tolerate feeling unloved. Because her parents—not unreasonably—don't want to reward her tantrums, they send her to her room alone to rage, which further "hardens her heart" and solidifies her working model of relationships into one of deprivation. She's wearing a backpack, so to speak, stuffed with the sadness and fear that she can't express. To keep it from sloshing over and flooding her without warning, she armors herself with anger. We can identify her by the "chip on her shoulder."

As she gets older, she's emotionally fragile, easily set off by the normal hurdles of daily life. When she sees another child crying, her mirror neurons fire and she can't help but feel a taste of what the other child is feeling. It's too raw for her, too uncomfortable. She may well scream at the crying child to *"Shut up!"*—or even slug him. Or she may simply wall herself off so that she can't feel the emotions of other people. If this wall against emotional connection is regularly reinforced, she becomes capable of inflicting pain on other people. Her working model of relationships is one of struggle and pain; she's experienced herself as the helpless victim—but she's learning to embody the other side of that relationship as well: the bully.

The lucky child who has been raised with empathy, however, will react to his crying classmate very differently. The other child's crying naturally makes him uncomfortable, as his mirror neurons fire and he feels a taste of what the other child is feeling. But he's more comfortable with these feelings. He's had them before, as all children have, and he knows things will be okay. It's a friendly universe and help will come. The feelings will pass. So he can tolerate his own discomfort and even strategize to soothe it. He may offer the other child his blankie, or tell the teacher the child is crying. It's the flowering of empathy we see in children who have themselves been treated with empathy. His working model of relationships is one in which people notice and accept each other's feelings, in which relationships can be repaired and wrongs righted. He's beginning to be able to embody both sides of that relationship.

Empathy isn't the only emotional intelligence skill your preschooler is practicing. He can soothe himself through most upsets, although he still climbs into your lap for comfort. His orbitofrontal cortex, still under construction during toddlerhood, is now mature enough to evaluate whether a given impulse is socially acceptable, so he can often stop himself from grabbing a toy or lashing out in rage. He can even put a name to his feelings, and more and more, he can use his words to manage his upsets, rather than acting them out with tantrums. That's a sign that the left side of his brain—the center of logic—is integrating more with the right side of his brain, which is more emotion-oriented. He's growing in emotional self-awareness.

ELEMENTARY SCHOOLERS (6–9 YEARS): EMOTIONAL SELF-AWARENESS

By the time children are six, their nervous systems are almost completely wired. Now the frontal cortex strengthens, prunes, and organizes its neural highways. We can expect our child to gain steadily in self-control, planning, organization, and other executive functions throughout childhood and into his twenties. In fact, scientists now believe that the brain has the potential to adapt and change throughout life, so it can always be retrained to some degree. However, by age six the brain's basic structure has been built for your child's ability to trust, to self-soothe, and to empathize. We know that children whose environments change for the better can still develop emotional self-regulation, but it takes tremendous love and patience from caretakers.

Children at age six have a very clear working model of relationships, meaning they've drawn conclusions from their experiences about what to expect. Based on those working models, they've developed a set of strategies that they use to manage their own emotions. The kids who aren't sure they can count on adults to help them self-regulate have "big feelings" that burst out easily. The kids who are now quite sure they can't count on adults may seem more controlled, but they're more fragile than they look; their hearts race even while they act nonchalant. The lucky kids who've had responsive parenting have become conversant with their own emotions and are able to regulate them much of the time, which means they can now often regulate their own behavior. These children have high EQ rooted in their brain physiology. Their internal highways have been built to deliver soothing biochemicals and regulate the fear and anger responses of the amygdala, so they can use their full brain power to function at a higher level. They feel comfortable in their own skin and with other people's emotions, so they're able to connect deeply with other human beings.

The task for children from ages six to nine is to put their maturing emotional intelligence to work so they can master the daily emotions triggered by the many challenges of growing up. Unfortunately, children who have difficulty regulating their emotions and picking up on the cues of others often have trouble mastering these everyday developmental tasks. When anxiety or anger keeps kids from negotiating these normal hurdles, their self-esteem suffers, and they often become rigid and demanding in an effort to manage their fears.

Children who are emotionally intelligent encounter the same difficulties but usually navigate them more gracefully. Mastering each of these normal developmental hurdles stretches children's emotional intelligence and builds EQ "muscle."

These years are often easier for parents. After age six, the brain confers much better impulse control. Because of this improved emotional control and the focus on school, many parents don't even notice their child's inner emotional struggles. Understandably, they breathe a sigh of relief and focus on keeping their busy lives together. Unfortunately, rather than seeing off-track behavior as a cry for help, most parents discipline with "consequences" and other punishment. They miss the opportunity to help their child process the fears and unmet needs that drive "bad" behavior and build EQ.

For parents who pay attention, the elementary school years—when children are still very connected to parents—are the perfect time to help children master the world of emotions. Our lucky child with the empathic parents is now benefiting from not only their warm acceptance of his feelings but their engaged listening, which helps him develop more understanding of his own—and others'—emotions and needs. These parents understand that a child who's acting out is signaling that he needs their help with his emotions, and they see misbehavior as an opportunity for growth. Since these parents can manage their own anxiety, they're also able to help their child problem-solve by listening, reflecting, and helping him brainstorm options. By the time he's nine, our high-EQ child may be years ahead of his classmates in his ability to manage his emotions—and therefore his behavior.

What can parents do to raise a high EQ child? Let's find out.

Emotion Coaching Basics

I worried that this approach might spoil my kids or cause more misbehavior, but it helps them to want to act better. Last weekend, my four-year-old son started crying and screaming at me. I took a deep breath and resisted the urge to make him be respectful and to tell him to get over it (my past usual reaction). I held him on my lap and let him cry. I told him I understood and that it was hard not to be allowed to do things you want to do when you want to do them and that I bet he would do that all day long when he got bigger. He cried for maybe one minute, got up, and said, "Okay, I'm done. Let's go to the park!" In the past, these incidents would turn into major battles and end in my feeling exhausted and like a horrible parent.

—Lara, mother of an eighteen-month-old and a four-year-old

HOW CHILDREN DEVELOP EMOTIONAL INTELLIGENCE

Every child is born wanting to connect deeply with other humans and to enjoy mastering the hurdles life presents. That's what makes humans happy. But some children stumble, or even give up on these goals. What gets in their way? Big needs that go unmet, and big emotions they can't manage. Our job as parents is to meet those needs and help our child learn to manage those big emotions, which is what helps children develop high EQ.

Have you noticed the hardest part of helping your child learn to regulate her emotions? Most of us were brought up thinking that emotions are dangerous. If we can't tolerate our own sadness or anger, we can't tolerate our child's. And if we can't accept our child's disappointment, or anger, or grief, we give him the message that his feelings are too dangerous to allow. Unfortunately, that doesn't get rid of the feelings. It just disables our child from learning to manage them.

This chapter will give you the nuts-and-bolts strategies you need to help your child develop a high EQ: offering empathy, understanding emotions and needs, and helping your child with her big feelings, including fear and anger.

EMPATHY, THE FOUNDATION OF EQ

I had a mom meltdown the other day, and was having a fit over something my four-year-old daughter was doing. She took a few steps back, didn't get flustered, and looked at me. She came over and offered me a hug, and said, "You look really upset." She has experienced my empathy for her and her meltdowns and she is able to become a partner in the quest for balance and carry me when I need a little help in my day.

—Candace, mother of a four-year-old

Empathy is more than the foundation of emotional intelligence; it's the foundation of effective parenting, according to John Gottman, the author with Daniel Goleman of *Raising an Emotionally Intelligent Child*. Why? Because it's essential to your ability to understand your child and connect with her. Because it will prevent you from visiting on your child all the issues from your own childhood. And because without it, your child simply won't feel loved, no matter how much you love her.

Empathy is often defined as seeing things from the other person's point of view. But empathy is actually a physical event, controlled by the insula in our right brain. Remember how the structure of the right brain was formed during the first two years of life, before your baby became verbal? Scientists suspect that the right brain is the orchestrator of intimacy. The insula connects the brain with the heart, digestive organs, and skin. So when our heart leaps, or our stomach turns, or our skin crawls, the insula is sending us a message. And when we feel deep empathy, we feel it in our bodies. That means a more accurate definition of empathy is "feeling" from the other person's point of view.

When a parent bestows the gift of empathy on a struggling child, that visceral connection changes everything. Empathy strengthens the relationship bond. Empathy helps the child feel understood, less alone with her pain and suffering. Empathy heals. And the experience of empathy teaches the little one about the deepest ways that humans connect, providing her with a launching pad for every future relationship.

How do children develop empathy? It happens naturally, as part of healthy emotional development, as long as children experience empathy from their caretakers. That's why parenting with empathy is a double gift to your child: In addition to your empathy helping him learn to manage his emotions, experiencing your empathy will also help him to develop empathy for others. This giving of empathy is also a gift to you, because children who feel your empathy are much more cooperative in accepting your guidance. Translation: It makes parenting a lot easier!

But most parents find the idea of parenting with empathy anxiety-producing. How exactly do you do it?

You already know. Every time you say, "I know how you feel" or "Looks like you had a hard day," you're being empathic. Every time you rise above your own feelings to see things from your child's point of view, that's empathy. Sounds simple, right? Then why is empathy so powerful? Imagine empathy as a mirror that you hold up to your child. Your acceptance and understanding of what he's feeling helps him recognize and accept his own emotions. That's what allows the feelings to lose their charge and begin to dissipate. We don't have to act on emotions or even like them; we need merely to acknowledge their presence to liberate ourselves from them.

Your acceptance of his emotions teaches your child that his emotional life is not dangerous, is not shameful, and in fact is universal and manageable. Everyone has felt this; there's even a name for it! He feels understood and accepted. He learns that he isn't alone to cope with the crush of his powerful emotions.

What Empathy Isn't

- **Permissiveness.** You can (and should) set limits. The key is to acknowledge your child's unhappiness about those limits. It's important to your child that you be able to tolerate his disappointment and anger at you, as well as all of his other emotions.

- **Solving the problem.** The point is to help him get past his upset feelings so that he can begin to think about solutions himself, not to solve the problem for him. When he expresses his feelings about something, you'll want to listen and acknowledge, rather than jumping in with solutions. That means you'll have to manage your own anxiety about the issue (which means breathe your way through your anxious feelings and resist taking action).

- **Agreeing.** Accepting his feelings and reflecting them does not mean you agree with them or endorse them. You're showing him you understand, nothing more, and nothing less. If you've ever felt understood, you know just how great a gift this is.

- **Probing.** "Tell me how you feel" is not empathy. Empathy is sitting with what she's showing you about her experience, not ripping off a scab to examine the wound.

- **Analyzing.** *"I think you're mad because you're jealous it's your sister's birthday."* Empathy is accepting and being with what someone is expressing, not making them squirm by digging into their psyche—even if you're right. A simple *"You seem so grumpy today, honey"* will be more helpful to her in noticing what's happening. Even the words aren't necessary, especially as children get older, because labeling feelings often makes people feel analyzed or judged. Just a simple *"Hmm . . ."* or *"Wow!"* or *"I'm so sorry"* said with warmth and compassion helps your child feel understood.

- **Catastrophizing.** Match your reaction with his mood. Being a bit downcast because his team lost the soccer game doesn't merit a reaction from you as if someone had died.

- **Arguing with the feeling.** That just invalidates him and makes him wrong for feeling it. And it pushes the emotion under conscious awareness, so he's carrying around a negative feeling that's ready to resurface at the slightest provocation.

- **Trying to cheer her up.** Of course you want to help her past her uncomfortable feelings, but you don't want to give the message that she needs to run from them. Once she has a safe opportunity to notice, accept, and express the emotion to herself or to you, it will naturally dissipate. Then she'll feel ready for "cheering up" in the sense of a change of scene and topic. And you've given her the message that *all* of her is acceptable, including her uncomfortable feelings.

What Empathy Is

- **Listening and accepting without the pressure to solve anything.** You don't have to solve anything. You don't have to agree with his views. You do have to accept that your child is entitled to his feelings. Don't take it personally.

- **Mirroring, acknowledging, and reflecting.** *"You are so mad at your brother"* or *"Wow! Look at you all the way up there!"* or *"You seem worried about the sleepover."*

- **Honoring healthy boundaries.** The fact that you empathize doesn't mean you lose your own sense of well-being. Your warm understanding communicates that you understand he thinks it's the end of the world, at the same time that your ability to stay emotionally regulated reassures him that there's a light at the end of the tunnel.

YOUR CHILD'S EMOTIONAL BACKPACK

Today, driving home, my son whined that he wanted to go a restaurant for dinner. Then he started to scream. I could feel my patience wearing thin, but I managed to stay calm and say soothing things like, "I know you really want to eat at that restaurant for dinner. . . . You're sad. . . . Now you're crying." We got home and I felt immediate pressure to start dinner since we were both hungry, but I knew he had to empty his emotional backpack, so I told him I'd hold him as long as he wanted. Funny thing was, it didn't take that long. He cried deeply and then let out a big sigh and said, "I really did want to go to that restaurant and I was crying so much about it." Miraculously, the whole evening went well.

—Heather, mother of a four-year-old

Human emotion can't be successfully repressed. When we ignore or "stuff" our emotions, we push them out of our consciousness and into our subconscious, where they're beyond our control. Unfortunately, that keeps us from regulating them, and they erupt, sometimes with disastrous results. Luckily, we don't need to repress our emotions to manage them. As we get older, we can use our words and stories ("I'm a bit grumpy today because I'm tired, so I'm overreacting") to regulate our feelings. Our rational mind makes us feel safe enough to experience those big emotions. As we let ourselves feel them, they wash through us and evaporate.

Like other humans, children also need to feel their emotions before those emotions will dissipate and vanish. But since young children's rational brains aren't yet fully online, they can't use them to feel safer. Instead, your child uses you. Your warm presence makes him feel safe enough to experience his tears and fears. If you're not there—or if he's feeling disconnected from you at the moment—he stuffs those feelings into a figurative emotional backpack, which he lugs around with him. Until the child feels safe enough to empty the backpack, he's tightly wound and emotionally fragile, trying to keep its contents from sloshing out. He doesn't have access to the internal resources he needs to handle the normal challenges of everyday life.

Unfortunately, your child usually can't tell you why she's upset. She's not very experienced with emotions yet, so she doesn't know how to ask for your help. All she knows is that she feels out of sorts and irritable. Luckily, that's your signal, because feeling bad makes kids act bad, or "act out." You've probably heard that term used to refer to a child who misbehaves. But we could also think of misbehavior as acting out a big emotion that the child can't express in words. So all "misbehavior" is a signal to us as parents that our child needs our help with an emotion he can't process, one that's driving him to misbehave.

Some signs that your child needs your help with her emotions:

- She becomes rigid, expressing a desperate need that must be satisfied. If you do meet her demand, she immediately makes a new demand.
- She's grumpy and generally unhappy, and you just can't please her no matter what you do.
- She "misbehaves," sometimes looking right at you while she breaks the rules, signaling her disconnection from you. (When children are in the grip of strong negative emotions, they feel disconnected and alone.)
- She "acts out" in a crime of passion, such as hitting or breaking something, showing you that her feelings are too strong for her to control.
- She seems like a bottomless pit, or she repeatedly engages in the same misbehavior, and all your love and attention can't seem to change this pattern.

How can you help your child with big emotions? Since both tears and laughter help us discharge anxiety and emotion, help your child to play when she can, and cry when she has to. In other words, regular doses of play—especially play that touches on whatever issues are up for your child developmentally—will help your child work through the normal fears and frustrations that accompany developmentally appropriate tasks. You can also respond playfully to "off-track" behavior that signals disconnection. For instance, when your child looks right at you and breaks a minor rule, try grabbing him for some affectionate roughhousing, playfully rekindling your connection with him. Shouldn't you let him know that you're serious about the rule he just broke? He already knows about the rule. He broke it because of some unmet need or overpowering emotion that he needs your help to handle. But before you can correct, you have to connect. Discipline will just make him feel less safe. Play, on the other hand, creates a sense of safety and releases the connection hormone, oxytocin.

So if your child looks right at you and dumps out his Cheerios, it's not because he thinks they belong on the floor. Maybe he needs to connect with you. Maybe he feels overlooked because you're always with the baby. Maybe he's worried about the field trip today or that fight you had with your husband last night. You don't actually need to know what's driving his behavior; your first step is always to reconnect. Exaggerate your outrage. "What happened to the Cheerios?!! Oh *no*! This is terrible! You come over here, you Cheerio dumper, you! I'll show you what happens to Cheerio dumpers!" Grab him up and sling him over your back and run around the room with him. Then stop near the Cheerios and kiss him on the belly ten times. You'll know you're on the right track by how much he laughs—the more he more he giggles, the more he's discharging the anxiety he feels about this issue. Often, just this little game will restore your child to his sunny self, ready to help you clean up the Cheerios.

However, at least some of the time when your child is signaling you with grumpiness, misbehavior, or rigidity, his emotions are intense enough that the time for play has passed, and you have no choice except tears. But often when humans need to cry, we're afraid of those raw, vulnerable feelings. To keep them at bay, we lash out. So when your child has feelings that really scare him, he tries not to feel them. Instead, he gets angry. He acts (those feelings) out. He almost certainly "knows better" and would like to "behave," but he's in the grip of strong emotions that he doesn't understand, being driven to behave badly, and he just feels like a bad person. His misbehavior is a cry for help.

What kind of help? He needs his rage accepted with compassion, so he can get past it to the tears and fears underneath. He needs to show you how much he hurts, to know that you hear his suffering. Yes, he'll get past these feelings, but first he needs to know he's not bad for feeling such anger, and he needs your loving attention to experience all the fear, disappointment, or sadness under the anger, so he can move past it.

UNDERSTANDING ANGER

Children need love, especially when they do not deserve it.
   —Harold Hulbert

One of the most important messages we can give our children about emotion is that anger is a universal human feeling that can be managed and controlled. How do we do that? By acknowledging and responding to their anger, rather than ignoring it or punishing it. Once children understand that their anger will be heard and responded to, they can express it more calmly, rather than defaulting to aggression. By contrast, kids who are given the message that anger is unacceptable or disrespectful try to repress it, which means the angry feelings go underground only to burst out unregulated by the conscious mind. Our attitude toward our child's anger can therefore either help him learn to manage it or push him toward aggression.

Although we don't usually notice it when we're in the flush of rage, anger is actually a defense against deeper feelings of fear, hurt, disappointment, or other pain. When those feelings are too devastating, we automatically lash out to keep ourselves from feeling the pain. We mobilize against the perceived threat by attacking, knowing instinctively that the best defense is a good offense. Sometimes attacking makes sense, but only when there's actually a threat. And while our children are often angry because they feel so vulnerable, actual threats are rare. Most of the time when children get angry, they want to attack their little brother (who broke their treasured memento), their parents (who disciplined them "unfairly"), their teacher (who embarrassed them), or the playground bully (who scared them).

You can help your child with her anger by remembering that an angry child is showing you that she's scared, disconnected, and hurting inside. Your job is to acknowledge both the anger and the emotions underneath it. Once children have a chance to feel the vulnerable feelings they've been avoiding, they no longer need the anger as a defense, and it melts away.

When children live in a home where anger is handled in a healthy way, they generally learn to manage their anger constructively. That means:

- **Controlling aggressive impulses.** As we accept our child's anger and remain calm, she lays down the neural pathways—

and learns the emotional skills—to calm down without hurting herself, others, or property. By the time they're in kindergarten, children should be able to tolerate the flush of adrenaline and other "fight" chemicals in the body without acting on them by clobbering someone.

- **Acknowledging the more threatening feelings under the anger.** Once the child can let himself experience his grief over the broken treasure, his hurt that his mother was unfair, his shame when he didn't know the answer in class, or his fear when his classmate threatened him, he can move on. He no longer needs his anger to defend against these feelings, so the anger evaporates.

- **Constructive problem solving.** The goal is for your child to use the anger as an impetus to change things as necessary so the situation won't be repeated. This may include moving his treasures out of his little brother's reach or getting parental help to deal with the bully. It may also include acknowledging his own contribution to the problem, so that he resolves to do a better job following his parents' rules or to come to class more prepared.

Obviously, it takes years of parental guidance for children to learn these skills. But by the time children are six, the brain should have developed to the point where the thinking centers can override the emergency messages of the lower brain centers. Children who can't control their aggressive impulses when they're very upset are signaling that they need help to process a backlog of emotions and the chip on their shoulder. If parents are able to help children feel safe enough to express anger and explore the feelings underneath, children are able to increasingly move past their anger into constructive problem solving during the grade school years.

MEETING YOUR CHILD'S DEEPEST NEEDS

We figure out a way to chauffeur the children to nine lessons a week, organize the vacation trip to Disney World, throw a birthday party for a dozen five-year-olds. So why does a quiet story by candlelight seem impossible to manage? In truth, the story is more nourishing for our child's soul.
   —Katrina Kenison

Sometimes our child's strong emotions are triggered by essential needs that go unmet, needs the child can't verbalize. Most parents focus on physical needs like sleep, food, and cleanliness. But often we forget their deeper needs:

- To know that their parents adore them, love to care for them, and care about their happiness. (*Worthiness, security, self-esteem*)
- To feel truly seen, known, accepted, and appreciated—even the "shameful" parts like anger, jealousy, pettiness, and greed. (*Unconditional love*)
- To stay connected with each parent through regular relaxed, playful, unstructured, affirming time together. (*Intimacy, belonging*)
- To work through challenging daily emotions. (*Emotional wholeness, self-acceptance*)
- To master new skills. (*Mastery, independence, confidence*)
- To act from one's own motivations to impact the world. (*Self-determination, power*)
- To make a contribution. (*Value, meaning*)

Children can't name these needs, but when they're not met, they don't thrive. They seem unhappy, uncooperative, insatiable. Nothing feels like enough to them. So they demand more, more, and more. More time before bedtime. More treats than their siblings. More material possessions.

But more of what we didn't really need to begin with can never fill our deepest desires.

Luckily, children let us know when their needs aren't being met. In fact, all "misbehavior" is an SOS from your child, alerting you to unmet needs or tangled feelings. If you listen to your child and let her know you're taking her needs seriously, you'll see her relaxing, not feeling like she has to fight with you to get her needs met. She'll feel the way we all feel when our needs are filled: comfortable, happy, open, appreciative. That's when kids are ready to cooperate.

When children feel powerless to convince us that their needs are legitimate, they whine, turn everything into a power struggle, or become apathetic or defiant. We usually call this "bad" behavior, but we could also think of it as a childish, dysfunctional strategy to meet the child's legitimate needs.

Does that mean you shouldn't get annoyed? You probably can't avoid it. But transforming your annoyance will make you more effective in changing your child's behavior. Remind yourself that your kid is just trying to meet a valid human need, and your help is essential in finding a better way for him to meet that need.

Of course, not all wants are needs. But when we meet children's deeper needs to be seen, appreciated, and connected, they're happier and more cooperative, so they can manage their disappointment when we say no to the fleeting desires they think will make them happy. Those desires aren't actually needs; they're strategies to meet needs. Some attention from you might meet her need for sweetness far better than that candy.

EQ COACHING WITH A DIFFICULT CHILD

Some children are born with a tendency toward anxiety or depression. Sometimes, these tendencies are severe enough to express themselves in negative thinking, compulsive behavior, phobias, or anxious behavior that are tough for parents to handle. As always, let's begin with our Three Big Ideas—Regulating Yourself; Fostering Connection; and Coaching, Not Controlling. If we can notice our own tight knot of fear and dismay about our child's problems, we can loosen it and give ourselves and our child some room to shift. If we can work to stay fiercely connected to our child, that sense of safety will do more to ease his symptoms than anything else we might try. For instance, research suggests that responsive nurturing can make the difference between a shy child becoming a leader or a recluse. Finally, coaching, not controlling, means thinking creatively and finding the outside support we need to meet this special challenge. In some cases, professional intervention is essential. In others, our child just needs extra help from us to work through an overlay of fear so that she can rise to her age-appropriate developmental tasks. What might this look like?

When Morgan started preschool, she clung to her mother every morning and howled so that she could be heard throughout the school. Her assistant teacher put special effort into connecting with her, so that Morgan eventually was able to let her mother leave in the morning, although never without tears. Throughout the day, however, Morgan shadowed the teacher. At home, Morgan was afraid of bugs, of going down the bathtub drain, of having her hair washed, of the dog in the fenced yard next door. She seemed to be a born perfectionist, insisting on getting things just right and crying if she felt criticized. She took forever to fall asleep, clutching at her parents if they tried to leave the room, and then woke repeatedly, screaming until one of her parents lay down with her. Her parents, who were both light sleepers, traded off night duty, so that each of them was up much of the night every other night.

While Morgan may have suffered some trauma earlier in her life, it's just as likely that she was simply born with a mild predisposition to anxiety. She's unlikely to star in the school play or even tell a joke at the school lunch table. But that doesn't mean she can't have a happy childhood, close friends, and a good life. Morgan will probably always be a bit anxious, but her parents can help her learn to manage her anxiety. Parents of anxious children can help their child by:

- Teaching her to notice her anxiety and calm herself.
- Teaching her to be aware of her own feelings and express them (stuffing emotions causes anxiety).
- Teaching her social skills.
- Teaching her relaxation skills.
- Helping her gain confidence with real achievement.
- Helping her work through fear by tackling physical challenges.
- Minimizing the stress in her life.

Morgan's parents began to use relaxation exercises with her every night to help her relax. They made time for daily roughhousing and wrestling to help her gain physical confidence. During Special Time, they played games to get her giggling about separation, perfectionism, and control. Finally, they decided to work directly to help their daughter off-load her pervasive fears, beginning with sleep.

First, her parents helped diffuse some of Morgan's anxiety about sleep by playing with the issue. Her father would pretend to drop off to sleep on the couch and then awaken frightened because no one was with him. Morgan laughed hysterically and told him not to act like a baby; Dad kept trying variations of his game as long as Morgan kept laughing. In one variation, Morgan would put her father "to bed" on the couch and tell him she knew he could sleep by himself while her father begged her to stay and Morgan giggled.

After a few weeks of this, her parents chose a weekend with no other obligations and explained to Morgan that they were going to help her learn to fall asleep by herself and sleep alone in her bed. Morgan's anxiety blossomed into full-blown panic. She cried, screamed, tantrummed, hit, struggled, and hid under the bed. Her parents helped each other stay calm and patient, each reminding the other that they weren't traumatizing their daughter but helping her to surface and conquer a fear that was old, deep, and debilitating. When bedtime came, they tucked Morgan in, reassuring her that they would always keep her safe, that they knew she could sleep by herself. Her mother didn't, however, actually leave the room when her father did. Instead, she held Morgan during the ensuing meltdown. Every time Morgan began to settle, her mother kissed her good night and got up to leave—and Morgan cried more, clinging to her mother. Finally, after four hours of crying, trembling, and sweating, Morgan told her mother that she could leave, as long as she promised to return if Morgan called her. Morgan slept through the night that night for the first time in her life. The following night, the process was repeated, but lasted only half an hour. Soon Morgan was falling asleep by herself and sleeping through the night.

Is this sleep training? It would be more accurate to say that Morgan was having a hard time separating from her parents to fall asleep and stay asleep, so her parents helped her surface and dissolve the fears that were causing her separation anxiety. Notice that they never left her alone to cry. Instead, they announced their plan to leave and then helped their daughter through her fearful reaction. Anxiety—another word for *fear*—is often at the root of children's sleep issues. While there is nothing wrong with a four-year-old sharing her parents' bed, four-year-olds are certainly capable of sleeping alone, once they get some help with their fears.

A success story? Absolutely. But the best part is that Morgan became more relaxed in general, and some of her other fears disappeared on their own. Fear has a way of spreading beyond its original source. When we give anxious children a chance to work through the past terror stored in their bodies, we help them move toward more courage and freedom in all aspects of their lives.

Action Guides

The change (since I began to accept her feelings) has been remarkable; she's extremely reasonable and cooperative. We still have tough days, but the tantrums are gone! I figure that if she's upset about something, she's entitled to her feelings—I'd rather step back (take a deep breath) and have her cry for five minutes and then crawl in my lap, and we give each other a hug and move on with our day. It takes about the same amount of time as a full-blown tantrum, but it's far less stressful and we don't walk away feeling angry and resentful!

—Renet, mother of a four-year-old

Ready to emotion-coach? Take a deep breath and restore yourself to a state of calm, as much as possible. Now, summon up all the compassion you can, to make it safe for your child to feel those upset emotions. As soon as he does, they'll evaporate. Over time, this befriending of his emotions will allow him to recognize and regulate them. Simple? Well, yes, but not easy. The Action Guides in this section will help you hone your emotion-coaching skills.

SEVEN STEPS TO NURTURE EMOTIONAL INTELLIGENCE IN YOUR CHILD

So you want to raise an emotionally intelligent child and you're wondering where to begin? Start with these basic steps to use with your child on a daily basis; then we'll talk about what to do when emotions run high.

1. **Acknowledge your child's perspective and empathize.** You don't need to "fix" whatever your child is upset about, but you do need to empathize. We all know how good it feels to have our position acknowledged; somehow it just makes it easier when we don't get our way. *"It's hard for you to stop playing and come to dinner, but it's time now."*

2. **Allow expression of emotion, even while limiting actions.** Your child's feelings are legitimate. What he needs from you is coaching on a better way to express them. *"You are so mad your brother broke your toy, but we don't hit. Come and I'll help you tell him how you feel."*

3. **Respond to the needs and feelings behind problem behavior.** "Troublesome" behavior signals big feelings or unmet needs. If you don't address the feelings and needs, they'll just burst out later, causing other problem behavior. So instead of scolding a child who's acting up or dawdling, you might say: *"You're having a hard time this morning. Starting school has been fun, but you miss time with Mommy. I will be right*

here to pick you up after school, and we'll snuggle and play together and have Special Time, okay?"

4. **When a desire can't be granted, acknowledge it and grant it through "wish fulfillment."** It's amazing how often you can get through an impasse by giving your child his wish via imagination. Partly this is because it shows you really do care about what your child wants. But there's another, fascinating reason. Imagining that our wish is fulfilled actually satisfies us for the moment, meaning our brain actually looks satisfied on a brain scan! Giving your child his wish in imagination releases some of the urgency behind it so that he's more open to alternatives. *"You wish you could have a cookie. I bet you could gobble ten cookies right now! Wouldn't that be so yummy?!"* Then find a way to meet the deeper need: *"I think you're hungry. It's almost time for dinner, but I hear you can't wait. Let's find a healthy snack that makes your body feel better."*

5. **Tell the story so your child understands his emotional experience.** When our child is emotional, she's acting from the right side of her brain. Those emotions need to be acknowledged and felt, or they hijack her. So the first step in emotion coaching is always to empathize with our child's feelings. But we then need to help her bring in the left, or logic-based, side of her brain as well. That helps her make sense of what's happening, so she doesn't feel simply at the mercy of emotions sweeping through her. To do that, name feelings (*"You are so disappointed"*), and tell stories: *"Yes, that's right. . . . When we went to the dentist you were scared at first and refused to open your mouth. . . . But you held my hand*

and were very brave and the dentist said you are doing a great job brushing!"

6. **Teach problem solving.** Emotions are messages, not mud for wallowing. Most of the time, once kids feel that their emotions are understood and accepted, the feelings lose their charge and begin to dissipate. This leaves an opening for problem solving. Sometimes, kids can do this themselves. Sometimes, they need your help to brainstorm. But resist the urge to solve the problem for them; that gives your child the message that you don't have confidence in his ability to handle it himself. *"You're so disappointed that Chloe can't come over because she's sick. You were really looking forward to playing with her. When you're ready, maybe we can work together to come up with ideas of something else to do that sounds like fun."*

7. **Play it out.** Play is how children process experience. Most any emotional issue your child is having will respond to play. It's useful to regulate behavior: *"You are Superman today! You are so powerful! Can you help me push the shopping cart carefully through the aisles?"* And when you notice a negative pattern developing, play is often the best medicine: *"Let's play the Bye-Bye Game. . . . See, Mommy always comes back!"* (For the Bye-Bye Game and other games for emotional processing, see Playing with Your Child: Games for Emotional Intelligence in this chapter.)

EMOTION-COACHING YOUR CHILD THROUGH A MELTDOWN

Last night my daughter had a meltdown after I removed a toy she was playing with roughly. She was screaming, "Give it back to me!" I knelt down next to her and held out my arms for her. She held on to me tightly and cried into my shoulder. When she had calmed a little, I asked her, "Are you feeling angry that I took the toy away from you?" "Yes, I'm angry," she nodded and sobbed a little more. After a short time, she looked up at me and said, "I love you." We kissed and moved on. Later that evening, I mentioned how big she is getting. She nodded and said, "I still cry sometimes." "I cry sometimes, too," I replied. She nodded again. "It's okay to cry."

    —Gis, mother of a four-year-old

When storm clouds brew, even the most well-intentioned parent can get triggered and escalate the upset rather than calm it. But that's when your child most needs your help to learn to regulate himself.

- **Choose a scheduled meltdown.** When you notice that your child's behavior is rigid, demanding, or off-track, it's time for a "scheduled meltdown." Ignoring his behavior and hoping he'll get into a better mood will result in an escalation of acting out until he ends up in a full-fledged upset, usually at the most inconvenient time for you. Instead, move into a "scheduled meltdown" on your own schedule—while you're still calm enough to stay compassionate.

- **Regulate your own feelings so you can welcome your child's big emotions and help him vent.** When we maintain our composure, it communicates to our child that there's no emergency, even if he feels like there is at the moment. This helps him feel safer.

- **Set a compassionate limit.** Get down on his level, put an arm around him, look him in the eye, and set your most compassionate limit: *"No cookie now, sweetie. It's almost dinnertime."* He will almost certainly launch into a meltdown.

- **Set whatever limits are necessary to keep everyone safe,** while acknowledging the anger. *"You are really angry, but no hitting. . . . I will keep us both safe."*

- **If he's angry instead of crying, help him surface his fears by lovingly confronting his defiance.** *"Sweetie, you just threw your toy at the cat. That scared the cat. Toys are not for throwing."* Look him in the eye. Stay calm. He will either go blank (numbing himself), look away in shame, or look straight at you in defiance. Regardless, reach out for him. *"Sweetie, I see how upset you are. But I won't let you hurt the cat."* At this point, your child will almost certainly refuse to meet your eyes. He may twist angrily away. That's because feeling the love coming from your eyes will melt his hardened heart and flood him with all those hurting feelings that he's been hiding away. Naturally, that scares him. He will either burst into tears (bingo!) or lash out angrily.

- **If your child gets angry, stay connected. Never send a child away to "calm down" by himself.** That just gives him the message that he's all alone in learning to manage his big, scary feelings.

- **Hold him if you can do so without getting hurt.** If not, but you can touch him, do so soothingly: *"Here's my hand on your arm."*

- **If you know what's going on, acknowledge it:** *"You are so angry that Dad won't let you do that."* If you don't know, say what you see: *"You feel so bad."*

- **Create safety.** You want the tears to come to wash the feelings away, like cleaning a wound. Try not to talk much during the meltdown, because it moves your child from his heart to his head and dries up the tears. Keep an occasional "voice bridge" of soothing sounds and safety-inspiring words: *"I will stay right here. . . . You are safe."* You definitely don't want to analyze him, evaluate him, or calm him down. In fact, you want to help him reach that hurting place inside, so you compassionately remind him of whatever triggered his upset: *"You really wanted _____. . . . I'm so sorry."*

- **If he yells at you to go away,** say, *"I will step back a little, to right here. But I won't leave you alone with these big, scary feelings. I'm right here and you're safe."* Since being close to you increases his sense of safety, it also increases the flow of upset feelings that are swamping him, so he may want to get away from you to stop those feelings. But just because he wants you to go away doesn't mean he doesn't need you there. When kids calm down, they invariably say they didn't really want us to go.

- **Ignore any rudeness during a meltdown; don't take it personally, and resist the urge to retaliate.** This is not the time to teach appropriate behavior. These feelings aren't about you, even when he's yelling, *"I hate you!"* When your son says, *"You NEVER understand!"* try to hear that as information about him—at this moment he feels like he's never understood—rather than about you. If he yells, *"I hate you,"* answer, *"I hear how angry you are, and how much hate you feel right now. I love you no matter how angry you are. I will always love you, no matter what."*

- **Remember that your child may be reliving something scary or painful.** When a child clears out fears he's been repressing, his body needs to move, to save itself as he wanted to do when the upsetting event first happened. This is true for both big traumas, such as medical interventions in which someone held him down, and smaller traumas, such as Mom or Dad yelling. Peter Levine, in his book *An Unspoken Voice*, describes this as the natural healing process by which the "body releases trauma and restores goodness." So if your child seems to be fighting for his life, it's because he's re-experiencing all that arousal of fight-or-flight that he felt in the original circumstance, and he may need to move his legs as if he's running, or struggle against those arms holding him down. You'll know his body is releasing if he gets sweaty, or cold, or suddenly needs to pee or vomit. Many kids really like to push against our hands. Sometimes it helps to hold the child in our arms with his back to us, so he is flailing away from us. He may arch his back and throw his head back against you. Obviously, don't let him hurt you, and move out of reach if necessary to stay safe. Use your soothing voice to keep an emotional bridge: *"You are safe. It's okay to let all those feelings out. Nothing can hurt you. I am right here."*

- **Keep breathing and stay calm.** When a child is working on old fears, he can go on like this for an hour or more. That's how big this fear was to him. You are giving him a tremendous gift. Remind yourself that *this* is the help your child was asking for when he acted out. Once these fears are cleared out, they're gone, and you and your child are liberated from them, free to go on together to a better life.

- **Honor his grief.** Sometimes kids will finish this hard emotional work, look up at you, and change the subject. That's fine; she's signaling that she's done for now. Don't worry; if there's more to get out, it will come up another time. You can say, *"What hard work you did, sweetie,"* and follow her lead into the new subject. But often after children express their fears, they collapse into your arms in tears. Crying in your arms is his chance to let out his deepest sadness and begin to heal it. Let him cry as long as he wants. If he stops, make eye contact. If he's able to hold your gaze, he's let out what he needs to. If not, you can help him release more pent-up emotion by reminding him of whatever upset him to begin with: *"I'm sorry I didn't cut the sandwich the right way, sweetie."*

- **Afterward, reassure your child of your love.** Kids often need your assurance that you still find them acceptable despite all their upsetting feelings. Once the storm passes, your child will be free of the feelings he was having to hold down with such rigidity, so he'll be more flexible. He may fall asleep, or he may go on to have a wonderful evening with you. He'll also feel more connected to you because you tethered him through his inner tornado.

- **Help your child make sense of the experience.** This is not so much "teaching a lesson," because your child already knows the expected behavior; he just couldn't control those big emotions. Your goal is to help him understand that he was swamped by emotions, but it's okay. Language is what helps us make sense of emotion. Eventually, the understanding provided by words will reassure him that he's safe even when swamped by emotion; that he can manage his big feelings. *"You were so sad when I said no. . . . You got very mad and threw your cup. . . . Then you cried. . . . That was hard work. . . . Mommy listened. . . . Everything's okay. . . . I am always here if you need to show me your feelings. . . . I love you so much."*

- **Wait to teach.** While your child is vulnerable after the melt-down is not the time to have a discussion about his transgression. If you feel you must teach, wait until after your child is calm to remind him about appropriate behavior, preferably with a light touch that acknowledges he already knows the rule: "What are cups for? Oh, right, to drink from! Not to throw, right? Let's get you a drink of water!" If the damage was more severe—he hurt a person emotionally or physically—the message needs to be more serious about the effect on the person, but the timing still needs to happen after he's calm and aware of his desire for "repair."

- **Expect to see more meltdowns for a few weeks,** now that he trusts your safe presence. If you can't take time at the moment he launches into a tantrum, tell him, *"I love you, but I can't listen now, sweetie. I will listen to all your feelings after dinner."* Just make sure to keep your promise to give him his scheduled meltdown. You may have to go through a month of this kind of "witnessing" to help your child free himself of the pent-up emotions that are driving his behavior. But because you're getting rid of the upsetting feelings that were driving your child to act out, you'll find him having fewer meltdowns over time, and in between you'll notice that he's happier and more cooperative.

Yes, it's a lot of work for you. But once you realize that you don't have to fix anything, it gets easier. Notice that what you provided was safety and connection. Your child did the hard work of releasing his emotions so he could heal and move on. You'll have to breathe your way through it each time, and probably repeat a little mantra to keep yourself calm. This will almost certainly bring up big feelings from your own childhood, so you may need to find an adult with whom *you* can vent and cry. But wait until you see how much closer you and your child feel to each other. It's worth every bit of sweat and tears. Gradually, your child will learn that while he can't always get what he wants, he can always get something better—someone who loves and accepts all of him, including the scary parts. And he'll have internalized the ability to weather disappointment and other deep discomforts, which is the beginning of stable internal happiness—otherwise known as resilience.

WHEN YOUR CHILD ACTS OUT BUT CAN'T CRY: BUILDING SAFETY

Dr. Laura . . . My son is wound tighter than a drum and everything makes him mad. I know there are tears under there, especially from having a new baby sister. But he won't cry, he just gets mad! He throws things, hits the dog. How can I help him?
    —Nicole, mother of two

There will be times when you embrace your acting-out child with your warm compassion and he bursts into tears, sobs his heart out, and is cooperative and delightful for the rest of the day. But more often, your child will be too frightened of that logjam of emotion he's been tamping down. The problem is, he needs to cry to release all those feelings. Otherwise, he'll spend the day bouncing from one angry incident to the next. How can you break through his anger to release the tears and fears underneath? By building safety through play when he "misbehaves." Here's how:

- **When you see your son trying to hit the dog, intervene in a playful way.** Grab him up and say warmly, *"What's that? Hitting the dog?!...Yes, yes, we can be mad, but no, we can't hit the dog!"* Take him to the couch to roughhouse a bit (kissing him all over or tossing him around), or run around the room with him, chanting, *"We're mad, we're mad, but we can't hurt the dog!"* When you put him down, he may simply bask in your warm attention, in which case that was what he needed—to feel reconnected with you. You've wrapped him in enough warm attention that you've melted some of those thorny feelings.

- **Play while he can.** But there's a good chance that his feelings are too big for even the sun of your adoration to melt them, and he will take your playfulness as "permission" or a dare, or what it really is—a lighthearted acknowledgment of his feelings. In this case, he will immediately head back toward the dog. That's good! Your goal is to help him feel safe enough to show you his feelings; being playful defuses the tension. So as soon as he heads for the dog, you grab him up and repeat your playful exuberant running around and chanting. After a few rounds of this, your son may relax and snuggle up to you. If so, great! He giggled a lot, and now he's feeling deeply connected.

- **Let him cry when he has to.** Or you may notice that your son is getting a bit frenzied, which means that his feelings are reaching a fevered pitch. Or you may just have had enough. That's a good time to take a deep breath and change your demeanor to one of calm compassion instead of playfulness. This is just like setting any other empathic limit, but you've increased your child's sense of safety by playing first. So you set the limit and support him through the meltdown.

- **Set a compassionate limit.** Stop and put him next to you on the couch or the rug, look him in the eye, and say compassionately and seriously, *"Okay, sweetie, no more playing . . . I won't let you hurt the dog."* Almost certainly, you will have built up enough of a sense of safety that your child will begin crying. Then you can support him as described in the previous Action Guide.

The good news is that you don't have to do anything to *make* your child "feel" his emotions. All you have to do is embrace him with warm compassion and adore him, messy, contrary feelings and all. In the safe embrace of your unconditional love, your child will open up to healing.

PLAYING WITH YOUR CHILD: GAMES FOR EMOTIONAL INTELLIGENCE

All young mammals play; it's their way of learning skills they'll need when they're full-grown, from finding food to getting along with others. It's also the way small humans explore, learn, and process their emotions. We can think of play as the work your child needs to do to build her brain and grow up healthy. Kids are also simply more "in their bodies" than adults. When they get wound up emotionally, their bodies need to discharge all that energy. That's one of the reasons they have so much more energy than we do.

Many parents tell me they're too tired and busy to play with their children. Mothers, especially, are often so focused on moving kids through the daily routine that they see play as an onerous task. But what if I told you that physical play with your child is the single best way to bond and help your child process emotion?

Kids use play to work through emotional issues so they can restore their equilibrium. Over and over, they act out going to the doctor's office, trade roles, give shots to their teddy bear. At least in their imaginations, they get to be the powerful one. That's an essential antidote to their daily experience of being smaller, dependent, often powerless. Giggling releases the same pent-up stress hormones as a good cry in a parent's arms. And roughhousing stimulates endorphins and oxytocin, the feel-good hormones, so physical play makes kids happy and helps them bond.[11] That's why it's one of the best ways to strengthen your relationship with your child.

The good news is that these games don't have to last long—maybe even as little as two minutes. And believe it or not, most parents find them energizing. That's because the tension and irritation we carry around makes us tired. When we play, we discharge stress hormones just like our kids, giving us a little more energy. And just as for kids, physical play triggers the release of endorphins and oxytocin in our systems, so we feel happier and more connected.

So when your child asks you to play, make a deal. Sure, you'll play Barbie, or build a train track for a few minutes. But first, will they play your game for a few minutes? Here are some ideas to get you started:

- **Wrestle, pillow-fight, let your child try to push you over.** All kids need a safe way to express their anger at their parents. Of course, let your child win, until he asks you to try harder.

- **Chase your child.** Toddlers, especially, need to run away from us and know we'll always re-collect them. You'd rather have her do it in your home than at the park, so make it a game. Chase after her, catch her, and let her go again. Or try to catch her but trip. This is both a power game and a separation game, like peekaboo.

- **Be a bumbling monster.** This variation of the chase game adds the elements of fear and dominance, and works with all ages of kids. Swagger and strut and roar at your child about how you'll catch him and show him who's boss, being just scary enough to trigger giggles as you trip and bumble and let him outsmart you or overpower you. Kids spend most of their time feeling smaller and powerless, so they need opportunities to feel stronger, faster, and smarter than we are. (*"You can't get away from me! Hey, where'd you go? You're too fast for me!"*) For timid kids, reverse roles: *"I'm the scary monster coming to get you.... Oh, I tripped.... Now, where did you go? EEK! You scared ME!"*

- **The Bye-Bye Game.** Kids in every culture of the world play separation games because the threat of losing parents is such a big fear for all children. *"Let's play Bye-Bye.... I'm going out the door. If you miss me, yell the silliest word you can think of, and I'll come back."* Walk into the closet or bathroom, but don't give your child a chance to miss you. Before you're fully through the door, jump out again, yelling *"Rhinoceros!"* or any word that will make your child laugh. Hug and kiss her, and say, *"I missed you so much, I couldn't leave.... Let's try that again!"* Exaggerate your own separation anxiety to get your child laughing, and very gradually increase the amount of time you're out of sight. Eventually, you can graduate to Hide-and-Seek.

- **The "I Need You" Game.** For separation issues, when your child is being clingy, or when there's a new baby and she's wondering if she's still loved, cling to her, being super-exaggerated and silly. *"I know you want me to let go so you can go play, but I NEED you! I only want to be with you. PLEASE be with me now?"* Keep holding your child's hand or clinging to her dress. She will like the feeling that *she* is the one in charge of letting go, rather than feeling pushed away. If you act silly enough, she will also giggle and let off some of the tension around good-byes. When she definitively pushes you away, say, *"It's okay. I know you will come back. We always come back to each other."*

- **The Fix Game.** I call this the fix game because it fixes what-ever's wrong by convincing the child he's deeply loved. Play the bumbler as you chase her, hug, kiss, let her get away, and repeat again and again: *"I need my Chelsea hugs. . . . You can't get away. . . . I have to hug you and cover you with kisses. . . . Oh no, you got away. . . . I'm coming after you. . . . I just have to kiss you more and hug you more. . . . You're too fast for me. . . . But I'll never give up. . . . I love you too much. . . . I got you. . . . Now I'll kiss your toes. . . . Oh no, you're too strong for me. . . . But I will always want more Chelsea hugs. . . . I'm coming after you . . ."* Both parents can even play at the same time, and "argue" about who gets to hug their darling child first. This game is guaran-teed to transform your child's doubt about whether she's truly loved (and any child who is "misbehaving" harbors that doubt).

- **"Are you out of hugs?!"** Use this when your child is annoying or in your face. *"Are you out of hugs again? Let's do some-thing about that!"* Grab your child and give her a *long* hug—as long as you can. Don't loosen your grip until she begins to squirm, and then don't let go immediately. Hug harder and say, *"I LOVE hugging you! I never want to let go. Promise I can hug you again soon?"* Then let go and connect with a big, warm smile, and say, *"Thank you! I needed that!"*

- **When your child has fears of any kind.** Let your child scare you, and be mock terrified. He'll giggle at your fearfulness, releasing his anxieties about his own. Or let her ride horsey on your back, and be just wild enough that she's a tiny bit afraid of falling off, so she's laughing and shrieking as she hangs on. Any games that help children dance with their fears physically give them an opportunity to giggle out pent-up fear, so they can be braver in real life.

- **When your child is reluctant about potty learning.** Sing ridiculous potty songs, wear a diaper on your head, pretend you just can't hold it but you're too scared to use the toilet, and dance around. The more your child giggles about using the potty, the more ready she'll be to actually do it.

- **When your child goes through a stage of whining a lot.** Remember that whining is an expression of powerlessness. Refusing to "hear" until they use a "big kid" voice further invalidates them. But you don't really want to reward whining by "giving in" to what they're asking for in that whiny voice, either. Lawrence Cohen, in *Playful Parenting*[12]—my inspiration for many of these games, and the book I recommend most often to parents—suggests that you express confidence that your child can use her "strong" voice and offer your assistance to help her find it by making it into a game: *"Hey, where did your strong voice go? It was here a minute ago. I LOVE your strong voice! I'll help you find it. Help me look. Is it under the chair? No . . . In the toy box? No . . . HEY! You found it!! That was your strong voice!! Yay! I love your strong voice! Now, tell me again what you need, in your strong voice."*

- **When you and your child seem to be having a lot of power struggles.** All children need a chance to feel powerful and to experiment with defiance; you'd rather this be a game than over something that matters. Try "I bet you can't push me over" or "Oh no, don't do *that!*" (*"Whatever you do, don't get off the couch! Oh no, now I have to give you twenty kisses! Okay, your turn to give me an order."*)

- **When your child is getting overexcited or too revved up.** *"You have so much energy right now. Do you want to spin around? Come over here (or outside) with me where it's safe to spin around, and I'll spot you."* Find a safe place where no other kids or parents are there to further stimulate him, and let him spin around, or jump up and down, or run in circles around you—whatever he chooses. When he drops in exhaustion, snuggle him and say, *"It's so much fun to be excited. But sometimes you get overexcited and you need a little help to calm down. Now, let's take three deep breaths to relax. In through the nose, out through the mouth. One . . . two . . . three . . . Good! Do you feel a little calmer? It's good to know how to calm yourself down. Now, let's go snuggle by ourselves and read a book for a bit."*

- **When your kids are fighting a lot.** When tempers are calm, say, *"Would you two please fight with each other now?"* When they begin to fight, pretend to be a TV commentator. *"We're on the scene tonight watching two sisters who can't seem to get along! Stay with us while we observe this behavior live! Notice how big sister is bossy, but little sister is provocative! Both girls want the same piece of salami! Are they smart enough to realize there's more salami in the fridge? Stay tuned. . . ."* Your kids will giggle and let off tension, and get to see how ridiculous they are.

- **To help a child who's coping with a challenging issue, like the start of school, or playground struggles, or being sick.** Have one stuffed animal be the parent, and one be the child, and act out the situation. Using stuffed animals removes it one step from reality so most kids find it more comfortable, but some children like to actually act the situation out themselves (as opposed to using the proxy of dolls or stuffed animals). *"Let's pretend we're in the sandbox and I want your truck but you don't want to share,"* or *"Let's pretend you're the teacher and I'm the student,"* or *"Let's pretend you're the doctor and I'm sick."* Playing out these situations that cause so much stress for kids helps them feel more in control of their own emotions and lets them be the powerful one in a situation where they might have felt powerless and humiliated in real life.

ADDITIONAL RESOURCES: SCRIPTS FOR SIBLING CONFLICTS

Sibling issues are beyond the scope of this book, but there's plenty of support on the Aha! Parenting website to help you foster sibling harmony. These scripts take you through the process of conflict resolution and teaching emotional intelligence with siblings. If you're reading this book electronically, simply click on the script to read on your e-reader.

Teaching Emotional Intelligence with Young Siblings
When the preschooler hits the younger sibling . . .

www.ahaparenting.com/parenting-tools/family-life/child-hits-baby

Teaching Older Siblings to Navigate Conflict
"She hit me back first!"

www.ahaparenting.com/parenting-tools/family-life/siblings_fight

4

Raising a Child
Who *Wants* to Behave

Dare *Not* to Discipline

> My son, now four, can be very controlling and willful, but
> I really did find that once I threw out the reward-and-
> punishment approach and took this new direction, the
> fighting and power struggles became less and less over
> time, and I no longer ever feel the need for things like
> time-outs. I am so glad that I turned my back on those
> methods.
>
> —JO, MOTHER OF TWO

What kind of human being do you want to raise? When I ask parents
this, most say they're hoping for a child who's happy, responsible,
considerate, respectful, authentic, and honest. A self-disciplined
child who acts right, whether or not you're there. A kid who thinks
for herself and doesn't bow to peer pressure.

Most parents worry about what kind of discipline works best to
raise that kind of child. After all, every child is different. And parents get so much conflicting advice about discipline. No wonder it's
a struggle.

So I won't just be giving you my opinions about how to raise a
self-disciplined child who wants to cooperate. As in the rest of this
book, I'll be sharing what the latest research tells us. Fortunately,

there's a lot of it, and it's consistent. The executive summary? This is a tough one for many parents, so stick with me. If you want a cooperative, ethical, self-disciplined child whom you can trust to do the right thing, even as she becomes a teenager, you should never punish. No spanking, no time-outs, no yelling, no parent-contrived consequences. Really. No punishment of any kind. The word *discipline* actually means "to guide" but virtually everything we think of as discipline is punishment. And punishment erodes your relationship with your child, which destroys the only motivation she has to behave as you'd like. This chapter will show you why punishment doesn't work, and why you don't need it to raise a child who will make you proud.

Throughout this chapter, we'll use our Three Big Ideas—Regulating Yourself; Fostering Connection; and Coaching, Not Controlling—to help you take the struggle out of guiding your child toward the behavior you want. What does connection have to do with raising a child who wants to behave? Everything. The only reason kids give up what *they* want, to do what *you* want, is that they trust you and wouldn't want to disappoint you. What does regulating ourselves as parents have to do with discipline? If you've ever found yourself yelling and then been stricken with remorse, you know the answer to that question. You'll be happy to hear that I've seen many, many parents who've used the tools I'll be giving you in this chapter to stop yelling. It's completely possible for you to look back a year from now and not remember the last time you yelled at your child. Coaching, not controlling, requires us to consider carefully how we guide, or discipline, our child. If your most important goal is obedience, then you won't mind using fear and force to ensure it. If, on the other hand, you want to raise a child who does the right thing whether you're there or not, then you need to think longer term. Instead of threatening and punishing, thinking long-term means teaching the right behavior, strengthening your connection so your child *wants* to meet your expectations, and then helping him with his emotions so he has the ability to behave well. Let's look at how to do that.

The Dirty Little Secret About Discipline and Punishment

I have stopped time-outs altogether and even consequences and now have very little need for "discipline." K is much more amenable to correction than she was before (now that we don't use punishment)—and this is a high-need, high-intensity, willful child!
—Alene, mom of two kids under age four

Punishment is defined as an action with an intent to hurt, either physically or psychologically, in order to teach a lesson. Punishment is effective only to the degree that the child experiences it as painful, so while parents may think they are using "loving punishment" to teach their child, the child will never experience punishment as loving.

The dirty little secret about punishment is that it doesn't work to teach children better behavior. In fact, studies show that punishment creates more bad behavior. Not just that children who behave badly get punished more, but that children who get punished more will behave badly more often over time.[1] That's because punishment teaches all the wrong lessons.

- Punishment models force. Just ask a child whose parents spank or yell to "play Mommy" and watch her discipline her dolls.
- Punishment convinces the child that he's bad. Bad for having the bad feelings that drove him to behave badly, bad for

behaving badly, bad for causing us to be angry at him, bad for getting mad when we punish him. Unfortunately, many studies prove that children live up or down to our expectations, meaning that children who think they're bad will act "bad."

- Punishment actually keeps the child from taking responsibility, because it creates an external locus of control—the authority figure. When a child is punished, she begins to see herself as incapable of "behaving" on her own. She no longer sees it as her job to "behave"—it's the authority figure's job to "make" her!

- Punishment makes the child angry that we're intentionally hurting her, so she resists seeing that the behavior we're promoting actually has some value to her. She becomes defiant, angry, more aggressive, and more likely to act out.[2]

- Punishment teaches kids to focus on whether they'll get caught and punished, rather than on the negative impact of their behavior. It actually impedes moral development by, as Alfie Kohn, author of *Unconditional Parenting*, says, "directing the child to the consequences of his behavior for . . . himself"[3] rather than taking responsibility for his impact on others.

- Punishment erodes our child's warm connection to us, which is his only motivation to choose to follow our rules.

The more painful the punishment, the more deeply the child learns these negative lessons, and the more his behavior suffers. But even time-outs and parent-imposed consequences are experienced as emotionally painful—punishment—by children, so they have the same effect as other punishment, although arguably to a lesser degree than physical punishment.[4]

I'm not advocating permissive parenting, or just letting children do whatever they want. Children are new on the planet, and they look to their parents for guidance. In fact, when they don't get that guidance, they feel unsafe, and they push for it. That's what we mean when we say a child who is acting out is looking for limits. But while limits are essential, it is never necessary to be less than kind and compassionate with children. Instead of enforcing limits with punishment, we can guide behavior in a way that makes it more likely that our child will accept our standards as his own. After all, teachable moments are only teachable if the student is ready to learn.

Although *discipline* means "to guide," in common usage it always seems to include an element of chastisement, or making the child feel bad, along with the guidance. To change our thinking, we need to change our words, so let's move beyond "discipline," which most of us associate with harsh teaching. Instead, let's offer our child loving guidance.

When our children are young and easily intimidated, loving guidance may be more work than using punishment to scare them into behaving. But there's no question that it's more effective and more rewarding, because it gets us out of the discipline business altogether by producing kids who *want* to behave appropriately.

In a moment, we'll examine exactly what kind of guidance works best to raise self-disciplined kids, age by age. But first, let's consider any fears you might have that discipline, or punishment, is necessary to raise good kids.

Most parents say they punish to teach their children how to behave appropriately. However, that's clearly not true. Children actually learn how to behave from what we model every day, whether it's *"Thank you for the present, Aunt Susan"* or *"That *#@*! just cut me off in traffic."* And if he doesn't actually know the appropriate behavior, then teaching is in order, not punishment.

The truth is that we punish when we think our child knew how he should have behaved, but he didn't choose it. We're not so much teaching good behavior as hoping that the punishment will be unpleasant enough that our child will be persuaded to do things our way. Unfortunately, it doesn't work to prevent a recurrence of the misbehavior, or we wouldn't need to keep punishing.

It's obvious why punishment doesn't work with children. Research has repeatedly proven that "crimes of passion" can't be prevented by punishing criminals, because when humans are driven by fierce emotion they aren't thinking rationally. So certainly a child under age six, whose rational brain doesn't yet have full control over his emotional brain, doesn't have the capacity when he's in the grip of strong emotions to consider the punishment he may suffer. Punishment doesn't help him with the fierce need or emotion driving his "crime of passion," so it doesn't get to the root of the problem and prevent recurrences. Instead, punishment has all the negative effects we've already considered.

From this rational perspective, punishment doesn't make sense. So why do we do it? We punish because:

- Even the threat of punishment stops misbehavior in the moment, as long as we're willing to follow through on our threats and keep escalating as necessary.
- We're told to punish, by "experts" who aren't informed about the most recent research.
- We're frightened; we feel powerless; punishment makes us feel we're doing something.
- When we're in a state of fight-or-flight, it feels like an emergency, and our child looks like the enemy.
- We're hurt or angry. We lash out.
- We don't know other ways to coax good behavior out of our children. Punishment alleviates our frustration and makes us feel like we're addressing the situation.
- We've absorbed the misguided view that children will be disobedient and manipulative unless we force them to "behave."

- We were punished, and since we learn both sides of every relationship, we think this is what parents do to guide children.
- We were punished, and because the emotional pain of being hurt by the most important person in our life was too much for us to handle, we've repressed the pain of it. But emotions that are repressed don't go away, they press to the surface, causing us to re-enact the situation that produced them—just shifting to the other role. This is why people who've been hit as children so often hit their own child. And people who were punished automatically punish, unless they reflect on how it felt to them.

So we punish because we've been taught that's how to stop bad behavior, and we see that it does work instantly in the short term. But we also punish to discharge our own upsetting feelings. In fact, I would argue that most of the time we punish our children not to regulate their behavior—since it doesn't work unless we keep escalating—but to regulate our own emotions. We punish our child instead of taking responsibility for our own anger and restoring ourselves to a state of calm. Punishing our child discharges our own frustration and worry, and makes us feel better.

Are you thinking, "But sometimes the child needs correction! It's not all our own baggage!"? Yes, that's absolutely true. But the guidance that works with children is always most effective when it comes from love, not anger. When we're in the grip of fight-or-flight arousal, our child looks like the enemy and we're out to win, not to teach. In our calm moments, every parent knows this.

I can understand if you're feeling a bit nervous right about now. If we think punishment is our only tool to raise well-behaved kids, the idea of losing it is scary. What on earth will we do to get compliance from our child without the threat of punishment?

You might be surprised to hear that there are thousands of parents like me, who have guided their children without time-out or any other punishments, and whose children have grown into wonderful teenagers and adults. These children aren't perfect; they make mistakes like any other immature human who's still learning. But they've never needed to be threatened into compliance. Why? Because these kids *want* to make good choices, the choices we've guided them toward over the years. All kids know what the right choice is, if parents are modeling and talking about those choices. These kids want to do the right thing because they've stayed deeply connected to their parents, whom they don't want to disappoint. And because they've learned to manage their own emotions, they can resist impulses that might take them off track.

Your goal in disciplining your child is actually to help him develop self-discipline, meaning to *assume responsibility for his actions, including making amends and avoiding a repeat, whether the authority figure is present or not*. Isn't that the lesson we're hoping to teach when we punish? Loving guidance actually accomplishes this goal better than punishment or discipline. Here's why:

- **Loving guidance increases our influence with our child.** Humans resist being controlled. That's a good thing, since it allows us to take responsibility for our own behavior. But it means that when we guide children with force, they resist. So the more loving our guidance, the more our children are open to seeing for themselves the wisdom of the rules and habits we promote, and the more likely they are to "own them."

- **Loving guidance helps children feel safe,** so they can concentrate on their developmental tasks, like learning. Authoritarian parenting keeps children in a state of stress, worried about the next punishment (which may explain why kids who are spanked have lower IQs[5]). Permissive parenting, on the other hand, can make kids feel like no one is in charge, which is also scary. When we set limits in an empathic, loving way, we help our child feel safe.

- **Loving guidance gives children the support they need to understand and regulate their own emotions,** so they can behave as their best self without being pulled off-track by the pressure of deep feelings. He learns that actions are to be limited, but he is okay, complete with all his complicated emotions. That feeling of "goodness" is what helps all of us make progress toward our good intentions.

- **Loving guidance strengthens our bond with our child.** Loving guidance shifts us from focusing on our child's behavior to focusing on our relationship with her. She learns that she can't have everything she wants, but she gets something better—someone who accepts her, messy emotions and all, and who will help her manage her actions.

- **Loving guidance strengthens our empathy for our child.** We all know that children need love most when they least deserve it. We may be annoyed by his behavior, but empathy helps us see beyond our annoyance to understand why our child is acting this way. We end up feeling compassion for this small person who is trying so hard. Punishment, on the other hand, requires us to harden our heart to our child and abandon him emotionally when he needs us most.

- **Loving guidance builds self-esteem.** Because loving guidance gets us out of the discipline business, parenting becomes more satisfying for us and we can enjoy our child more. When your child sees himself as someone who consistently inspires your delight, he feels good about himself as a human being.

- **Loving guidance creates a more peaceful home,** which gives kids (and adults!) the safe refuge they need from the pressures they encounter in the outside world.

Are you wondering how you can actually get your child cooperating without the threat of punishment? Let's look at how you can move beyond discipline in each developmental stage.

Guidance as Your Child Grows

BABIES (0–13 MONTHS): EMPATHIC REDIRECTION

The bad news is that babies often want everything they see. The good news is that they're generally distractible during the first year. Appropriate "discipline" for babies consists of offering guidance and setting limits for your child's safety—*"Hot! The fire is hot!"*—as well as for the protection of the kitty and those shiny breakables.

Should your baby start learning the meaning of the word *no*? Sure, for emergencies. But your baby's job is to explore; that's how babies learn and build smart brains. She needs to pull the pans out of the cupboard and put everything in her mouth. Babies who are told "No!" all the time learn to think inside the box. Does that mean you should let her put her fingers in the light socket? Of course not. You'll need to set limits to ensure her health and safety. But it does mean that babyproofing is better than trying to teach limits at this age. If it's important—the fire, for instance—you can't risk a young child following your limit, because she doesn't yet have the intellectual capacity to understand the danger. If it isn't important, why fight about it? Either way, the answer is to babyproof and supervise your child, rather than to punish transgressions.

There is increasing evidence that moods in infancy lay the groundwork for mood tendencies later in life. A baby who spends a lot of time unhappy will develop a brain neurologically primed for unhappiness. When a baby is upset and doesn't get help to regulate himself, his brain will wire itself so that his "base level" of anxiety is higher, and so that he moves from calm to upset more quickly. Given this, we want to minimize our baby's frustration when we set limits. Having a comforting adult to hear her, soothe her, and help her "switch gears" is essential: *"I know, you want that light, but the light is hot. Yes, you're mad. . . . I hear you. . . . When you feel better, we can go find the doggie and pet her."*

TODDLERS (13–36 MONTHS): SIDESTEPPING POWER STRUGGLES

By thirteen months, many parents are drawn into power struggles, as the toddler becomes a vocal advocate for her own desires. This is the age that takes parents by surprise. But it's completely appropriate for your toddler to have her own opinions and develop a sense of her own power in the world. That's her developmental task right now.

Toddlers are famous for saying "No!" but it turns out that we teach it to them. A UCLA study cited by Claire Lerner of the research center Zero to Three found that the average toddler hears the word *no* or its equivalent about every nine minutes.[6] Toddlers want to assert their will, which is a healthy part of toddler development, but they're stymied at every turn: *"No, you can't have that pen near the couch; give me the pen. . . . No running. . . . Get in the car now. . . . No, you can't have candy. . . . No, that's fragile. . . . No hitting!"* Reasonable requests and limits, all. But the toddler doesn't see the reason for them, so most toddlers rebel and test at every turn. This new belligerence is her first step toward taking responsibility for herself. If she's not allowed to say *no* to you now, she won't be able to say *no* to an inappropriate advance from her soccer coach or to her peers as a teen. Let her say *no* whenever you can do so without compromise to safety, health, or other people's rights.

You can always use your size advantage, and sometimes you need to, but every time you overwhelm her by force and make her "lose," you're increasing her tendency to be oppositional. Skip the long explanations. Instead, see yourself as the guide for a brilliant, joyful being who is still learning the rules here and can't yet reason the way you do. If you can remember that his brain isn't fully wired yet, so his cerebral cortex can't exert much control over his upsetting emotions, you'll find it a lot easier to see things from your toddler's perspective. Empathy works its magic by defusing emotion, even at this age: *"You are crying. You really wish you could have that, but that's not for babies."* He will cry harder for a few moments (as we all do when we feel understood and the floodgates open), but then he'll be able to let it go and move on to other things.

So what kind of "discipline" is appropriate for your toddler? Empathic limits! Let's examine this in action.

Olivia, age two, is splashing water right out of the tub. Her father calmly explains that water belongs in the tub and asks her to stop. But Olivia persists. What should Dad do?

We need to start by checking our expectations against our child's age and capacity. Not many two-year-olds could resist splashing in the water. When a child has a good relationship with her parents and still won't cooperate with their requests, it's because her needs and feelings are stronger than her frontal cortex (which is, after all, just beginning to take shape in two-year-olds).

A two-year-old's job description is to explore the world, which includes throwing water around at every opportunity. Our jobs are to keep her safe, to clean up the wet bathroom, and—yes—to let her explore when she can do so safely and without making our lives too difficult. (Resentment makes for lousy parenting, as we have all discovered at times.)

So if we start from the premise that our two-year-old is not being bad, but is a young human exploring the world who really doesn't understand why Dad cares so much that the water is getting all over the bathroom, then we're seeing things from her perspective. That empathy changes everything. We may even be willing to let her splash water all over, at least for today. But we may also be tired and have too much laundry to do already and simply can't bear the idea of more water getting splashed, so we may decide to set a limit on the splashing.

In this case, Dad has already asked Olivia once to stop splashing, but she couldn't do it. Now, let's try to redirect that splashing energy. Get in her face in a friendly way, with your hand on her splashing hand, and say, *"Olivia, water stays in the tub. . . . Can you splash gently, like this?"* Stir the water with her. Maybe she'll start stirring instead of splashing. Or maybe not, and it's time for one more kind but clear warning, and then take her out of the tub. Too many warnings before we follow through teach the child that she doesn't have to pay attention until the third or fourth warning. Instead, say kindly, "Can you stop splashing the water out, or do you need to get out of the tub now?"

Then, set your limit in a compassionate way. Gently take her out of the tub, empathizing with her upset: *"You're mad! You don't want to get out. You love the tub. You love splashing. But that was too much splashing for me, and it was just too hard for you to stop splashing. Tomorrow night we'll try again. And now that it's getting warm, you can splash all you want outside in your pool."* (That's meeting her natural need to splash.)

"But that's all the splashing I can handle for tonight. I know, that makes you so sad and mad; you're crying now. Come here, sweetie. Let's get you wrapped in this warm towel and snuggle a bit. Whenever you're ready, we'll get dressed and read your book."

Because we're calm and kind as we set our limit, our child doesn't get distracted by having to fight back or prove she was right. She may be mad that we got her out of the tub, but she is *much* less angry than if we were mad about it. In fact, she feels loved, understood, and convinced we're on her side, even though she doesn't get what she wants. Our relationship has deepened, rather than eroded.

Because we don't make her wrong, she doesn't internalize the sense that she is a bad person, either for splashing or for getting mad about being removed from the tub. That's important, because when humans feel like bad people, they're more likely to act like bad people.

Because we didn't take it personally, and empathized with her upset even while we took care of our own need to avoid a flooded bathroom, our child gets the message that there is nothing bad or scary about her feelings. It is just sadness, and after sadness we can feel better and read a story. So we're supporting her development of emotional intelligence.

Because we soothe her distress, the neural pathways in her brain that send soothing biochemicals are strengthened and her ability to self-soothe is strengthened.

Because we set a limit, our child learns that indeed there are consequences to her actions. We will enforce our limit on splashing by removing her from the tub. But that is not a consequence in the way most parents use it, as a punishment. It is simply a firm limit. So she is free to learn rather than getting distracted by punishment. She is actually empowered by the fact that she can choose. Of course, her brain development hasn't quite caught up with her desire to manage her splashing impulse. But now she *wants* to manage her splashing, rather than getting distracted by fighting with us or "proving" she can win or testing our limits. She's headed in the right direction.

PRESCHOOLERS (3–5 YEARS): LEARNING SELF-MANAGEMENT

By the time your child is three, he seems to know the rules (*"Don't hit the baby!"*) So if your preschooler knows what's right but doesn't choose to do it, then what's stopping him? He can't quite regulate himself to choose what's right. Because:

- **He's curious.** Preschoolers are natural scientists. How do you make lipstick swivel up and how does it look on the wall? Would a washcloth flush down the toilet? He isn't trying to be bad, just learning how the world works, and he doesn't realize that seeing if your tax forms float in the bathtub qualifies as an emergency.

- **He's busy, and he doesn't understand why your agenda is important.** No four-year-old would agree that brushing his teeth *this minute* is more important than finding his lost action figure. Repeating ourselves is unavoidable: We help our children create positive life habits by working with them, over and over, to brush their teeth, hang up their jacket, and put their toys away. That's just part of the parents' job description, best accepted with grace, like doing the laundry. Try expressing your requests as an invitation to play: *"Climb on my back for a bucking bronco ride to the bath, cowboy!"* No preschooler can resist a good game, even if it eventually leads to the bathtub or someplace else he might rather avoid.

- **She feels disconnected from us, either temporarily or persistently.** All young children feel disconnected from their parents when they're fighting off fear, frustration, and the many other uncomfortable emotions that build up in the course of their day. Preschoolers often "store up" fear and hurts, waiting for a safe opportunity to feel and express them. And if they spend the day away from us, you can count on them arriving home with a "full backpack" of negative feelings that they don't feel comfortable letting themselves feel while they're trying so hard to be "big kids" at school. Until your child has a chance to be heard, those feelings will be looking to spill out, disconnecting her, driving misbehavior and keeping her from being her usual sunny self. That's why the single best thing you can do for your preschooler is to prioritize reconnecting with her when you're reunited at the end of the day. Special Time and happy roughhousing help kids discharge the feelings they've been storing up, reconnect, and regulate themselves. The parent functions almost as an external regulating system, giving the child a safe haven to process the complicated feelings that would otherwise push him to choose misbehavior.

- **His brain is still developing.** He's still learning to soothe himself when he gets upset, so when his temper flares, he can't rein it in quickly. He may be able to use four-syllable words, but don't be fooled, his anxious amygdala can still overwhelm his higher brain functions (*"Does she love the baby more? Take that, baby!"*) It's critical to remember that he isn't bad, just little. His rational brain functions aren't fully online yet.

But preschoolers have much more control of themselves than toddlers, so these are the crucial years to teach the fundamental lessons of behavior. We do this—you guessed it!—by regulating our own emotions to stay calm, keeping our connection with our preschooler strong so he's more open to our influence, and coaching rather than controlling to help our child develop self-management skills.

ELEMENTARY SCHOOLERS (6–9 YEARS): DEVELOPING POSITIVE HABITS

By age seven, the brain has done some serious rewiring and settled down to the task of learning. By now, most children who have been raised with respectful listening and empathy can manage their emotions well enough to avoid tantrums. And because they're better at managing their emotions, they're better at managing their behavior.

That doesn't mean six-to-nine-year-olds always behave, however. They need repeated reminders to do simple things. They're sore losers. They fight with their siblings. They worry about peer interactions and take it out on us. Some of these issues come from their increasingly complex social worlds. Some—sibling squabbles, famously—come from the big feelings they're still learning to manage. But most of the conflicts we have with elementary schoolers come from our differing needs. We're focused on them doing homework, brushing teeth, doing chores, following the hundreds of directives we give them every day. They're focused on mastering that soccer ball kick, or making friends, or whether their sibling is getting more favorable treatment. No wonder we so often find ourselves frustrated.

Many of our conflicts with school-age kids can be solved with more structure and more hands-on interaction. Pointing to the chart on the wall reminds your six-year-old that he has to brush his teeth and put his lunch in his backpack before he heads for school.

A consistent daily routine of a snack and homework as soon as he gets home helps your seven-year-old learn to sit himself down to tackle an unpleasant task. Working with your eight-year-old every Saturday morning to pick up her room while you have a nice chat helps her solidify the habit.

If your child has been supported to notice relationship ruptures and repair them, rather than being forced into grudging apologies, he probably does it automatically by now. If not, it's time to start using the Three Rs of Making Amends: Reflection, Repair, and Responsibility (see the Action Guides in this chapter). Instead of parent-prescribed consequences, empower child-chosen initiatives in which your child takes responsibility for something he's done that has caused damage. When he breaks an object, he helps to replace it. When he hurts a relationship, it's his job to repair it. But remember that if you think up the reparation and force it down his throat, it only makes sense that he'll reject it. Instead, let this be an empowering opportunity for him to learn that we all make mistakes—and we can always take action to make things better.

Setting Limits with Empathy: The Basics

THE SWEET SPOT BETWEEN STRICT AND PERMISSIVE

Human behavior doesn't fit neatly into boxes, and parenting styles are no exception. But almost fifty years ago, a team of researchers headed by Diana Baumrind observed families and developed four descriptions of the parenting approaches most parents use. Updated versions of these same four descriptions are still used by most child development experts as a useful way to understand parental behavior to this day. Can you see yourself in one of these four parenting styles?

1. **Authoritarian.** Authoritarian parents have high expectations of their children, which is a good thing, research shows.
   That's how children get good grades, learn to manage themselves responsibly, and stay out of trouble. The problem is
   that these parents don't offer their kids much support. It's
   pull up your socks, straighten up and fly right, my way or the
   highway. These parents were usually raised this way themselves and usually think they came out fine, but research
   shows that their kids often end up rebellious during the teen
   years. They're also more vulnerable to the pressures of the
   peer group, because they're not used to thinking for themselves and taking responsibility for their own behavior, and
   because kids who don't get enough support end up looking
   for love in all the wrong places.

2. **Permissive.** Most permissive parents are trying hard not to
   repeat their own parents' tough-love parenting style, so they
   go overboard in the other direction. These are parents who
   offer their children lots of support, which is essential. But
   there are two problems with this parenting style. First, parents who use this style often give their children the message
   that disappointment, frustration, and other upsetting emotions must be avoided at all costs. It's harder for their kids to
   learn they can face unhappiness and bounce back, which
   is crucial to developing resilience. Second, the permissive
   style avoids setting limits and high expectations. Some
   parents believe that's a good thing—they wouldn't want to
   get in the way of their child's natural development. Others
   just can't bear their child's suffering because they can't regulate their own anxiety. But kids who never need to "manage"
   themselves to accommodate limits and rise to expectations
   have a harder time developing self-discipline. Don't get me

wrong—there's no such thing as too much respect and empathy. But if you let your child walk all over you or other people, what are you teaching him about relationships? This parenting approach tends to raise kids who are self-centered, anxious, and not very resilient.

3. **Neglectful.** There have always been parents who can't give their children the love and attention they need, whether because of alcoholism, narcissism, or simply needing to work two jobs to support the family. But this style of parenting seem to me to be even more prevalent today, at least in some communities, where we rationalize putting children into daycare at ever-earlier ages, and then as they grow up we leave them to their own lives with their peer group, so that we have little or no influence on them by the time they're teenagers. The most obviously neglectful parents sometimes vanish into drug addiction or abandon the family, but I also see caring, "normal" families where the parents are too distracted by their own work or social lives to engage deeply with their kids. It's not unusual to see these parents lavish money on their children instead of attention. This is always a message to the child that he isn't worth loving, and if both parents are uninvolved, the lack of connection often results in a child with anxiety, substance abuse, or other issues.

4. **Authoritative.** The final parenting style is the one that Baumrind's research showed raises the best-adjusted kids. Her authoritative—as opposed to authoritarian—parents offer their children lots of love and support, like the permissive parents. But they also hold high expectations, like the authoritarian parents. Age-appropriate expectations, of

course—they aren't expecting a three-year-old to clean up her room by herself. But they may well be working with that three-year-old to help her clean up, over and over and over, so that by six she really can clean up her room herself. These parents are involved—even demanding. They expect family dinners, lots of discussion straight through high school, good grades, responsible behavior. But they also offer their children complete support to learn how to achieve these expectations. Importantly, these parents aren't controlling like the authoritarian parents. They listen to the child's side of things, they make compromises, and they cede control where possible. Their kids, not surprisingly, stay close to them—they often describe one of their parents as the person they would most trust to talk to about a problem. These kids usually do well in school, and they're also the ones that teachers describe as responsible and well liked, simply nice kids who are a pleasure to have around.

Because the term *authoritative* is so close to *authoritarian* and often confuses parents, I prefer to call this style "empathy with limits."

It's essential to note that this is *not* just a matter of finding a happy medium between strict and permissive. Actually, the brilliance of Baumrind's vision was that she integrated two continuums: demandingness and responsiveness. Stay with me here, because you're about to discover the answer to many of your parenting dilemmas. Here's how these two continuums—demandingness and responsiveness—create our four parenting styles.

As you can see on the next page, permissive parents are low on demandingness, but high on responsiveness. Authoritarian parents are the opposite: high on demandingness, but low on responsiveness.

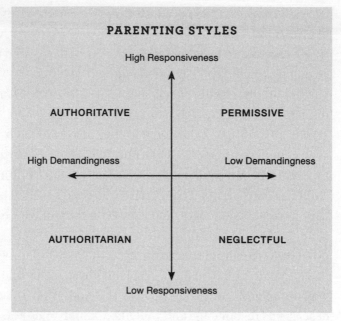

PARENTING STYLES

High Responsiveness

AUTHORITATIVE   PERMISSIVE

High Demandingness   Low Demandingness

AUTHORITARIAN   NEGLECTFUL

Low Responsiveness

Neglectful parents are low on both. And (authoritative) parents who use empathy with limits—no surprise!—are high on both responsiveness *and* demandingness.

Can you see how this might play out in daily life? For instance, what do parents do when their eight-year-old brings home a bad report card?

- **Authoritarian.** Yells at kid and without any discussion grounds him until the next report card, which had better have improved grades. End of discussion. Maybe a tutor is hired, which is presented as a punishment, and maybe substituted for an activity the kid loved, like playing basketball. The child is left demotivated and angry and has to figure out any improvement for himself.

- **Permissive.** Listens empathically. Accepts the child's excuse that it's all the teacher's fault and asks the child to please try to do better next time. She may tell the child she believes in him or even make a suggestion about working harder—but she doesn't give him any real help in figuring out how to change things, in the form of new structure so he can actually learn the necessary information and skills. If the child tries to express something vulnerable, like his fears that he just *can't* do math or get organized, the permissive parent can't tolerate the anxiety, so she reassures him that he has what it takes. Her son is left all alone with his worries.

- **Neglectful.** What report card?

- **Limits with empathy.** Asks the child whether he's surprised by the report card, what he thinks created this situation, and what he thinks he can do to learn the material and bring his grades up. Agrees on a plan with the child, one with a ton of limits and high expectations, because there's lost ground to make up. But this isn't just a boot camp. This parent is completely empathic with how hard this change will be for her son. What's more, she sees herself as partly responsible and an essential part of the remedial work. She lends him her calm hopefulness, so he can manage his anxiety as he climbs out of the hole he's dug for himself.

See how this works? The parent who uses empathy with limits has expectations that are just as high as those of the authoritarian parent and is just as much of a leader with her children. There's more partnership, understanding, listening, and respect, however, so the child doesn't go on the defensive and is more likely to step into the responsibility. The difference between permissiveness and empathy with limits is the high expectations and better regulation of our own anxiety, so that our child is supported to tackle what's hard. And the difference in parental involvement should be obvious—parents using empathy with limits are the most involved of any of the parenting styles. Which is probably why they're happier parents.

SHOULD YOU SPANK YOUR CHILD?

I loved my mother dearly, but I was afraid of her. To her dying day less than two years ago (I am in my forties) I was still afraid of saying the wrong thing or "getting in trouble," as much as I loved her. I vowed that my children, while respecting me, would not be afraid of me. I think I am succeeding, thanks in no small part to what I have learned from your encouraging us to love our children fully and wholly instead of parenting from a place of fear and worry.
   —Alene, mother of two

I've heard many stories from adults who've never forgiven the parents who spanked them "for their own good." And yet, in the United States, most parents still use physical punishment. As recently as 2007, 85 percent of adolescents said they had been slapped or spanked by their parents at some point in their lives.[7]

If your parents used spanking as a discipline method growing up, you may have reconciled yourself to their behavior by justifying it. You may even think there is no other choice for managing children who are "a handful." I often hear *"I got hit when I was a kid and I turned out okay,"* or *"I was spanked as a child, and I deserved it."* It's very hard for us to believe that people who loved us would intentionally hurt us, so we feel the need to excuse their behavior. But repressing that pain just makes us more likely to hit our own children. If

SPANKING: THE RESEARCH

Researcher Dr. Elizabeth Gershoff examined sixty years of research on corporal punishment in a 2002 meta-analytic study that is still considered the state of the art in the field.[8] This meta-analysis found that the only positive outcome of corporal punishment was immediate compliance. In other words, children who were spanked immediately stopped the offending behavior.

Unfortunately, however, corporal punishment was also associated with less long-term compliance, meaning that in the long term, spanking actually made children more likely to keep engaging in the offending behavior. Worse, corporal punishment was linked with nine other negative outcomes, including increased rates of aggression, delinquency, mental health problems, problems in relationships with their parents, and likelihood of being physically abused by parents whose punishment got out of hand.

A 2012 study reviewed the previous two decades of research and confirmed Gershoff's findings, reporting that kids who are spanked have less gray matter in their brains and are more likely to exhibit depression, anxiety, drug use, and aggression.[9] Spanking has repeatedly been shown to lower intelligence, while it increases tantrums, defiance, bullying, sibling violence, adult mental health problems, and later spousal abuse. *No* studies show that kids who are spanked are better behaved or grow up to be equally healthy emotionally. This may surprise you if you've heard that some studies show positive results from spanking. The press likes to create controversy because a good fight makes news, but *every* study of this issue that is considered scientifically credible (meaning it is peer-reviewed and meets scientific standards for publication) shows that spanking damages kids' psyches and worsens behavior.

you were willing to reach deep inside and really feel again the hurt you felt when you were physically punished as a child, you would never consider inflicting that pain on your own child. And the pain does not end in childhood, even if we repress and deny it. The scientific consensus of hundreds of studies shows that corporal punishment during childhood is associated with negative behaviors in adults, even when the adult says that the spanking did not affect them badly. Even a few instances of being hit as a child are associated with more depressive symptoms as an adult. While most of us who were spanked "turned out okay," it is clear that not being spanked would have helped us turn out to be healthier. I suspect that one contributing factor to the epidemic of anxiety and depression among adults in our culture is that so many of us grew up with parents who hurt us.

IS YELLING THE NEW SPANKING?

Since you're reading this book, you probably try to avoid spanking in favor of more positive discipline. But yelling? Most parents yell. It's just something we assume happens when we live with kids, like the flu. Afterward, we're often regretful, hoping we haven't done any damage. Or, if we yell a lot, we may rationalize: How else can we get that kid's attention? And it's not like it hurts her. . . . She barely listens; she rolls her eyes.

It is usually true, as we reassure ourselves, that our children know we love them, even if we yell. But it isn't true that yelling doesn't hurt children.

Imagine your husband or wife losing their temper and screaming at you. Now imagine them three times as big as you, towering over you. Imagine that you depend on that person completely for your food, shelter, safety, protection. Imagine they are your primary source of love and self-confidence and information about the world, that you have nowhere else to turn. Now take those feelings and magnify them by a factor of a thousand. That's something like what happens inside your child when you lose your temper at her.

If your child does not seem afraid of your anger, it's an indication that she has seen too much of it and has developed defenses against it—and against you. The more often we get angry, the more defended our child becomes, and therefore the less likely to show that it bothers her. Anger pushes children of all ages away from us. It practically guarantees that they'll have an "attitude" by the time they're ten, and that yelling fights will be the norm during their teen years. The unfortunate result of yelling is a child who is less likely to want to please you and is more open to the influences of the peer group and the larger culture.

Luckily, yelling doesn't have to be part of your parenting. When you shift your approach, you'll find that your child changes, too, and you won't feel like yelling so often. And as you use our Three Big Ideas—Regulating Yourself; Fostering Connection; and Coaching, Not Controlling—you'll find yourself more mindful and able to intervene constructively with your child before you lose control. For a plan to stop yelling, see Part 1 of this book.

TRANSFORM YOUR TIME-OUTS TO TIME-INS

To me, it is not about "avoiding" or "preventing" these emotional explosions; rather, it is about how we help our child understand their emotions and work through the distress. As a child, it was comforting and secure to know that I could have a meltdown with my parent there to guide me and be with me as I felt so confused.
   —Eileen, mother of two kids under age six

Compared to spanking, time-outs seem like a humane, sensible approach to discipline. They interrupt the bad behavior. They give everyone a chance to calm down. They're nonviolent (except when you have to drag your child to his room kicking and screaming).

But the fact that time-outs are better than spanking doesn't mean they're optimal discipline. You don't seriously think he's sitting on the naughty step considering how to be a better kid, do you? Like any normal human, he's feeling ashamed and angry and reviewing why he was right. Time-outs don't actually work to create better behavior. Here's why:

- **Children need our help to learn to calm themselves.** Sure, a child will eventually calm down if confined to "the naughty step" or his room, but what he's learning is that he's all alone with his most challenging feelings.

- **Time-outs make children feel bad about themselves.** Any child can explain to you that time-outs *are* punishment, no different from when you were made to stand in the corner as a child. Like all punishments, time-outs make him see himself as a naughty person, which means he's more likely—not less likely—to act like a naughty person again.

- **Time-outs create a power struggle** by pitting you and your authority against the child. Kids don't want to go to time-out. So either you threaten them, or you drag them. It's true that as long as the parent is bigger than the child, the parent wins this power struggle, but no one ever really wins in a parent-child power struggle. I frequently hear from parents of seven-year-olds that they can no longer drag their child to time-out and now have no way to discipline their defiant child.

- **You're breaking your child's trust in you by triggering his fear of abandonment.** Time-outs are symbolic rejection. They create compliance only to the degree that they trigger your child's abandonment panic.

- **Because you have to harden your heart to your child's distress during the time-out, time-outs erode your empathy for your child.** Yet your empathy is the basis of your relationship with him, which is the most important factor in whether he behaves to begin with.

No wonder parents who use time-outs find themselves in a cycle of escalating misbehavior! If you're using time-outs to deal with your child's outbursts and meltdowns, your answer is *time-in*. With time-in, we see our child's "bad" behavior as a cry for our help. We step in to reconnect and help our child with the emotion or need that's driving his behavior.

How? When you realize your child is approaching that dangerous overwrought place, suggest that the two of you take a time-in. Grab your cranky, belligerent little one and find yourselves a cozy corner. Snuggle up. Make it a game and laugh if you can. But if your child continues to act out those miserable feelings that are upsetting him, recognize that the most healing thing you can offer him at the moment is a chance to cry and get those feelings off his chest. Set whatever limits are necessary as compassionately as you can: *"I won't let you throw that cup, sweetie."* When he bursts into tears, welcome them and stay close. You'll find that your child is very different after a good cry. (See "Emotion-Coaching Your Child Through a Meltdown" in Chapter 3.)

Are you wondering if that's rewarding "bad behavior" with attention? No more than you're rewarding hungry crankiness with food if you feed your hungry child. Kids need connection with us to get through their day, especially at difficult times. If you suddenly notice from your child's behavior that she needs some connection time to refuel emotionally, why would you withhold it? Of course, if she's demanding a treat or to climb onto something dangerous, you hold firm to your limit; you don't "reward" a child's off-track behavior by giving in to something you've already said *no* to. But your attention isn't a reward, it's a lifeline.

And yes, if her behavior was inappropriate, you'll want to discuss it after she's calmed down. *"We feel better now, after a nice snuggle. . . . You were mad before, weren't you? You threw your cup. . . . That's dangerous; cups are not for throwing. . . . When you're upset, you can say, 'Mommy, I need help!' and I will help you."* Notice you're not scolding. You're reviewing what happened and describing an alternative behavior—one that you model, so your child has lots of opportunity to learn it.

What if you're using time-outs to keep yourself from getting more upset and smacking your child? Removing yourself when you're losing it is a terrific self-regulation technique and models self-management for your child. But you don't have to send your child anywhere—which makes him feel like he's "bad." Instead, just take a break yourself!

THE TRUTH ABOUT CONSEQUENCES

Throw the word consequence entirely out of your vocabulary and replace it with the term problem solving.

   —Becky, mom blogger and mother of two boys

Natural consequences are effective teachers. It's better to learn at five that harsh words rupture friendships than to learn it at fifteen, and it's better to learn early on that if he doesn't think about what books he needs at home to study for the test, he won't be able to get them after the school closes.

Building on this, most parenting experts suggest that when children "misbehave," the best response is "consequences." Letting children experience the consequences of their poor choices will teach them to make better choices in the future. Makes sense, right? Not entirely. This works only if it's a natural consequence that the parent doesn't have anything to do with creating. Here's why.

When parents use consequences for discipline, they aren't the natural result of the child's actions (*"I forgot my lunch today, so I was hungry"*). Instead, consequences for children are the threats they hear through their parents' clenched teeth: *"If I have to stop this car and come back there, there will be CONSEQUENCES!!"* In other words, *consequence* is just another word for *punishment*. As with all punishment, when we mete out consequences, our child goes on the defensive, leaving him less free to learn the desired lesson. Even if we haven't created the consequence, but our child sees that we have the ability to ameliorate it and choose not to, he might well conclude that we aren't on his side, which makes him less cooperative with us.

I'm not suggesting that you move heaven and earth to protect your child from the natural outcome of his choices. We all need to learn lessons, and if your child can do so without too much damage, life is a great teacher. But you'll want to make sure these are actually "natural" consequences that your child doesn't perceive as punishment so they don't trigger all the negative effects of punishment. What's more, you'll want to be sure that your child is convinced that you aren't orchestrating the consequence and are firmly on his side, so you don't undermine your relationship with him. Consider the difference in these responses to our child's request that we bring him the lunch he's forgotten:

- **Response A:** *"Of course I will bring your lunch to the school, sweetie. I don't want you to be hungry. But try to remember it tomorrow."* The child may or may not remember his lunch tomorrow. There is no harm in doing this once or even twice, if you can do it easily. We all have forgotten things like lunches, and it is not a sign that your child will be irresponsible for life. But it is a signal that you need to help your child with self-organization strategies.

- **Response B:** *"I'm certainly not going to drop everything to bring you your lunch. I hope this will teach you a lesson."* The child will probably learn to remember his lunch. *But* he concludes that the parent doesn't care about him, and he becomes less cooperative at home. Notice that while this is a "natural consequence," the parent's attitude transforms it into a punishment.

- **Response C:** *"Okay, I will bring your lunch, but this is absolutely the last time. You would forget your head if it weren't glued on and don't expect me to always drop everything to bail you out."* The child does not learn to remember his lunch but does learn that he's a forgetful person who irritates his parent. In the future, he acts like a forgetful, irritating person by forgetting his lunch and expecting his parent to bring it to him.

- **Response D:** *"I'm so sorry you forgot your lunch, sweetie, but it just doesn't work for me to bring it to you today. I hope you won't starve, and I will have a snack waiting when you get home."* The child learns to remember lunch *and* feels cared about *and* his self-image stays intact.

Does that mean you can never step in to help your child learn lessons from the events in her life? Of course not. If you're having daily conversations with your child about her life, you'll find constant opportunities to ask questions that invite her to reflect and learn. Just remember to focus on problem solving rather than blame.

What about situations when we want our child to make amends—for instance, when she's hurt her brother's feelings? The natural consequence in such a case is that she's damaged the relationship. If you can give her the space to calm down and the help to work through whatever feelings drove her to attack her brother, she'll be more free to appreciate the cost of her harsh words and the truth that she loves her brother, even if he does drive her crazy sometimes. If your family has rituals in place that encourage showing appreciation and making amends, and you model from the time they're little how rifts can be repaired, your child will follow your example. It's fine to set the expectation that people in your house make amends when they hurt each other. Just resist the temptation to force your child's apology, or you'll find it sticks in her throat. You want your child to feel empowered to repair her relationship with her brother, not resentful that you prefer him yet again and are making her take the blame. (See "Empowering Kids to Make Amends with the 3 Rs: Reflection, Repair, and Responsibility" in the Action Guides in this chapter.)

DOES POSITIVE PARENTING WORK WITH A DIFFICULT CHILD?

The truth is, these kids push us to be better parents. We have to acquire skills to make it work and to meet their needs. They can teach us loads about ourselves if we hang in there and keep trying.

—Patience, mother of a special-needs son

If you've been reading this book thinking, "These ideas might work for other kids, but not for *my* child. She doesn't understand what it's like with my child," then I want to speak directly to you. Maybe your child is strong willed. Maybe he has challenges regulating his impulsivity. I know from talking to parents that many children are especially challenging and difficult to parent, and that you need an extra dose of patience to raise them. Everything I describe in this chapter about relying on positive parenting rather than punishment will be harder to implement for your child.

But that doesn't mean that everything I've been saying doesn't apply to your child. In fact, it applies more to your child than to kids who fit into the continuum of what we think of as "typical." Parents of typical kids can probably use any reasonably consistent, loving child-raising philosophy and their kids will come out more or less okay. But for challenging children, parenting matters even more. Authoritarian parenting isn't optimal for any child, but it will drive a strong-willed child into risky behaviors and right out of your life. If you have a temperamentally more difficult child, the only way you can parent effectively is through connection, empathy, and helping your child process emotion, which is what this book is about.

Action Guides

Kids raised from birth on to feel safe expressing their emotions, who feel their parents are on their side, aren't perfect. They're easier to parent, though, because they're better at managing their emotions, and therefore their behavior. They're more willing to accept our guidance.

But what if you're transitioning from punishment to loving guidance? And lo and behold, your child has not suddenly turned over a new leaf and become the little angel you were hoping for?

The answer is that you're learning emotional regulation, and so is your child. You're learning to keep your composure and breathe your way through your upsetting feelings. Your child most likely has a backpack full of old tears and fears, and now that he feels safer, all those feelings are bubbling up to be healed.

As with any transition, changing your parenting will include an adjustment period, during which you deepen your relationship and learn to work together. The hard part is regulating your own feelings so you can stay calm and welcome your child's emotions. Luckily, you'll see positive changes very quickly, so you'll have incentive to keep going. Don't worry about changing your child. If you change what you do, your child will change. Use these Action Guides for quick reference.

HOW TO SET EMPATHIC LIMITS

One of the first things we learned from you was how to set empathic limits and hold our son while he cried (and screamed, and flailed). I remember the first time we did this as a particular turning point. It was 5:00 a.m., and he had come into our room again. I said, "It's still sleeping time. Let's go back to your bed," and he fell apart in tears and screaming. My husband and I held him, told him we loved him and he could be as mad and sad as he wanted, through about thirty minutes of one of the worst meltdowns we had seen. At the end, we held his little tired body as he snuggled into my husband. That day, he was a different child. He was loving and cooperative.

—Cassi, mother of two

Setting limits is an essential part of parenting. Limits keep our children safe and healthy and support them in learning social norms so that they can function happily in society. And if we set limits empathically, kids are more likely to internalize the ability to set limits for themselves, which is otherwise known as self-discipline.

How are you at setting limits?

- **Does your child immediately jump up to comply with every request, even though you never raise your voice, threaten,**

or punish? If so, give thanks, and please write to me with your secret.

- **Does your child usually comply eventually, after some repeated reminders, negotiations, and occasional frayed tempers?** Your family is in the completely normal range. Some brushing up on your technique will help you get less irritated.

- **Does your child ignore your every request, leaving you screaming far too often?** That's a symptom of a relationship issue, not a limits issue. Start with some relationship repair work so that your child *wants* to cooperate with you.

And that's the biggest secret of setting limits. You can't really *make* anyone do anything. Your child complies with your requests because of the strong relationship of trust and affection between you. The other option, of course, is fear, which is an effective motivator in the moment. But because you have to keep escalating your threats, fear becomes less and less effective over time. Love, by contrast, becomes a more effective motivator over time.

So how *do* you set effective limits?

- **Start with a strong, supportive connection** with your child so he knows you're on his side and wants to please you.

- **Don't start talking until you're connected.** Look your child in the eye. Touch him to get his attention.

- **Join with her as you set the limit.** *"This looks like so much fun . . . but I'm afraid someone's going to get hurt here."*

- **Set the limit calmly, kindly, and with genuine empathy.** *"Ouch! I don't yell at you, so please don't yell at me. You must be really upset to use that tone of voice. What's the matter, sweetie?"*

- **Acknowledge her point of view as you set the limit.** *"It's hard to stop playing and come inside. But now it's time for your bath."*

- **Help your child feel less "pushed around" by offering a choice.** *"Do you want to come in now, or in five minutes?"*

- **Get agreement so your child "owns" the limit.** *"Okay, five minutes, but no fuss in five minutes, right? Let's shake on it."*

- **Follow through, pleasantly.** It's much easier to stay pleasant when you follow through before you lose your temper. It's also easier to get cooperation from your child if she knows you won't keep moving the deadline if she fusses. Most of the time, you'll need to move in physically close and make eye contact for her to take your limit seriously. This is much more effective than raising your voice. *"It's been five minutes. Time to come in now."*

- **Keep joining and empathizing.** *"You're having so much fun out here! But now it's time for your bath."*

- **Limit the negotiations.** *"I know it's hard to stop playing, but we agreed five minutes and no fuss. It's been five minutes. Let's go."*

- **Don't expect him to like it.** No kid will always comply cheerfully, and that's okay. You can empathize with his unhappiness without changing your limit. *"I hear that you hate coming inside when some of the other kids get to stay out later. That must be hard. But you need a bath tonight and I want to be sure we get time for a story before bed."*

- **When you can't grant a wish in reality, grant it in fantasy.** *"I bet when you grow up you'll stay up and play outside all night every single night, won't you?"*

- **If your child cries or rages at your limit, listen to her feelings.** Once children feel heard, they're much more cooperative. *"You wish you could have candy. . . . Now you're crying. . . . I'm right here, sweetie, with a hug when you're ready."*

- **Respond to the need or feeling that's driving the behavior.** *"You're bugging your brother because you want to play with him, aren't you? Let's go ask him, instead of wrecking his game."*

- **Resist the temptation to be punitive in any way.** Setting the limit is sufficient to teach the lesson, as kids will eventually internalize our rules and routines as their own. Criticism makes it more likely that our child will rebel against our rules.

- **When your child defies you, focus on the relationship, rather than on discipline.** A child who is rude is either very upset or expressing her need for a better relationship with you. In either case, consequences will make the situation worse. I'm not suggesting you put up with rudeness, just that you see it as a red flag to do some repair work on the relationship.

- **When all else fails, try a hug.** No, you're not rewarding your child for bad behavior. Children act out when they feel disconnected; you're reconnecting so she has a reason to behave. You're giving her the safety to move through her turmoil faster. And you're helping her relax into her best self.

HOW TO HELP KIDS WHO TEST THE LIMITS

Any child in his right mind will test the limits. That's his job. He's pretty new on the planet, after all, and he's figuring out the rules. The most common reason that children test the limits is that they really want to find out where those limits are. Children need the security of knowing that someone more experienced and knowledgeable is looking out for them. They don't feel safe when we don't guide and nurture. That's why we often say that children will keep pushing until they find our limits.

But what if we set clear, empathic limits and our child still tests them? Even once he's noticed that certain limits seem solid—for instance, dinner comes before dessert, Mom won't let him hit his brother, and Dad stops him every time he jumps on the couch—sometimes he can't help testing those limits. Why?

1. **He *really* wants something,** like dessert *now,* and he hopes that maybe we'll change our mind. He knows that many of our limits are open to negotiation. Maybe if he keeps asking, we'll make an exception about dessert, too. What does he have to lose? We can help him by:

    • Being as consistent as possible with rules that are most important to us.

    • Empathizing.

    • Giving him his wish in fantasy: *"I bet you'd like to gobble up the entire cake right now, wouldn't you?"*

- Helping him distract himself, which is a critical skill for impulse control: *"You really want that dessert. But your body needs healthy food first. Let's find something healthy AND delicious to snack on while we make dinner together. And do you want to help me wash the lettuce?"*

2. **He has feelings he needs help to manage** that are overwhelming his awareness of the limit, and in this case also his affection for his brother. He doesn't think, he just lashes out. We can help him by:

- Being aware of triggers that usually set him off and intervening before he loses it. *"Let's move your project onto the kitchen table, where it's safe from your very curious little brother."*

- Noticing the small signals that he's out of sorts, and helping him off-load his big feelings with giggling or connection before they come crashing out in a total meltdown.

- Spending fifteen minutes of unstructured Special Time with him every day, so he's more emotionally resilient when things inevitably go wrong.

3. **He has needs he can't express that aren't being met.** If he's been sitting in school much of the day and he's cooped up inside waiting for dinner, the couch starts to look a lot like a trampoline. Sure, he knows the limit, but he'll burst if he doesn't move. What's a kid to do? We can help by noticing our child's needs and responding preemptively:

- An active child needs a small trampoline, or a mattress in the basement.

- A child who's easily overstimulated needs plenty of downtime.

- Every child who has a sibling needs daily private time to bond with each parent.

WEAN YOURSELF OFF CONSEQUENCES: TWELVE TERRIFIC ALTERNATIVES

My three-and-a-half-year-old was sitting on the couch after her bath wearing her towel and said "No" about five times when I asked her to get into her PJs. I was busy with the baby and I heard my husband threaten, "Okay, fine—no books, then," and your quote popped into my head and I said, "Hey! We've got a problem—it's bedtime and you need to be in your PJs. How do you think we should solve it?" And just like that, she got a big grin her face, suggested we all clap our hands and march our feet, and we formed a line right into her room—happily! Same thing for teeth brushing and potty later! Each time I said, "Hey, great problem-solving skills! Thank you!" And her response? "You're welcome, Mama—no problem!"
—Carrie, mother of two

Worried about what you'll do without the threat of consequences to keep your child in line? Next time your child refuses your guidance and you find yourself about to blurt out a threat, try one of these responses instead. Remember to start by taking a deep breath to calm down, so everyone can think.

1. **Let your child solve it.** *"You haven't brushed your teeth yet and I want to be sure we have time for a story. What can we do?"* Children love to help and to solve puzzles. Sometimes they just need to be given the chance—and a little respect.

2. **Partner for win/win solutions.** If your child doesn't offer a solution that works for you, explain why and help her come up with one. *"You think you should just skip brushing teeth tonight? Hmm . . . That doesn't work for me because your poor teeth would stay germy and they could get little holes in them. What else could we do to get your teeth brushed and time for a story? Want to put your PJs on, and then brush?"*

   Once your child believes that you're serious about win/win solutions, she's much more likely to work with you to find a solution that works for everyone.

3. **Invite cooperation with your phrasing.** Consider the difference in these approaches:

   - *"Go brush your teeth now."* Since no one likes to be told what to do, a direct order like this often invites resistance, either direct or in the form of stalling.

   - *"Can you go brush your teeth now?"* Many kids will reflect on this and just say *no.* Don't phrase your request in the form of a yes-or-no question unless you're willing to accept *no* for an answer.

   - *"Do you want to brush your teeth now, or after you put your PJs on?"* You're extending your child the respect of giving him some control, at the same time that you retain the responsibility of making the decisions you need to as his parent. Only offer options you can live with, of course.

   - *"You may brush your teeth now."* Almost sounds like a privilege, doesn't it? This is a command, but a respectful one. Works especially well with kids who get overwhelmed by choices.

4. **Offer mastery.** Let her take charge of as many of her own activities as possible. Don't nag at her to brush her teeth; ask, *"What else do you need to do before we leave?"* If she looks blank, tick off the short list: *"Every morning we eat, brush teeth, use the toilet, and pack the backpack. I saw you pack your backpack; good for you for getting that out of the way! Now, what do you still need to do before we leave?"* Children who feel more independent and in charge of themselves will have less need to rebel and be oppositional. Not to mention they take responsibility early.

5. **Ask for a do-over.** *"Oops. I told you to brush your teeth and you ignored me and then I started to yell. I'm sorry. Let's try a do-over."* This is a great way to interrupt things when you're headed down a bad road. Get down on your child's level and make a warm connection. Look in her eyes. Touch her. *"Okay, let's try this again, sweetie. It's teeth brushing time! How can we work as a team here to get your teeth brushed?"*

6. **Make it a game.** *"You don't want to get in your car seat? This is your pilot speaking. This rocket ship is ready for blastoff. Please buckle up! Ten . . . nine . . . eight . . . seven . . . six . . ."*

7. **Divert the oppositional energy with physical, playful reconnection.** *"What do you mean you don't want to put on your PJs? Come here, you won't-wear-PJs-boy! I'll show you who's boss around here! Where do you think you're going? You'd better get over here and put on your PJs! I'm the PJs enforcer and I always get my man! Hey, you got away!"* Bumble, trip, and fall. Put the PJs on your own head to get him giggling even more. When you finally catch him, roughhouse until you collapse in each other's arms. Now that the mood

has changed to one of connection, assume compliance and offer a choice: *"Do you want to put your PJs on while you listen to the story, or are you getting cold enough to need them on first?"*

8. **Give her what she wants with a wish.** *"I bet when you're grown up you'll stay up all night, every night, won't you?"*

9. **Give her what she wants for real.** Many disputes are not worth a power struggle. *"I hear that you don't want to wear your jacket today. But I'm afraid that you'll be cold once we're outside. How about I put your jacket in the backpack, and then we'll have it if you change your mind?"* She's not going to get pneumonia. As long as she won't lose face by asking for the jacket, she'll put it on when she gets cold.

10. **Put your child in charge.** *"You don't want to get in your car seat? That's okay, we have time. You get in when you're ready. I'll read my book while I wait."*

11. **Engage the rational brain.** Move past fight-or-flight by telling the story: *"You were having so much fun playing with Daddy. Then he told you to go brush your teeth. You were mad, right? . . . Then Daddy said no story tonight. Right? . . . Now you are sad and mad. . . . I am right here. I love you. Daddy loves you. Daddy was upset, too, but now he is here to hug you. . . . Let's find a way that we can all have a good evening and feel good when we tuck you in to bed. Maybe we all need a do-over?"* This builds emotional intelligence in your child—and in your partner. And even if it doesn't get you all on the same page, at least it gets you into the same book!

12. **Get to the root of the problem.** Often when kids defy us, they're asking for help with their emotions. You'll know this is happening when your child seems unhappy and is making you unhappy; when whatever you try just doesn't work. At those times, your child is showing you that he has some big feelings he needs to express, and he needs your help. So if you set a limit and your child defies you, forget about punishment and consequences. Move in close, look him in the eye, and restate your limit with as much compassion as you can muster. Help him have his meltdown. After your child gets a chance to dissolve that hard knot of unhappy emotion, you'll find him much more cooperative.

If we're in a rut of threats and consequences, retraining ourselves can be tough. The key is to eliminate the word *consequences* from your vocabulary and replace it with *problem solving*. You'll be amazed at the difference.

HOW TO INTERVENE IN THE HEAT OF THE MOMENT

When I get down on my knees and empathize with my three-year-old, it defuses a tantrum and makes her feel loved. Sometimes she needs a tight squeeze, or to really push or fight against me, like head-butting a pillow. And sometimes the tantrum is insurmountable and it seems like we'll never get through it. But she's starting to mirror my deep cleansing breaths, in through the nose, out through the mouth. And she says things like, "Mommy, we don't yell, right?" Baby steps. As a single parent I still lose it, but when I see her taking deep breaths and trying not to have fits, I know it's making a difference.

—Carrie, mother of a three-year-old and a baby

There's a major storm brewing, or maybe it's already hit. What can you do in the heat of the moment?

- **Keep everyone safe physically.** That means stopping the car, separating the fighting kids, removing yourself from flailing fists, or even holding your child's hands as she tries to hit you. Kids need to know that parents will keep everyone safe.

- **Keep everyone safe emotionally so that learning can happen, by modeling emotional regulation.** We keep kids safe emotionally by staying connected, empathizing, refraining from attacking. By contrast, when we move into fight-or-flight, we lose the chance to calm our child.

- **Limit the behavior and provide guidance for what needs to happen.** Kindly, calmly, firmly take whatever action is necessary to address the situation. Pick your child up from the supermarket cart and carry him to the car, leaving the cart behind and saying, *"We'll go back when you're ready."*

- **Help your child work through her emotions so she can manage her behavior.** How do we teach kids to manage their emotions? In the heat of the moment, we listen, with as much compassion as we can summon. When your child yells *"I hate you!"* just listen and reflect so your child feels heard: *"You must be very angry to speak to me that way. . . . What's going on, sweetie?"* Then listen. Reflect: *"So you were mad when . . . I understand. . . . Let's all try a do-over."*

Notice that "holding your child accountable" isn't on this list? That doesn't happen in the heat of the moment; that happens after everyone has calmed down. (See "Empowering Kids to Make

Amends with the 3 Rs: Reflection, Repair, and Responsibility," next in this chapter.) He'll be able to learn better then. And you'll be able to teach a lot better, too.

EMPOWERING KIDS TO MAKE AMENDS WITH THE THREE Rs: REFLECTION, REPAIR, AND RESPONSIBILITY

While kids always resist apologizing on the field of battle, they generally want to reconnect and rejoin the warm bonds of the family once their feelings have been heard. How can you empower your child to take responsibility for and repair any damage he's done, whether to a relationship or to property? Use the three Rs of making amends: reflection, repair, and responsibility.

- **Reflect.** When you ask open-ended questions and help your child "narrate" what happened, her rational brain gains understanding. This gives her more control over her emotions and behavior in the future. *"You were so worried when Eliza took your doll that you hit her. . . . She was hurt and cried. . . . So Mommy put the doll away and you were even more scared and cried, too, right? But then everyone finished crying and you and Eliza had fun with the teddy bears, right? Sometimes you worry when other children touch your special toys. But no one will take your doll home. That is your doll and it lives here with us. If you get worried, what could you do instead of hitting?"*

- **Repair.** When your child damages a relationship, empower him to repair it. Can he get an ice pack for his sister? Draw her a picture? This should not feel like a punishment, but a way to repair a valued relationship that was inadvertently damaged. Young children usually prefer this to a coerced apology, which feels humiliating rather than empowering. *"You hurt your brother's feelings when you knocked over his tower. What could you do to make him feel better? You want to help him rebuild his tower? Great! Why don't you offer that to him, and see what he says? Do you think he might also like a hug?"*

- **Responsibility.** The beginning of responsibility is seeing that his choices have a big impact on the world, and that he can always make a choice: "response-ability." Offer observations as he goes through his day to help him notice the choices he's making and the results: *"You sure made Michael happy when you gave him a turn with the truck."* This works better than praise or punishment to empower him to make wise choices.

Unlike punishment or forced apologies, the three Rs of making amends give your child the foundation to manage both her emotions and her behavior. Worried that your child won't learn to apologize? If you apologize to her, she'll learn from your example how to apologize to you and to others.

PREVENTIVE MAINTENANCE

My four-year-old has stopped having the meltdowns where she kicked and hit. Instead, when she gets cranky, she can now say, "I need a hug"!
    —Julia, mother of two

When we ignore routine maintenance like oil changes, our car runs badly. Once we find ourselves in a broken-down car, our options are limited. So think of these strategies to prevent problems and misbehavior as preventive maintenance for your child, and you won't find yourself in the breakdown lane as often.

- **Special Time.** Special Time is your most important tool to stay connected and help your child express his emotions.

- **Routines.** Minimize your job as head cop.

- **Set only the limits you really need to set.** Saying *no* too often convinces him you aren't on his side.

- **See problem behavior as a cry for help.** Maybe she needs more warning before transitions. Maybe he fights with his brother in the car because he's overstimulated from school and he needs a little time to himself. Maybe she's getting out of bed twenty times because letting you go at night is just so hard for her, on top of other separations during the day or her jealousy of the baby. Notice that in each of these situations, it would be hard for your child to understand what's happening inside her and articulate it to you, but you can address the root cause to change the behavior.

- **Connection before correction.** Of course your child needs guidance. But he can't accept the guidance if the relationship isn't there to support it. Ninety percent of your interactions with your child should be about connecting, so he can accept the 10 percent that are about correcting.

WHAT IF YOUR CHILD CROSSES THE LINE?

I don't understand why a transgression shouldn't be punished. . . . What if they really cross a line? Yesterday my three-year-old threw a book because he got mad. It hit my husband in the eye and cut his skin—yikes! I removed him from the room, told him that was not allowed ever, and put him in a thinking spot. Yes? No?
   —Jamie Lynn, mother of three- and five-year-old boys

Yikes, indeed! Most three-year-olds try throwing things, with no idea how much damage they can do.

The problem with removing a child to a thinking spot and leaving him alone there is that it doesn't help him with the feelings that drove him to throw the book to begin with. Behind aggression we almost always find fear—and every small person has fears we can't even imagine. A three-year-old who is grappling with fear may well get enraged about something and may well throw whatever is at hand. That's normal behavior, although of course it can be dangerous, as this child learned, and of course we tell him that throwing things at people is not allowed, ever, just as these parents did. But this child knows by now (and certainly after hurting his dad) that throwing hurts. What he needs is help from his parents to manage the feelings that drive him to throw.

I'm wondering what happened inside this three-year-old once he was in the thinking spot. If I were him, I would have felt very afraid for my father, worried that I was a terrible person who was capable of horrific harm, unable to control myself, so bad I had to be removed and could not even make up with my dad. I would see myself as so powerful that I could bloody my invincible father, which would be a terrifying idea. That shame and fear would be so much that I might well push it away (as we all do with those uncomfortable feelings) by getting angry. I might well sit there justifying what I had done, telling myself why I was right.

As you can see, isolating this child isn't going to help him learn to manage the feelings that pushed him "over the line." He's so scared he can't think straight, so he isn't drawing logical conclusions. While he may follow our directive to apologize after his time-out, he won't be in better shape to manage his aggression next time. Or, he may never again lash out at his dad, but he may begin to act out in other ways, like hitting his brother, peeing all over the house, or having nightmares.

What if, instead, we immediately tended to the person who is injured, which gives the clear message to the child that this hurt is a big deal. We even let him help. Hopefully, the focus on his father would be enough to shift him out of his anger and into concern for his dad. *"Oh my! Your dad is hurt. Sweetie, go get a washcloth and let's help your dad."* We're inviting him in, so that he's part of the solution. He may have done a monstrous thing, but we're communicating to him that he isn't a monster. This is the foundation of his being able to face that he did something that crossed a line—and to forgive himself. It starts with our forgiving him.

Are we forgiving him too easily? No. He can't simultaneously feel like a bad person and act like a good person. He acted in a way that was clearly out of the bounds of loving family relationships. Rather than shunning him, which fortifies his position as the bad kid, we step out to get him and bring him back into the embrace of the family. Without that reconnection, we can't reach him, and any "discipline" will only teach him that he's bad.

Once the wounded parent is okay, we take a deep breath so we aren't acting out of anger. We remind ourselves that the best way to prevent this from happening again is to help our son with his feelings, not to punish him.

We gather him close, very seriously and kindly, look him in the eye, and say, *"Books are not for throwing. That really hurt Daddy, didn't it?"* Our child will most likely burst into tears, which releases all the turmoil going on. We hold him while he cries. When he calms down, we say, *"You were mad, so you threw the book, but that really hurt Daddy. That was scary. Daddy will be okay, but that's why we don't throw things at people."*

After he's calm, we ask him what he could do to make Daddy feel better. We give him a chance to redeem himself, to become a good person in his own mind, the kind of person who is able to control his anger so he doesn't hurt other people. This transformation would be unlikely if he were removed to the thinking spot, because he would sit there isolated like a criminal, hardening his heart. But he has been in the middle of the emergency, as one of the helpers, so his heart is open. He feels our kindness, and also our firm expectation that he become someone who helps, not hurts. He feels safe to show us all the fear behind his anger. Once he expresses all those feelings, they evaporate, and stop driving his behavior.

What has our child learned?

- Throwing things can badly hurt someone.
- I *want* to control myself better next time so this never happens again.
- Feelings don't have to be an emergency if you don't act on them.
- Mom and Dad understand my big feelings. I can trust them to help me.
- I am capable of hurting someone badly, and I never want to do that.
- I am capable of making things better, of repairing rifts, of making things right when I make a mistake.

Maybe most important, instead of feeling like he has crossed a line that leaves him disconnected, beyond the love of his parents, he has learned that he's loved unconditionally. His parents didn't give up on him. They know that at core he is good and wants to "do right," and they never stopped believing in him. That belief will strengthen his belief in his own goodness, and help him grow into your trust.

Because the healing miracle of unconditional love is that there is no line. There is only love.

ADDITIONAL RESOURCES: SCRIPTS

Want more help on what to say when you're setting limits? These scripts are available on the AhaParenting.com website. If you're reading this book electronically, simply click on the script to read on your e-reader.

When Your Child Hits You
This script takes you through the process of handling your child's aggression.

www.ahaparenting.com/parenting-tools/positive-discipline/Child
-Hits-parent

Leaving the Playground
This script takes you through the process of setting a limit for your child and handling the resulting meltdown.

www.ahaparenting.com/parenting-tools/positive-discipline/How-to
-set-Empathic-Limits

5

Raising a Child Who Achieves with Joy and Self-Esteem

Mastery Coaching

Most parents say they want their children to succeed. But what do we mean by success? In our culture, it's often reduced to achievement. Do well in school, get into college, get a job with a high standard of living and prestige. But while that kind of success may make you feel proud as a parent, it won't necessarily make your child happy. Happiness has little to do with success as traditionally defined. It depends instead on connecting deeply with others (one of our Three Big Ideas) and on what the psychologist Abraham Maslow called "self-actualization," which we can interpret as developing our full potential by accessing our unique gifts, honing them, and sharing them with the world. Not everyone can be a star, but each of us—if we're lucky—can engage in the cycle of exploration and self-expression that psychiatrist Edward Hallowell calls "mastery." If we think of raising children with mastery as helping them grow wings, then this is the pinnacle of parenting for the long term by coaching, not controlling. And as we'll see in this chapter, raising a child with mastery depends on our ability to regulate our own anxiety and foster connection (our Big Ideas).

A master carpenter. A master teacher. A master guitar player. The word itself is a powerful one. We raise children and hope they will have the motivation and courage to tackle challenges and master them, as that is the source of true success. Different things matter at different times, but we always want to master the challenge before us, whether that's running a fast mile, creating a loving marriage, enjoying a career that provides for our family, or giving back to others through volunteer work. The ability to accomplish our personal goals is what allows us to create fulfillment throughout our lives. So mastery is essential to happiness, to achievement, and to being happy while achieving.

What's more, practicing the cycle of mastery is the most reliable way to enter that fulfilling state called *flow* in which time disappears. Mihály Csíkszentmihályi, the originator of the idea of flow, defines it as being so involved in an activity that we're transported into pure focus and joy. Athletes call it "being in the zone," but it's not just for world-class athletes. The passionate pursuit of a goal blesses any one of us with joy if we're willing to wholeheartedly apply ourselves to learning and creating. Flow and mastery go beyond conventional ideas of achievement and happiness to give our lives deeper meaning.

Mastery is also the source of self-esteem. Because humans sometimes compensate for feeling bad about themselves by adopting an arrogant, inaccurate view of their talents, asking people whether they feel good about themselves doesn't accurately gauge their self-esteem. That's led to some confusion about whether self-esteem is a positive quality. But let's set aside the challenges of measuring self-esteem and define it simply as the knowledge that we are more than enough exactly as we are, on our own terms, regardless of external circumstance. That faith in ourselves—that self-esteem—is essential for emotional health.

As we discussed in earlier chapters, self-esteem begins with unconditional love, which convinces us on a deep level that we have intrinsic worth as people regardless of what we accomplish. But as children grow, their self-esteem is built on real accomplishment. All humans find themselves tested by their environments; all of us have tasks to master throughout our lives, growth that is demanded of us, practice and training and hurdles and tests. These challenges shape who we are, bring the gifts we share with the world into expression. So self-esteem as we grow derives from the experience that we have what it takes to bring our dreams and talents into reality—in other words, mastery.

Mastery isn't a one-time feeling. It's a way of approaching experience that through repetition becomes an acquired trait, a way of living life. It describes a person who loves to explore, learn, grow, apply himself, practice, master something, take joy in the whole creative process whether he "succeeds" or "fails" in the eyes of others, and move on to his next goal. Sometimes we assume these children are simply more talented, or self-motivated, or achievement-oriented. But those are results, not causes. Every child is born with latent talent. Any child who enjoys the process of mastery has the internal motivation to polish his natural abilities to achieve—as long as the achievement he's aiming for matters to him. The achievement is secondary, a side benefit of the mastery.

What Is Mastery Coaching?

Your responsibility as a parent is to work yourself out of a job. You start with a helpless infant who can't even control his hands. Over the years he learns to crawl, walk, run, feed himself, get along with other humans, read, navigate the neighborhood, drive a car, pass his high school exams. At each stage he's propelled by biological instinct and the human spirit toward the next developmental hurdle. He struggles, sweats, clears it, regains his equilibrium, and hurtles forward again. Is it graceful? Rarely. Can you trust Mother Nature to help your child get it right? Yes.

But what about the glitches? Certainly there are children who have a harder time learning to read, or get along with other kids, or make transitions, or control their temper, or remember their backpacks. Every child needs extra support from us in some area at some time. That's the scaffolding part of helping your child develop mastery, and this chapter will show you how to give that help to your child.

But many of the challenges our children face in normal development are completely avoidable. In fact, we as parents often inadvertently create them. The irony is that out of our desire to help our children succeed—and our own anxieties about whether we, and they, are good enough—we try to mold them using techniques that backfire and destroy the joy they take in developing their own mastery. We overstimulate, overassist, overprotect, overschedule, and overcontrol, all of which we'll talk more about in this chapter. Luckily, there are three basic guidelines that provide an antidote to these impulses and save us from our own anxieties:

1. **Unconditional love.** Some parents assume that unconditional love removes the child's desire to work hard, because she's accepted just as she is. So they try to encourage mastery by pushing their child to achieve, inadvertently giving the message that their love depends on whether the child does well. The tragedy is that to help their child succeed, these

parents are destroying the foundation of their child's happiness—the belief that she's deeply lovable just by being herself. The irony is that fear saps the joy that children need for mastery. The hard work that creates mastery requires a passion that can only spring from within the child, a joy in each step of the practice and exploration.

2. **Respect.** We show respect by appreciating our unique child wherever he is in his development. We respect our child's natural process of exploration and discovering for himself, rather than feeling we must rush in to teach and rescue. We respect her play, daydreaming, and other interests as her essential work, rather than interrupting her or directing her play. We don't insist that he play a sport or instrument that we love when his interests lie elsewhere. We respect our child's agenda and passions as they unfold at each age. We may expect our child to apply himself in school to the best of his ability, but we don't force him to sacrifice his own curiosity and personal interests in order to "achieve" on standardized tests. We see ourselves as our child's partner or even assistant, rather than his boss, as he sets his course, making ourselves available as a resource. Rather than evaluating him against some imagined developmental norm and setting him up for failure by pushing him to achieve things he cannot yet do, we support him to develop from where he is, regardless of what other kids his age may be doing.

3. **Scaffolding.** What's scaffolding? It's that structure around a building as it's being built. After the building's up, the scaffolding is dismantled—outgrown, no longer needed. But the

building couldn't be built without the scaffolding. The scaffolding we provide for our child is what allows him to build his own inner structure to become successful at a given behavior. It includes the following:

- Routines and habits ("We always put things back in their place as soon as we're done with them.")

- Expectations for behavior ("In our family, we think anything worth doing is worth doing well.")

- Modeling ("See, if you push it here, it opens!")

- A safe environment (babyproofing)

The best way to help a child experience mastery is to respectfully observe him, so we see where he needs support, and then build scaffolding in those places. For instance, we might teach a child who loses his possessions some specific habits to keep track of things. Or when our six-year-old has a conflict with another child, we might listen empathically to her woes and then help her brainstorm what she could say to the other child, rather than immediately calling the other child's parents. Respectful observation and strategic scaffolding take more effort from us than stepping in to do things ourselves or just expecting our child to master things on her own. But the result is a confident, self-motivated child who sees herself as able to tackle new things, and succeed.

How do our respect, unconditional love, and scaffolding help our children develop a love of mastery? Let's trace this process through childhood, beginning with your newborn infant.

Building Mastery as Your Child Grows

BABIES (0–13 MONTHS): THE BUDDING SCIENTIST

A parent's job is to help the newborn make the transition into the world. How can this be done in a respectful manner? . . . Observing your baby in order to understand her, helping her form attachment by talking to her and telling her what you are going to do, and waiting before intervening.

—Magda Gerber

"Now I'm going to pick you up. . . . Let's take that wet diaper off. . . ." Why does Magda Gerber suggest that parents talk to their preverbal baby as they handle her? It's basic respect, rather than treating her like an object. But does it matter to her development?

We don't know. But over and over, we see evidence that babies are budding scientists, researching their worlds and drawing conclusions. While we once thought that preverbal babies wouldn't remember a given event and thus wouldn't be affected by it, researchers are increasingly concluding that babies "record" everything that happens to them, on a nonverbal, visceral level. Preverbal experience may be even more important than what comes later in shaping our attitudes, moods, and beliefs about life.

Remember the lucky baby from our earlier chapters? His parents naturally take pleasure in their baby's learning, but since they know that when he first sits or walks has no bearing on his eventual happiness or success, they try to ignore developmental milestones, trusting Mother Nature to help their son blossom on his own timetable. Are they being irresponsible? Not one bit. They see their pediatrician on schedule, and she's trained to notice any red flags. It's the parents' job simply to love, nurture, and enjoy their unique baby as he develops.

Like all babies, our lucky little guy is self-motivated to roll over, to grab the rattle and shake it, to sit up, to crawl. His mom resists her impulse to help him learn to roll over. Instead, she sits with him, gently giving him feedback: *"Yes, you're pushing yourself up. That's a lot of effort. You're building those muscles."* Does he understand her? Maybe not yet, but he will understand more than we assume much sooner than we think. What is he learning?

- Because his mother acknowledges his efforts, he learns that they have value.
- Because she doesn't jump in to help, he learns that this work is his own.
- Because her tone remains relaxed, he learns that there's no emergency and that his mom has confidence in his ability to master this valuable work if he just keeps practicing.
- Because she responds to his vocal and physical expressions, he knows that she's available to help if he needs it.

This lesson will be repeated in various forms throughout his infancy and his childhood and will become part of his most basic belief system about himself and his world.

This wise mom talks to her son because she's in a relationship with him, right from the start. But she also talks to him to manage her own anxiety. Like most new parents, she wants desperately to give her son a good start in life. But she knows that the best start consists of his finding and developing his own inner resources. By talking to her baby, she reminds herself of how capable he is and keeps herself from impulsively rushing in to "rescue" him. Of course, she's paying attention. If he rolls on his arm and tries to get it out and cries, she will begin by soothing him with her voice, talking him through what's happening: *"You're on your arm. It's twisted. Ouch, that hurts."* Her calm communicates that this isn't an emergency, just part of the normal process of learning to roll over. So he tries again, experiments a bit, adjusts his position, and succeeds in pulling his arm out.

But what if he just doesn't have the internal fortitude today to keep trying, and looks to her for help? Naturally, Mom steps in. Our child needs a chance to try on his own—so we soothe our own anxiety to wait and give him that chance without rushing in—but he also needs to know he has backup. Now, Mom offers her little one the smallest amount of support possible to help him sustain his "work" toward his goal. She lightly touches his body, showing him how his arm is pinned. Maybe that's enough for him to shift off it. Or maybe not, and he insists that he's done, for now, with this exploration. She listens to her child, and responds. *"Is that enough for today, sweetie? Here, come to Mama. You can try again tomorrow."*

That lesson, like every lesson, will return on another day until he masters it. Over time, little ones can endure the discomfort of "trying" longer, and even begin to take joy in it, knowing that those uncomfortable moments are just part of the larger cycle of mastery that allow us to create. This confidence that he can endure the discomfort of pushing through obstacles is a cornerstone of his developing resilience. Our lucky baby has a mom who observes him as he engages with the world and takes her cues from him. When she intervenes, it's because she sees he needs a bit of assistance, rather than out of her own anxiety or her need for him to achieve. Does she feel those things? Of course; she's a parent. But she knows they're her own needs, not his, so she breathes her way through those feelings without taking action.

This baby is enjoying his own self-paced curriculum, which consists of direct experience. He explores, using all his senses. He masters new things, beginning with moving his own body. He builds his capacity to concentrate as he swipes at the rattle, finally seizing it. He learns about cause and effect as he drops his spoon, over and over, off his high chair. As his parents allow him to explore and experiment, as they respect his independent play without interfering, as they share his delight in discovery, our baby begins to enjoy the process of mastery. He's also laying the foundation for high IQ.

Babies don't need artificial stimulation like DVDs and electronic toys to develop smart brains. In fact, babies who frequently watch DVDs actually lag behind in verbal ability. Some researchers theorize that screen time hampers brain development because it's over-stimulating, while others think that it simply gives babies less time for the human interactions from which they truly learn. Babies are designed to learn language not by watching it, but by engaging with a person speaking directly to them. Research has shown that it's those Eureka! moments when the baby puts two and two together that cement a connection in the child's mind: "Oh, *that's* what Daddy means by *up*!" Mastery isn't just about mastering the world of things, or even about managing ourselves, but also about complex human interaction—calling for help, enticing a smile, sharing excitement about a toy.

What can parents do instead of baby DVDs and flash cards to give their child's learning a boost and lay the foundation for mastery?

- **Babyproof to minimize saying *no*.** We all want our baby to learn that the garbage is off limits—and she will. But she isn't capable of that for some time yet. In the meantime, she needs to physically explore—that's her job, and essential for her developing brain—so ensuring that she has a safe environment for exploring offers her the support she needs for learning.

- **Respectfully observe.** Listen to what your baby is telling you. True, he can't speak your language yet, but babies are good at making themselves understood, if we pay attention.

- **Don't rush to teach. Instead, let your child learn by experimenting.** As the developmental psychologist Jean Piaget observed, "Every time we teach a child something, we keep him from inventing it himself."

- **Respond with targeted support.** This may mean picking your baby up. It may mean using your voice to let her know you're there. It may mean narrating the story of what's happening for your child: *"You're batting at the mobile. . . . You can almost reach the blue duck."*

- **Help your baby develop his emerging safety sense.** For instance, as babies become mobile, most will scoot to a stairway or the edge of a bed to look over but won't crawl off. Instead of scooping her up to prevent her going near the edge, we can spot her so she can't actually hurt herself and observe her as she explores. Babies who feel "in charge" of their own safety learn more quickly how to keep themselves safe.

- **Never interrupt a happily engaged baby.** Okay, there may be times when you must. But in general, when a baby or child is focused on something, he's working. Interrupting him is disrespectful, implying that what he was doing isn't important. It keeps him from solving that particular problem, at least for now, but more importantly it interferes with his concentration and "attention span" muscle building. This is how he learns to play by himself, which you'll be very happy about when he's three.

By the time your baby passes his first birthday, he's drawn many conclusions from his experimentation in the world. Is the world a fascinating, safe place to explore? Can he make things happen? Is he able to respond effectively? Can he get help when he needs it? The answers to these questions provide the foundation for his ongoing pursuit of mastery.

What does mastery look like as your baby passes his first birthday and begins to toddle around? Let's find out.

TODDLERS (13–36 MONTHS): DO IT MYSELF: DEVELOPING RESPONSE-ABILITY

Everything in the toddler is geared toward mastery: learning, understanding how things work, seeing what effect she can have on the world. How do our tools of unconditional love, respect, and scaffolding help our toddler master daily life?

Unconditional Love

Because toddlers don't yet have much information about the very real dangers of the world, they need fairly constant supervision and guidance. But since force creates resistance, every time we choose to use our physical advantage to control our toddler, we create a less cooperative child. Unfortunately, we also create a child who sees "control" as outside her, so she's less likely to see her self as "response-able," which undermines the internal discipline she needs for mastery. In the chapters on emotion coaching and discipline, we talked about encouraging the development of internal discipline by staying connected with unconditional love while we set limits. The same approach encourages our child's development of mastery. So when our toddler tries to twist away from us in the parking lot, we might remind ourself that she isn't being defiant, she just has no idea of the danger and wants the autonomy to run.

We might let her run in the nearby park before we shop, or ask her to help us push the shopping cart across the parking lot.

Respect

Respect means that when we can cede control, we do. When our toddler is struggling to dress herself, we make ourselves available to encourage, make suggestions, or assist if asked, but we don't interrupt her to take over the task ourselves. And respect means that while we take pleasure in our toddler's rapid learning and attempts at mastery, we don't make him perform or show off his achievements.

Scaffolding

Scaffolding for a toddler includes the following:

1. **Modeling.** "We pat the dog *gently* like this."

2. **Offering tools and strategies.** "You may climb on this stool to wash your hands in the sink."

3. **Sequencing.** "When we get home we'll have lunch, and then it will be naptime."

4. **Support in emotional regulation.** "We have to wait our turn for the slide; I'll stand with you and help you wait."

5. **Reminders.** "Balls are for throwing *outside*."

6. **Encouragement.** "You're pushing that heavy door so hard. . . . You've almost got it!"

Let's consider how these tools work in the daily life of a toddler. David's parents know that toddlers need to move, so they've created a safe play space in their home with a soft climbing structure, and they often roughhouse with him, tumbling and wrestling. Although they live in an apartment, his father, who is home with him three days a week, takes him to the nearby playground every day so he can run, swing, and climb as much as possible. Dad wants to encourage his son's curiosity and love of learning, so he creates plenty of opportunities for his toddler to open and shut, dig and dump, splash and throw, sort and push. It can be frustrating to have to put all the pans and plastic back in the cupboard every day, but Dad wants his son to learn to think outside the box, so he prides himself on saying *no* as little as possible, even while he guides his son and keeps him safe.

David's parents offer scaffolding in the form of patient, repetitive step-by-step guidance for all the many routines and life rules that their toddler needs to learn. His mother also controls her own impulses so she can simply appreciate her child's efforts. That means she's trained herself to bite her tongue or grab hold of her own hands to avoid taking over when her son's trying to figure something out or master a new skill. Instead, she sits near him, watching with interest and encouragingly acknowledging his efforts when he looks at her for help. When he can't jam the cylinder through the square hole in his shape sorter, for instance, she might observe, "It doesn't fit through that hole.... Hmm..." When he begins to try the other holes, and discovers, with delight, which one works, she shares his excitement.

Why even be present? If she's not "doing" something, why not be in the other room washing dishes, or next to him in the playroom on her computer? That's fine, of course, at times. Toddlers don't need 24/7 engagement. Learning to focus on their own work near us but without interacting with us is an important developmental task, one that we encourage by noticing when they're engaged with something and moving ourselves out of the interaction for short periods. But this mom *is* doing something; she's lending her calm strength to her son. Particularly when a little one is tackling something that requires him to regulate his own frustration ("This won't fit!"), it's helpful to have our warm, supportive presence communicating that it isn't an emergency, and that we're confident he can solve this problem. If he wants our help, is there anything wrong with asking, "Hmm . . . It won't fit. . . . I wonder if it would fit in the other hole?" No, of course not. But think about the times when you solve a puzzle on your own, versus the times someone else helps you. The learning, satisfaction, and confidence all come when you do it yourself. So of course we give our child help when he needs it, but we give the minimal amount required for him to take the next step himself.

Like all toddlers, David is learning mastery when he fiercely insists that he "do it myself!" There are days when he experiments to see how much power and "response-ability" he has by answering *no!* to almost every question. He often tests to be sure the limits are solid, by looking right at his parents as he does something they've previously forbidden. When he's tired, sometimes his emotions overwhelm his still-under-construction frontal cortex and he sometimes throws himself down on the floor and wails in frustration. But as he learns more and more words, he's increasingly able to use them to understand and communicate his experience, which allows him to master his emotions more often. And because David's parents offer constant, tailored support, and respect his preferences while offering empathy when they must set limits, David is convinced that his mom and dad are on his side. Therefore, he isn't locked into resisting his parents, as so many toddlers are, so he can constantly evolve more effective strategies to master himself, and his world. He's confident in his ability to respond to what comes his way, and he trusts that his parents are there for backup. David is on his way to developing mastery.

PRESCHOOLERS (3–5 YEARS): SELF-MASTERY THROUGH PROBLEM SOLVING

A famous child development study designed by Walter Mischel at Stanford University found that when young children are offered a choice between one or two cookies, they always choose two. Mischel then told the children in his studies, "Here is one cookie on this plate where you can reach it. I need to leave the room for a few minutes. If you don't eat this cookie while I'm gone, when I come back I will give you an additional cookie. If you can't wait to eat this one, that's fine, but you won't get a second cookie. If you can wait, then when I come back, I will give you the second cookie as well as this one."

Virtually all toddlers eat the cookie while the researcher is out of the room. They can't wait, no matter how much they want the second cookie, for the same reason they can't always follow your rules at home. They may very much want to, but their brain development isn't sufficient for them to control their own impulses, even to meet a goal that is important to them.

Even once they're preschoolers, 70 percent of kids can't control their impulses enough to avoid eating the first cookie, no matter how much they also want the second one. But David, our high-mastery toddler, has grown into one of the 30 percent of preschoolers who can wait. All those experiences mastering his own attention span and emotions have given him practice managing himself. He knows how to work hard in pursuit of something he wants. And many experiences in problem solving have taught him some useful strategies. So when the researcher leaves the room, David distracts himself. After one longing look at the cookie, he leaves the table with the cookie, pulls out the most interesting toy from the shelf, and focuses on it completely. David successfully regulates his own impulses to avoid eating the first cookie while the researcher is out of the room. When the researcher returns, David gets the second cookie he wanted.

I admit that when I first heard about this cookie experiment I thought it was a bit cruel, and I wondered why we read so much into it. After all, what if the child doesn't *want* the second cookie? And who cares if they can resist eating the first one? But virtually all young children say they want the second cookie, so the question becomes whether the child can manage his impulses in order to meet his own goals. The cookie experiment is useful because it shows us whether the child has developed his rational frontal cortex sufficiently to regulate his emotions, anxiety, and impulses. This huge accomplishment is an indicator of the child's emerging self-mastery, which allows him, in turn, to master the world. Studies show that four-year-olds who can manage themselves well enough to not eat the cookie do better in school, do better with peers, and are rated by parents as more cooperative. They're better at concentrating, at screening out distractions. As they grow, they're more competent, confident, and happier. They even score an average of two hundred points higher on the SAT, which isn't really surprising given that they're higher-achieving students and better at regulating their own anxiety. It's easy to see why impulse control helps kids become more responsible and well-behaved. Because they can regulate their emotions, they can control their behavior.

Virtually all children eventually develop the ability to resist the first cookie as their frontal cortex solidifies the neural pathways to soothe anxiety and regulate emotions, which was discussed in the chapter on emotion coaching. Parents help their children reach this relatively mature stage faster every time they soothe anxiety and reflect feelings. But this ability to self-regulate also develops as a result of the child's increasing experience in problem solving as he attempts to master the outside world. The children who are able not to eat the cookie are proficient at refocusing their attention to concentrate on something else. Let's look at how parents of pre-schoolers can use scaffolding tools to support their preschooler as an emerging problem solver.

1. **Modeling.** "I'm trying to figure out what this key goes to. Want to help me try it in the front and back doors?"

2. **Offering tools and strategies.** "When two people share one piece of cake, how can we make it fair? How about Jenna divides it in two, and Jacob picks who gets which piece?"

3. **Sequencing.** "When we get to pre-K, I'll read you a story. Then we'll find your friend Christopher, and you can play in the block corner with him when I say good-bye."

4. **Support in emotional regulation.** "You're so frustrated with that. Here, I'll hold this side for you, so you can push that side into place."

5. **Reminders.** "We always clean up our own messes. Come, let's get the paper towels and I'll help you."

6. **Encouragement.** "It can be frustrating to get your shoes on by yourself. . . . I love how you keep trying and don't give up!"

All of these scaffolding practices, first introduced with toddlers, remain essential to support preschoolers in mastering their world. But preschoolers also need encouragement to practice solving problems at a higher level. This requires us as parents to give up some control and encourage every tendency toward self-sufficiency. For instance, Ethan, age three, wants a drink of water. His parents have equipped the bathroom with a stool and unbreakable cups so Ethan can help himself to water whenever he wants. This isn't an easy process for Ethan, who still has to pause to remember which way to turn the faucet, but he takes great joy in the problem solving necessary to get himself a drink. Does he sometimes spill water in the bathroom? Yes, but that's a small price to pay for a more self-sufficient child and not having to "serve" your preschooler every time he's thirsty. He's even learning to clean up his own messes!

Similarly, Haley's parents tell her that she can be in charge of her own clothing. They keep only in-season clothes on the shelves in her closet, so the four-year-old can choose her own outfits. Do her plaids and flowers often clash? Of course. But not only are her parents avoiding power struggles and giving their four-year-old some essential autonomy, she's also learning which clothes she feels good in and how to get them onto her body by herself.

Kira wants to wear her red dress, but her mother has hung it up in the closet out of her reach. "Can you figure out how to get it down yourself?" she asks Kira. The intrepid five-year-old pulls the bathroom stool into her closet and climbs up. She can touch the dress but not tug it off the hanger. Undaunted, Kira drags the chair from her mother's desk into her closet and climbs up on that. Victory! Kira is learning to keep trying different strategies until she finds one that works—a fundamental of mastery.

As you've probably noticed, mastery often results from parents summoning up the patience to step back and let the child "do it myself," even when it takes twice as long. But parents can also teach mastery skills directly. Cameron's mother wants to help her three-year-old learn more impulse control, so she plays fun games to give him practice, like "Red Light, Green Light" and "Mother, May I?" When James gets frustrated because his tower falls, his dad helps him experiment with a larger base to support the taller tower. Emma's mother brainstorms with her when she has to choose between a friend's birthday party and her older sister's recital.

How does this support build mastery? The process of mastery depends on our ability to evaluate problems, consider approaches, experiment with solutions, and manage our impulses and emotions through the inherent frustrations. From the three-year-old's attempts to build a tall tower to the four-year-old's negotiations with his peers about which game to play to the five-year-old's proficiency at his computer game, preschoolers must manage themselves if they want to master their worlds.

By age six, the human brain takes another leap forward as the reasoning parts of the brain take charge, and children enter the age of mastery.

ELEMENTARY SCHOOLERS (6–9 YEARS): EXPLORING PASSIONS

Middle childhood . . . is a time of great cognitive creativity and ambition, when the brain has pretty much reached its adult size and can focus on threading together its private intranet service—on organizing, amplifying, and annotating the tens of billions of synaptic connections that allow brain cells . . . to communicate.
    —Natalie Angier

Around age six, the adrenal glands begin bathing the brain in DHEA and other hormones, signaling the beginning of adrenarche, or middle childhood. The accompanying changes in the brain are associated with a huge leap forward in rationality, including the ability to override emotional impulses, plan, and evaluate consequences. These capacities will continue to mature into young adulthood, but the six-year-old, compared to his younger self, is notably more able to use rational thinking to manage himself. While the brain has stopped growing, the neural system retains its elasticity and gears itself toward learning of all kinds: reading, math, languages, physical skills, music, values, and even habits. As the brain shifts from growing to organizing itself, kids gain the self-control and determination they need to strive toward goals that are important to them. Although their interests will evolve and change right through the teen years, their confidence in exploring and mastering those passions takes shape now. These are also the years when kids learn the joys of contribution and autonomy as they take on age-appropriate responsibilities and self-care. Ages five through nine are the years when children begin to see themselves as being capable of mastery.

Let's observe how parents can evolve the scaffolding practices we've been using since babyhood to encourage the development of mastery in their school-age kids.

1. **Modeling.** The emotional self-management and "how to's" you've been modeling all along get more complicated now, as you explicitly teach your child more complex skills, from how to refuse a social invitation to how to do household chores.

   This is also a terrific time to begin consciously modeling your values for your child as explicitly as possible: "I felt a little jealous that another parent gets to be the soccer coach and I'm the assistant coach, but I'm a good sport, so I'll congratulate her sincerely. And since I value doing a good job of whatever position I'm in, I'm looking forward to helping with the soccer practice drills and in every other way I can."

   What do values have to do with mastery? Values shape our view of the world and how we act in it. They include both what we hold dear, such as spiritual teachings, and what we think it's important to be, such as honest. Some values—love of learning, listening to our inner guidance, working hard, persistence, being curious and playful—contribute directly to the development of mastery. Our children learn values by observing what we do and drawing conclusions about what we think is important in life. Regardless of what we consciously teach our child, she'll understand and shape her values based on what she sees us do. If you tell her that soccer is about fun, skills, exercise, and teamwork (all hallmarks of mastery), but your first question is about who won the game, she'll learn that winning is what really matters.

2. **Offering tools and strategies.** The self-discipline made possible by the brain in middle childhood makes this the ideal time to help children develop habits and strategies that will serve them throughout life. Think in terms of both routines—doing homework and writing thank-you letters—and ways of being, such as persisting in the face of difficulty, curious exploration, and interpreting the world optimistically. All of these habits contribute to mastery.

3. **Sequencing.** "First snack, then homework, *then* you can play outside, just like every day. We always finish our work before we play." In addition to helping children learn to self-regulate and establish productive habits, sequencing helps them develop the "executive function" skills of planning, staying organized, following through, and completing a task in accordance with certain standards. Some people are born with more abilities in these areas, but routines and other forms of sequencing help children hone this capacity.

4. **Support in emotional regulation.** While tantrums usually fade into the past as children make their way through elementary school, we can help them refine their self-regulation by getting the higher brain involved. Consider how this might work with Zack, who is starting second grade and beginning to find homework more challenging. He resists sitting down

to do it and often ends up yelling or in tears. Some experts recommend that parents simply bow out of this power struggle, giving the child the responsibility for completing the teacher's assignments. But Zack's parents see that he needs help managing whatever feelings are causing his outbursts before he can apply himself to his studies. Bowing out would just leave him unsupported. Using the tools in the emotion coaching chapter, they intensify their play connection with him over the weekend to strengthen his trust in them. Then, on Monday, when Dad repeatedly suggests that Zack start his homework and Zack resists, Dad playfully wrestles with him: "Get over here, you never-do-homework-boy, you! We'll see about that!" Finally, Dad looks his son in the eye and kindly but firmly announces, "Okay, Zack. We're done playing. Time to sit down and start your homework." Zack bursts into angry tears. Dad stays with him while Zack shouts that homework is stupid, his teacher is stupid, and his Dad is stupid. When Zack flails at him, Dad says "Whoa, buddy, I don't want those hitty hands near my face. Here, I'll hold out my hands for you to push against," and while Zack protests, "I don't *want* your hands!" he struggles to push against them. Finally, Zack collapses into Dad's arms, sobbing. After five minutes, he looks up. "Dad, I just can't do that homework. I'm just dumb!"

Whether Zack needs glasses or some extra help in learning to read, his homework problem is on the way to being solved. More important, Zack has learned how to face the emotions that sometimes block every child's progress. As time goes by, he'll become comfortable enough with his feelings that he can breathe his way through them, skip the struggle, and confront his fear. Facing our fears is essential to solving our problems and to gaining the emotional confidence that's essential to mastery.

5. **Reminders.** Because we see that our kids are now capable of so much more, we expect more. We're often frustrated, therefore, by the ongoing need for reminders. It helps to keep in mind that there's no reason our child should share our priorities. *We* know that teeth need to be brushed every day, but at any given moment, his agenda will hold ten competing priorities that are more attractive and feel more urgent to him. If you have a child who easily develops strong habits, you may not have to remind him about routines like teeth brushing or hanging up his jacket, but you'll also find him less flexible when it comes to change. Most kids? They need your patient reminders for a long time while their habits solidify. Since that's part of your job description, you might as well find a way to accept it and enjoy it, instead of resenting it.

6. **Encouragement.** Giving helpful feedback gets increasingly complicated as our children become more sophisticated. Consider how most of us would respond to this common query from our six-year-old:

Zoe: Mom, look! Do you like my drawing?
Mom: I love your drawing!
Zoe: You do? Do you like my trees?
Mom: They're great!
Zoe: [*studying them*] I guess. . . . It's a witch forest.
Mom: Awesome.
Zoe: Can we hang it up?
Mom: Sure, after I finish cooking.
Zoe: Okay. . . . I'll make another one.

Zoe spends two minutes producing a less elaborate version of her first drawing.

Zoe: Mom, look! Do you like this one?

Mom: It's great!

Zoe: [*studying her drawing in frustration*] I don't like it. . . .
     It isn't good.

Mom: Of course it's good! Don't say that!

Zoe: Am I a good artist?

Mom: Of course, honey, you're a great artist! Want to draw
     some more while I finish dinner?

Zoe: No. . . . I'm tired of drawing. I'm bored. . . . Can I
     watch TV?

Zoe's mother is trying hard to praise her daughter and give her positive feedback. But what has Zoe learned? That every time she dashes off a drawing and shows it to her mother, she can depend on a momentary good feeling from her mother's praise, but not necessarily a good feeling about her work. That she can't trust her own judgment; her well-intentioned mom will decide whether her work is good enough. That her mom is too distracted to discuss the inner world (the witch forest, in this case) that inspires, or worries, her. That although she herself has doubts about her trees, her mother thinks she's a great artist—maybe her mom doesn't know enough to help her? That she secretly suspects she can't draw trees, and she doesn't know how she could learn, so maybe she had better not even try, which will just create more evidence of her inability. The pressure to maintain her reputation as a "good artist" is already undermining her interest in drawing. Zoe's mom, of course, is doing what most of us would do, trying hard to encourage her daughter. She's proud of her child's natural talent, which really does seem unusual. She would be crushed to realize that she's lessening her child's emerging interest in art. Unfortunately, kids who don't gain confidence in their mastery begin to shy away from exploring and practicing, and they seek solace in the comparatively shallow (and less rewarding) pursuit of screen entertainment, as Zoe does here when she decides to stop drawing and watch TV.

Let's contrast this to a more thoughtful use of feedback from Grace's mother:

Grace: Mom, look! Do you like my drawing?

Mom: I noticed you working for a long time on that drawing! Tell me about it.

Grace: It's a forest where a witch lives.

Mom: Wow!

Grace: She's a mean witch, but if you stay on the path she can't get you.

Mom: So there's a way to stay safe in the forest?

Grace: Yeah, see, there's the path.

Mom: That's a relief. Is the witch scary?

Grace: Of course; she's a witch. Do you like it?

Mom: I loved watching you work on it because you were concentrating so hard and it looked like you were enjoying it. Do *you* like it?

Grace: I like the path. It's easy to follow and stay safe. But the trees don't look right. I just made round tops. Trees are hard to draw.

Mom: Yes. . . . Trees can be tough. . . . Lots of artists spend their whole lives practicing trees. We can look at some next time we go to the art museum, okay? We can see all the ways that different artists draw trees. It's okay to draw them any way you want to. And you can try different ways.

Grace: Okay. I'm going to do a new picture and practice my trees.

Mom: [*smiling*] I love how you keep practicing at things you
want to get good at!

What has Grace learned? That her mom values "concentrating so hard" and enjoying working at something. That her
mother is interested in the witches of her inner world. That
her mother values the work she does, but that *she* is the one
to evaluate it. That even skilled adults practice. That her own
work has some relationship to the work hanging in a museum.
That she can try different ways, and do things the ways she
wants to. That whether to practice more is her own choice but
will give her the results she wants in her work. That she can
take joy in sharing her inner life through the creative process.
Grace is accessing her unique gifts, honing them, and enjoying the process of sharing them with the world. She is well
on her way to developing mastery.

Mastery Basics

ENCOURAGING MASTERY

Children are motivated toward mastery when they experience the
pleasure of pursuing an interest and overcoming the inevitable
challenges of mastering it. Beyond respect, unconditional love, and
scaffolding, how can you help your child discover the joy of mastery?

- **Affirm the value of joy for its own sake.** Mastery is not pri-
  marily about achievement. Mastery is about the joy of exploration and learning, which gives the child the motivation to keep
  practicing enough to master something. Drudgery derails the
  joy kids need for mastery. If she loves swimming, let her swim,

support her in swimming—but don't get overly invested in coaching her for the Olympics or you'll take all the joy out of it. Follow her lead.

- **Affirm your child's ability to impact the world.** The sense of power essential to mastery derives from a child's experience of herself as having an effect on the world. *"If I stand on the stool, I can flip this light switch and light up the room!"* All children will experience reasonable limits to their power (*"I can't make the rain stop, and neither can Mommy"*), but the more your child has opportunities to make a difference in the world, the more she will see herself as capable.

- **Help her build confidence by tackling manageable challenges** with you as backup. Knowing you're there gives her confidence. If you do it for her or intervene to show her how, you're implying that she isn't capable enough to do it right. Don't worry about whether she does it right; if she does it at all today she'll be so excited, she'll want to keep practicing so she can do it even better in the future.

- **Praise effort, not results.** *"Wow! You didn't give up!"* or *"You've almost got it!"* Of course her "product" won't be perfect. She's a child. And even if it is great, the point is never the product—you don't want her resting on her laurels at age six, or sixteen. Your goal is for her to keep trying, practicing, improving, and learning that hard work pays off in her own satisfaction.

- **Teach self-encouragement.** As Peggy O'Mara of *Mothering Magazine* says, "The way we talk to our child will become their inner voice." Use mantras to encourage your child when the going gets tough. *"Practice makes perfect!"* and *"If you don't* *succeed, try, try again!" and "I think I can, I think I can!"* are time-honored maxims because they're helpful when we're frustrated. When your daughter strikes out with the bases loaded, she needs an automatic internal comforting voice to encourage and motivate her. Otherwise the harsh criticizing voice steps in, triggered by the disappointment. This kind of self-talk has been shown to improve our ability to master difficult tasks, as opposed to the self-disparaging comments many of us automatically make.

- **Support her in discovering her own passions.** Like the rest of us, children are motivated when they pursue something that's important to them rather than a goal we generate for them. And kids discover their passions through self-directed exploration, which can look a lot like wasting time to adults. His passions will change over time, but they always deserve your respect. They're his work. If you want him to take initiative and not need your constant engagement, support him in his interests.

HOW KIDS DEVELOP RESILIENCE

In previous generations, parents were often counseled to stand back and let their child find his own way, rather than "coddling" him. This sink-or-swim approach motivated many kids to dog-paddle, but I doubt that a near-drowning gives anyone the joy they'd need to develop mastery as an Olympic swimmer.

On the other hand, the impulse of most caring parents to rush in and fix it may keep our children from experiencing pain, but it can sometimes also prevent them from developing the resourcefulness essential to mastery.

What's the happy medium that facilitates resilience?

- **Appreciate the value of struggle as a learning experience.** There is nothing negative about struggle. That's how we develop mastery muscles and the confidence to tackle the next hurdle.

- **Don't set your child up for failure.** Offer scaffolding to help him succeed. Should you step in when you see failure ahead, or let him "learn a lesson"? Always a hard call. Rescuing children can prevent them from learning important lessons. But children who see their parents stand by and let them fail experience that as not being loved. Instead of learning the lesson that they should have practiced that clarinet or read the directions on that science kit, they learn the lesson that they're not smart enough, talented enough, good enough—and that their parents did not care enough to help them figure it out.

- **Support, don't "rescue."** If you take over the science fair project the night before it's due, that's worse than rescuing; not only does your son learn that you'll bail him out if he goofs off, he learns that he's incompetent. But if you help him each step of the way to organize his ideas and his work, *but* resist the impulse to improve on the project yourself, he completes the job, hugely proud, having learned something about how to plan and execute a complex project.

- **Help your child learn from failure.** There's a common misconception that children develop resilience by failing. Actually, children who fail often and don't see a way out are learning they can't win. Children develop resilience only when they successfully weather failure, which requires two realizations: *"I know what to do to avoid failing next time, and I can do it,"* and *"No matter what happens, I can handle it!"*

- **Empathize when your child experiences frustration.** Yes, kids need to experience disappointment, cry, and realize that the sun comes out the next day—but this process works best with plenty of parental support. That solid foundation of knowing you're always there, in her corner, is what allows your child to risk disappointment and come out the other side—in other words, to develop resilience.

GIVING CONSTRUCTIVE FEEDBACK

Our children need our positive affirmation on a fairly constant basis. I sometimes think of kids as little energy Geiger counters, parsing our moods for our passionate *yes!* to loving and protecting them. In fact, because their survival depends on our continued commitment to them, this is an evolutionary insurance policy.

But giving our child a constant flow of *yes!* unconditional love does not mean praising him. In fact, praise as we usually offer it to children is not unconditional at all. Conventional praise—*"Good job!... I'm proud of you!... Beautiful painting!"*—evaluates our child against standards that we determine. Studies show that children who are frequently praised in this way conclude that someone is constantly evaluating their performance. They become more insecure about expressing their own ideas and opinions, worried about whether they'll measure up. Instead of taking pride in their own behavior and achievements, they look outside for affirmation. Praise kills the joy we take in our own accomplishments and makes us dependent on emotional handouts from others.

Maybe worse, praise works only while you're there to dispense it. For instance, children who are praised for sharing begin to share *less* unless adults are watching, apparently because they've learned from the praise that no one in their right mind would share out of the goodness of their heart.

It's also well established that giving kids rewards robs them of the inherent pleasure of their achievements. For instance, children who receive money for grades no longer enjoy learning but operate in single-minded pursuit of the monetary reward, even to the point of being more likely to cheat. So it's not surprising that praise, given its potency as a reward, has similar effects. Children who are praised for eating vegetables learn that vegetables aren't inherently delicious; children who are praised for reading learn that reading isn't inherently rewarding—in both cases because "you have to be rewarded for doing it." So, ironically, when praise is overdone, it makes the behavior it rewards less likely to happen!

But this doesn't mean you can't positively, joyously, constantly affirm your child. In fact, your child needs that affirmation to thrive. The key is unconditional positive regard—noticing your child and affirming him, his activities, his *self*, and your love for him—rather than evaluating him with conditional praise.

Let's see how this works in practice by considering how we might respond to our child who is working on a puzzle. Researchers have repeatedly found that if we tell a child how smart he is to have figured out the puzzle, he'll shy away from harder puzzles. After all, he doesn't want to risk your seeing him as anything but smart. And he knows perfectly well that smart people don't get stumped by puzzles. So well-meaning praise can easily create a child who avoids situations in which he may not appear smart, such as learning new things he might have to work at.

Instead of labeling or evaluating our child, what if we simply connected with him, using our empathy, our willingness to be fully present and notice him, our joy in the relationship? What might we say?

- *"You really like doing that puzzle. . . . It's the first one you took out again today."* (Empathize with his feelings.)

- *"You're trying all the different pieces to see what fits in that spot."* (Notice what he's doing, which helps him feel seen and valued. In this case, we're also articulating the strategy we see him using, which helps him be more conscious of what he's doing, so he can evaluate whether this particular strategy is effective.)

- *"I love doing puzzles with you!"* (Communicate your enjoyment of sharing a task or project with him.)

- *"It's frustrating, isn't it? But you've almost got it!"* (Effective encouragement. By contrast, if we show him, we imply that he can't figure it out for himself, which lessens his self-confidence.)

- *"You did it! You got all the pieces to fit! You must be so proud of yourself!"* (We're mirroring his joy in his accomplishment, but notice we're not telling him *we're* proud of him, which implies that pride in him is something we can also withhold. Instead, we empower him by acknowledging that pride in himself is *his*, something he can take action to create.)

What about *"You're working really hard on that puzzle"*? That's clearly a value judgment—we're letting him know we think it's a good thing, especially if we often comment on it. You'll notice that virtually every choice we make about what to say to our child subtly communicates our values. For that reason, I don't believe that it's possible to be completely objective in our feedback, and I'm not sure it's even a good idea. We are, after all, guides to our child, and there are values that we want to communicate. For me, taking joy in working hard and doing a good job is one of them.

In fact, research shows that when we comment on kids' efforts—
"You are really working at that"—they do work harder, find more
enjoyment in the task, and ask for harder tasks. I think that's
because children want so much to be successful and master whatever they encounter. When they notice the behaviors that make
them more successful at their chosen activities, they're more likely
to choose to do more of those behaviors.

But notice that we're letting our child decide for himself whether
this is behavior he wants to repeat; we aren't saying "Good girl for
working so hard." That implies that if she wants to take a break,
she's a bad girl, which (if repeated often during childhood) could set
her up for a workaholic life in which she can't take care of herself.
Instead, she herself notices the connection between her sustained
focus (upon which we've commented) and her success at the puzzle.
She decides how to use that information. Our comment is empowering because it's a specific observation (*"You are working hard"*)
rather than an evaluative or global one (*"You are a good girl for
working hard"* or *"You always work so hard"*).

Still wondering about the difference between praise and appreciation? Children, like the rest of us, need to feel noticed and appreciated. Your child needs to hear your authentic feelings; the danger
is when she gets the message that she's good enough only if she does
things your way.

- **Praise** evaluates: *"You're a good boy for helping me carry in the
  groceries."*

- **Appreciation is an "I" statement** that expresses your truth
  and empowers your child by letting him know the effect of his
  actions on you and thanking him: *"Thanks for helping me carry
  in the groceries. . . . I love having your help when I get home tired
  after shopping."*

HOW TO AVOID HELICOPTER PARENTING

Why do grown-ups have to take over everything?
   —Kindergartener, age five

What's a helicopter parent? Someone who hovers more than you do.

Seriously, nobody tries to be a helicopter parent. But parenting is the toughest job in the world, so most of us obsess sometimes. And we want to be responsive to our child's needs, so sometimes it's a hard call to make. The irony is that so many of the ways we overdo it as parents actually sabotage our child's healthy development.

Wouldn't it be nice if we had a guiding framework so we know what's appropriate versus what's helicoptering? We do. Decades of research have confirmed what kids need to grow into happy, resilient, confident adults. In fact, it isn't usually our concern for our child that triggers our tendency to helicopter; it's our own fears. Here are some antidotes to help even confirmed hoverers avoid the most common anxiety-induced pitfalls:

Overprotecting

Clucking anxiously as he climbs that play structure may make you feel better, but it cripples your child's confidence. Just ask if he's keeping himself safe, then spot him. Breathe, smile, and exclaim, *"Wow, look at you!"* If he falls, you're there to catch him—which is, after all, what allowed him to try.

Overreacting

When we're worried, we usually feel an urgent need to take action. That alleviates our anxiety, but it doesn't necessarily give our child what he needs. So the first intervention is always becoming aware of and regulating our own emotions. Then we might realize that what our son actually needs is some role-playing with us about how to approach his baseball coach, rather than for us to pick up the phone ourselves.

Overcontrolling

Nobody wants to be the dad who's more invested in his son's basketball success than his son is, or the stage mom who lives through her daughter. That's pathetic. But each of us is faced with more minor versions of overcontrolling our kids, often beginning at potty training and continuing through college. Do you feel the need to redo your preschooler's misbuttoned clothes? Do you support your six-year-old son's interest in soccer but regard his drawing as childish? Would you let your nine-year-old give up piano? Whose life is it, anyway?

Overscheduling

Unstructured time gives children the opportunity to imagine, invent, and create. If we keep them too busy with structured activity or screen entertainment, they never hear the stirrings of their own hearts, which might lead them to study the bugs on the sidewalk, make a monster from clay, or organize the neighborhood kids into making a movie. These calls from our heart are what lead us to those passions that make life meaningful, and they're available to us even beginning in childhood, if we take the time to explore our inner worlds.

Overtigering

Okay, you want your child to go to Harvard. But at what emotional cost? Children learn through self-motivated exploration and play, which is a foundation of creativity and happiness throughout life. You may be proud if your child learns to read at age four, but the research shows that children in play-based preschool programs do substantially better academically than those who attend academic preschools. Likewise, pressuring your child to make As in third grade to help her college odds almost certainly decreases her chances at happiness in life. And if she's feeling shamed or not good enough, you're doing active harm.

Notice that overnurturing isn't on the list? That's because there's no such thing as too much connection, support, and love. Helicoptering comes from fear. Nurturing comes from love. Every choice we make, at core, is a move toward either love or fear. Choose love.

WHAT IF YOU HAVE A CHILD WHO DOESN'T DEVELOP MASTERY NATURALLY?

Humans are born curious, because learning makes survival more likely. For the same reason, humans are designed to pursue goals; "chasing" rewards triggers the release of dopamine in the brain. So human children naturally seek mastery, meaning they explore, learn, practice, and enjoy getting good at things. Parents sometimes tell me their child is lazy or unmotivated, but I don't believe there is such a thing as a lazy child. With a little conversation, we always uncover one or more deeper reasons for the child's lack of motivation, such as the following:

- The child has learning disabilities.
- The child is expected to do something he really doesn't find interesting and is being forced to do, such as piano lessons.
- The child is locked in a power struggle with the parents and is resisting in every way he can.
- The child has disconnected from his parents and is orbiting around his peers, who discourage academics or other parental goals.
- The child is depressed.

- The child is perfectionistic, anxious, afraid of making a mistake.
- The child's natural interests are not valued by the family and are discouraged (for instance, his athletic passion isn't valued in a more bookish family, or vice versa).

In any of these cases, our Three Big Ideas—Regulating Yourself; Fostering Connection; and Coaching, Not Controlling—will help moms and dads support their child toward a healing solution for everyone. The first step is always for the parent to dissolve her own knot of anxiety (self-regulation) so she can stop adding pressure to what her child is already feeling. A stronger connection will always allow the child to begin to work through his upsets around the issue, and it may well provide him with the motivation to pursue goals that are important to his parents, such as doing well in school. Then, coaching, not controlling, will help the parent support the child to explore his own interests. If the child is being asked to master something that doesn't come naturally to him, and is nonnegotiable—for instance, schoolwork—the parent usually needs to think outside the box about what her child needs to help create a breakthrough in a difficult situation.

Let's consider how we might support a challenging child to develop school mastery. Henry was always *more*—more active, more energetic, more persistent, more challenging. His parents joked that his brain didn't work quite like other children's brains—he had some extra flashes of lightning inside. Keeping him on track with tasks seemed impossible. But Henry was also cute and affectionate, so his kindergarten teacher found herself charmed by him despite his tendency to run around the room and forget what she'd instructed the children to do. His first-grade teacher quickly became frustrated, however, and suggested that Henry be evaluated for attention deficit/hyperactivity disorder (ADHD).

Henry's parents decided to postpone using the medication rec-ommended by the doctor, and instead work intensively with Henry at home for a year. His father, Sean, had struggled with ADHD him-self, resulting in a series of school experiences that undermined his natural love of learning. Sean happened to be between jobs, so he decided to take advantage of the opportunity to dedicate himself to homeschooling Henry for the rest of the year while teaching him to manage the symptoms of his ADHD.

Sean focused first on connecting with Henry through rough-housing, cuddling, and empathizing when his son was upset. That gave Henry the motivation to want to please his father by doing the very hard work of focusing on academics. Sean sat with Henry to teach him reading and arithmetic, following his son's lead, getting him excited, and coaching him when he faltered. After reading that many ADHD kids are kinesthetic learners who have a hard time learning from the usual auditory and visual teaching in classrooms, Sean encouraged Henry to move around while he was learning. Henry found that when he jumped rope as he spelled or added num-bers together, he remembered better. They also experimented with various structures and tools until Henry became more comfortable organizing himself and was even able to work independently at times.

Sean noticed that Henry was especially excited about engineer-ing and building projects. When Henry worked on them, he seemed motivated to be more patient and careful. So Sean kept the focus of their academic work on such projects, using them to teach math, reading, and history. He had found a doorway into Henry's drive for mastery, and they were both rewarded to see Henry's academic skills surge beyond grade level.

Sean also experimented with other ways to support Henry in man-aging himself. He located a center that offered biofeedback and video games to develop Henry's attention skills, as well as a counselor to coach Henry on social skills. To give Henry more experience learning social rules, Sean enrolled him in several low-key sports teams and classes. Henry learned that active daily outdoor play was essential to his ability to feel comfortable in his own skin. They tried various kinds of music to help Henry calm down and concentrate.

In researching strategies to help his son concentrate and organize himself, Sean came across new studies showing that some children's ADHD symptoms can be dramatically improved with changes in diet. Over several months of diet experimentation, Henry's impulsivity, explosiveness, and frenetic activity level diminished but did not disappear.

Maybe most important, Sean framed his son positively, as creative, excited, energetic, and persistent. Henry's challenges in focusing did not just vanish, and he remained extremely active. Sean often saw the same behaviors that had frustrated Henry's teachers. But by the time Henry was in third grade, he was ready for the new school his parents had located, which welcomed him and seemed able to support his learning style. His parents continued to stay very involved with his schoolwork, but Henry had learned how to manage his ADHD symptoms so that he could learn with other children his age. Henry was well on his way to mastery, because he had learned to manage himself. The silver lining? Sean's hard work not only helped his son handle the demands of school and enjoy learning; it created a foundation of closeness with his son that would last for life.

Action Guides

CREATE A NO-BLAME HOUSEHOLD

We all feel the urge to blame someone when things go wrong, as if fixing blame prevents a recurrence of the problem. In reality, blaming makes everyone defensive, more inclined to watch their back—and to attack—than to make amends. When kids feel blamed, they find all kinds of reasons it wasn't really their fault—at least in their own minds—so they're less likely to take responsibility and the problem is more likely to repeat. Worse yet, it teaches them to lie to us. Blame is simply anger looking for a target, and it never helps us toward a solution. We might even say that blame is the opposite of unconditional love.

So why do we do it? To help us feel less out of control, and because we can't bear the suspicion that we also had some role, however small, in creating the situation. Next time you find yourself automatically beginning to blame someone:

1. **Stop. In midsentence, if necessary. Breathe. Stop fighting against the situation,** which is what's driving you to blame someone. Instead, accept the situation. You can always come up with better solutions from a state of acceptance than a state of blame.

2. **Accept any responsibility you can.** It's a good practice to overstate your responsibility—without beating yourself up—even if it's just to note your lack of involvement. For instance, when your four-year-old gets mad because the toddler ruins his fort, protect the toddler but add, *"Oh, sweetie, I'm so sorry I wasn't here to help."* The truth is, we always have more responsibility than we'd like to admit. And the more responsibility you take, the less defensive your child feels, so the more responsibility she's likely to take in her own mind and, eventually, aloud. (You're modeling, remember?)

3. **Find a solution.** Instead of finding fault, train yourself to find solutions. Your household will run more smoothly because

you'll be focused on making things work better instead of making someone wrong. And you'll be training your child to be a problem solver and a person who steps up to the plate and takes responsibility to make things better. What more could you ask?

DEVELOPING RESPONSIBILITY

My little guy does not like it when I cook or do laundry or do the dishes. Why am I not paying attention to him? But I soon realized that he loves to help. He puts clothes in the washing machine, gathers potatoes to bring to the kitchen, brings me clothes hangers. And yes, it takes much longer than if I had done it all myself. But he actually squeals with delight at being given his next task. And I end up being much less frustrated.

   —Wendy, mother of a toddler

We all want to raise responsible children. And we all want to live in a world where others have been raised to be responsible, a world where adults don't shrug off their responsibilities as citizens. As my son said when he was four and surveying a littered park, *"Don't grown-ups know they have to clean up their own messes?"*

So how do we raise our kids to take responsibility for their choices and their impact on the world? Children don't want just to be doted on. They need, like the rest of us, to feel that they matter to the world, that their lives make a positive contribution. Children need to see themselves as response-able—meaning able to respond to what needs to be done. They need this for their self-esteem, for their lives to have meaning, and also so that they can learn to handle themselves responsibly in the world. The bottom line is that kids will be responsible to the degree that we support them to be with our scaffolding. How?

- **Give your child an opportunity to contribute to the common good.** Acknowledge her contributions, even if it's just cheering up the baby when he fusses. As your children get older, they need to grow into two kinds of responsibilities: their own self-care and contributing to the family welfare. Research indicates that kids who help around the house are also more likely to offer help in other situations than kids who simply participate in their own self-care.

- **Work with him.** Remember that your goal isn't getting this job done; it's raising a child who will take pleasure in contributing and taking responsibility. Make the job fun. Give as much structure and hands-on help as you need to, including sitting with him and helping for the first thirty times he does the task, if necessary. Know that it will be much harder than doing it yourself, but eventually, he will be doing it by himself. That day will come much faster if he enjoys it.

- **Rather than simply giving orders, ask your child to do the thinking.** For instance, to the dallying child, instead of saying, *"Brush your teeth! Put your clothes in the hamper!"* you could ask, *"What do you need to do to get ready for bed?"* The goal is to keep her focused on the list, evening after evening, until she internalizes it and begins managing her own routine.

- **Model responsibility and accountability.** *"It's a pain to carry this trash till we get to the car, but I don't see a trash can and we never litter."* Your child learns responsibility from your role modeling. If you don't follow through when you promise to pick up that notebook he needs for school or play that game with him on Saturday, why should he be responsible about keeping his promises?

- **Hold your child accountable for damaged goods.** If kids help pay for lost library books and cell phones, the chances of a repeat infraction are slim.

- **Don't rush to bail your child out of a difficult situation.** Be available for problem solving, helping him work through his feelings and fears, and to ensure that he doesn't just sidestep the difficulty, but let him handle the problem himself while you support him through each step.

- **Never label your child as "irresponsible," even in your own mind,** because the way we see our kids is always a self-fulfilling prophecy. Instead, teach him the skills he needs to be responsible. If he always loses things, for instance, teach him to stop anytime he leaves somewhere—his friend's house, school, soccer practice—and count off everything he needs to take home.

- **Teach your kids that as Eleanor Roosevelt said, they not only have the right to be an individual, they have an obligation to be one.** Studies show that people who take responsibility in any given situation are people who see themselves as willing to be different and stand out. That's the kind of child you want to raise.

DEVELOPING GOOD JUDGMENT

No one is born with good judgment and the ability to make wise decisions; those develop from experience combined with reflection. Your goal is to give your child decision-making experience, and make sure she has the opportunity to reflect on the results of those decisions. Here's how:

- **Practice makes perfect.** Give your child practice making choices even before she begins talking, and she'll find it easier to make decisions. (Who cares if the stripes and flowers clash? She looks like a rainbow. And if others can't figure out that she dressed herself, you don't really care about their opinion of your parenting, do you?)

- **Be clear about his span of control.** Emphasize what he has the right to make decisions about, and over what areas you as the parent retain the right to exert control. *"Yes, I guess you may wear your Superman outfit again, although you've worn it every day this week. But you'll need to change before we go to services, because there we dress up to show respect. And you'll need to brush your teeth. Do you want to do it now or right before we leave the house?"*

- **Help your child to think through the possible repercussions of her choices.** *"I wonder if you'll feel too pressured about getting your homework done if you add another after-school activity."* Just as important, offer her the opportunity to reflect on how her decisions worked out, which is what develops good judgment. *"I know you were worried about playing with two kids at once this afternoon. Are you glad you invited Clarisse to join you and Ellie for the playdate?"*

- **Model decision making.** Share how and why you make decisions from the time your child is tiny. *"I'd like our family to help with the drive for school supplies; all children deserve a good education, and this is one way to help."*

- **Know that it's okay for your child to make bad decisions.** Every poor choice is an opportunity for reflection and the development of good judgment, as long as you help her consider afterward how things could have been different if she had made different choices. Your child is still learning about herself as well as about life; she's bound to make some bad decisions. And if you can resist the universal impulse to say, *"I told you so,"* she'll be more able to accept the lessons she's learning.

HOMEWORK WITHOUT TEARS

Education expert Alfie Kohn makes a powerful case that homework doesn't actually improve learning in the early grades. Unfortunately, most of our children are in schools where they receive homework. Parents are expected to ensure that the homework is done, and children who don't do their homework are penalized. Most parents find it challenging to motivate their child to do homework at least some of the time, which isn't surprising, since it can be hard for a child to see the value of this often unpleasant task. Since homework is an intrinsic part of school, it's essential that our children find something about the experience that gives them satisfaction. How can we do that? By setting it up as a daily household expectation in which our child can take pride in a job well done. That requires our involvement. Here's how:

- **Stay informed.** "What homework do you have tonight?" should be a daily question. Young children can't be expected to find homework important if you don't seem to care what they're doing. Sometimes children need your help to understand the assignment, so you can avoid a meltdown at bedtime when it becomes clear they need to start over. I'm not suggesting that you step into the teacher's role and correct their work, but rather that you understand what's being asked of your child and support him to complete it. This also allows you to help your child learn to prioritize and manage projects he needs to work on over time.

- **Make homework a routine.** At the very least, homework teaches kids the valuable skill of sitting down to do an unpleasant task. Like all habits, it works best if it's at the same time every day. Since active outdoor play increases blood flow to the brain and helps kids learn, you may want to let your child play for an hour to let off steam after school, and then begin homework. Kids who have a hard time making that transition, though, may need to get homework out of the way first. Leaving homework until after dinner when kids are tired sabotages them because it keeps them from focusing easily and doing their best work.

- **Be aware that your child will have feelings about homework from time to time that she'll need your help to process.** Emotion-coach your child using the tools from that chapter, so that she can move past her fear and frustration to focus on the schoolwork.

- **Keep kids close while they work, not in their own rooms.** Staying near you helps your child stay focused. Most kids work best at the dining room table, or at a desk in the family room while you're close. Be available to answer questions but without being a distraction to your child by interrupting or engaging in phone conversations nearby. You may need to sit with your child to keep her on task, working on your own paperwork but lending your steady focus.

- **Eliminate technology while kids work.** Minimize distraction by keeping the TV and radio off, even if you enjoy them. When kids get older, they'll be using the computer for homework, which poses the same problems with distraction that it poses for adults, magnified by their inexperience. Delay that day as long as you can, at least until your child is self-motivated in regard to homework.

- **Offer as much support as necessary without taking over the work.** Parents often ask how much to help their child. My advice is to intervene as little as possible and as much as you need to, until your child is successfully mastering the work. I don't mean that you would ever *do* the homework, of course, but that you need to support your child with whatever scaffolding is necessary until he can do it himself. For instance, you might well help your child learn her spelling words and test her every week, until she can master that skill herself. If you need to start by sitting with your seven-year-old as she writes each spelling word ten times, do it. It's not an intrinsically interesting task, but as it gets easier for her, she'll be able to sustain her focus to do it herself. It's our job to give our child the support necessary to achieve a desired behavior, so he thinks of himself as a kid who can succeed, rather than a kid who is always failing. Kids want to succeed, but if we don't support them to do their best, they may conclude they just can't.

TRUST YOUR CHILD—AND MOTHER NATURE

Throughout this chapter on mastery, I've cautioned that our own anxiety often gets in the way of our child's developing mastery. But what can you do to manage that anxiety? It's only natural that we worry about our children. It's part of the job description. But when we say, *"Be careful!"* to our child, we're not giving the message that we care, even though that's what we feel. We're giving the message that the world is an unsafe place and we don't have confidence in our child to navigate it. Could you say, instead, *"Have fun!"*? Could you just move closer to the climbing gym to spot him and say, *"Wow, I see you climbing so high!"*?

Studies show that people who worry more don't actually gain insight or solve problems any better. They simply make themselves more unhappy. That's because although worrying is our mind's way of trying to protect us, we're actually negatively programming our subconscious. The subconscious thinks in pictures, and it believes whatever we tell it. So all those anxious thoughts looping though our minds are actually giving our subconscious the message to create those scenarios. At the very least, those worried thoughts stimulate feelings of fear and stress that keep us from being peaceful parents. And it's tough for kids to engage in the exploration necessary for developing mastery if we communicate anxiety every time they take initiative.

Want to break the worry habit and reprogram your subconscious for happiness?

- **Start noticing every time your mind goes into worry.** Every time you observe yourself worrying about something, stop. Breathe. Shake your hands out to let go of that fear.

- **Reassure yourself.**
    - *"Kids need to explore and experiment."*
    - *"The risk here is very small. . . . It's okay for him to fall down."*
    - *"I don't have to be perfect. My child will be fine, even though I make mistakes."*
    - *"It will be okay. He'll be okay."*
    - *"He's acting like a kid because he IS a kid."*

- **Reprogram your subconscious.** As you say your new mantra, show your subconscious a picture of your desired outcome, whether it's your child smiling and safe while she rides her bike, or happily flushing the toilet. Don't worry right now about how to achieve your goal—that will get your mind involved again, which brings up fear. Instead, summon up a feeling of happy gratitude along with your picture. The longer you can hold that feeling and picture, the more quickly your subconscious starts finding ways to help you create it. Keep revisiting your picture throughout your day, and make sure you summon up a feeling of happy gratitude each time.

- **Take action.** Ask yourself: *"What is one thing I can do right now (or today) to make this positive outcome more likely?"* Then do it. Here's where this technique differs from positive thinking. We have to feel good to know what action to take. But we have to take the action to change our lives.

Every time your worry surfaces, repeat these steps. Our minds tend to follow certain tracks repeatedly, like grooves on an old vinyl record. Each time you interrupt a worry and send your subconscious a picture of a happier outcome, you're carving a new path for your mind—a path of happiness instead of anxiety. Soon you'll find yourself in a whole new landscape, one in which you can see your child ahead of you on the road, leaping joyfully.

When to Seek Professional Help

Parents often ask me whether their child needs professional help. While every situation is unique, the answer depends on how well the child is meeting the age-appropriate demands of his life. If her anxiety is so pronounced that she can't go to school, she needs to be evaluated. If he's so aggressive that every playdate ends in fisticuffs, he needs help.

Often, parents can read a good book and/or get some expert coaching and help their child themselves. I've seen parents work with their child more effectively than any professional. But there are times when our anxiety as parents gets in the way and our child is better off with a skilled therapist who is warm but impartial. And there are times when expert help or even medication really is essential.

If you're torn, you might come up with a plan and give your own program a try. But remember that in some cases, early intervention matters. For example, if your child has a sensory processing dysfunction, it's important to get help while the brain is taking shape at age three or four, rather than waiting to see how big a problem it becomes. So make a deal with yourself that after a short period of time, you'll re-evaluate and, if necessary, get professional support.

Even if your child receives a diagnosis and professional intervention, you have something to offer your child that no expert can. You know your child as a human being, not just a collection of symptoms. You are connected to her like no one else in the world. Whatever other support you arrange to help your child overcome the challenges

life has given her, your love is the essential ingredient. Never under-
estimate the power of that love.

The Future Is in Your Hands

Nobody can go back and start a new beginning, but anyone can start today
and make a new ending.
　　—Maria Robinson

When your child looks back, this will be the childhood he remem-
bers. The foundation of everything she accomplishes in the world.
Of course, our kids will remember little of what we say to them. The
memories that color their lives will be about how we made them feel.
They'll be living those, every day.

Want a glimpse of the legacy you're creating today?

1. Shut your eyes and imagine your children grown and happy.
   Thriving.

2. Now imagine they're raising their own children. Your grandchildren. See how they're flourishing? That's because your
   children are such great parents. That's because of the way
   you parented your children.

3. Next time things get hard with your child, revisit this feeling. See your children, your grandchildren, and their children, and their children—all thriving. All smiling at you in
   gratitude.

ACKNOWLEDGMENTS

I am so grateful for the opportunity to support parents and children by sharing these ideas more broadly. This book would not have been possible without the contributions of thousands of people: the team at Perigee, my colleagues in the field, and my readers—the parents who get up every morning determined to do their best for their children. My deep appreciation to every one of you.

The birth of *Peaceful Parent, Happy Kids* relied on two inspired midwives:

Rebecca Friedman, my agent, who convinced me that parents needed a deeper understanding of my approach to parenting than my blog could provide and encouraged me to write this book. She has been an invaluable advisor, enthusiastic sounding board, and good friend from start to finish.

Marian Lizzi of Perigee, who took a chance on an idea that scared other editors, then took a rambling manuscript and crystallized it into an organized book. She's the editor every author deserves: the perfect combination of astute reader, deft editor, deep listener, effective communicator, cheerleader, and lovely human being.

I would also like to thank the staff at Perigee, the unsung heroes who took a Word file and with great care and a tremendous amount of work put it into your hands as a book.

I learn so much from the parents who share their experiences with me every day—Thank you! And a warm shout-out to all the readers of my blog and newsletters, for your dedication to your children, your willingness to open your hearts and minds, and the steady flow of love and appreciation that keeps me going.

To the busy mothers who read the initial disorganized manuscript and offered me such helpful, heartfelt feedback—Jennifer, Stacy, Kristina, Letitia, Sarah, Lorraine, Elaine, Deidre, Bonnie, Victoria, Laura, Emily, Karissa, Sejal, Laura, Diane, Jeannette, Mandy, Cathy, Kimberlee, Nancy, and Sandra—you helped make this book more useful to parents, and I will always be grateful.

My parents: Emerson, who gave me the gift of books and taught me how to play, and Joan, who gave me the gift of connecting with others and taught me how to work. Thank you for bringing me into the world and encouraging me to help heal it.

My children, Alice and Eli, who taught me most of what I know about parenting and proved the theories every day. You would make any parent proud. Thank you for transforming my life.

My husband, Daniel Cantor, my biggest fan, who remains my greatest source of love, support, and encouragement. Without you, this book would never have been written. Thank you for every single day.

Finally, I stand on the shoulders of so many brilliant thinkers in this field, past and present. Without them, my small contribution would never have come to be. While I can never adequately express my gratitude to them, the Further Reading section that follows will introduce readers to their work and hopefully provide inspiration for further reading.

FURTHER READING

John Bowlby, author of *Attachment and Loss*, first lured me into this field with his seminal work on attachment. Jean Liedloff (*The Continuum Concept*), Mary Ainsworth, Jay Belsky, Mary Main, and Gordon Neufeld (*Hold On to Your Kids*) further developed my understanding of the parent-child relationship.

My thinking about emotion, which remains the big unexplored territory in the parenting literature, is deeply indebted to Daniel Goleman (*Emotional Intelligence*), John Gottman (*Raising an Emotionally Intelligent Child*), Joseph Ledoux (*The Emotional Brain*), Peter Levine (*In an Unspoken Voice*), Aletha Solter (*The Aware Baby*), and Patty Wipfler (founder of HandinHandParenting.org), pioneers all.

I began to understand how parents can heal themselves and interrupt the automatic cycle of transmitting our wounds from my graduate school mentors Lawrence Aber and Arietta Slade, and from my idol Dan Siegel (coauthor, with Mary Hartzell, of *Parenting from the Inside Out*, and of *The Whole-Brain Child* with Tina Payne Bryson).

Allan Schore (*Affect Regulation and the Origin of the Self*), Alan Sroufe, Sue Gerhardt (*Why Love Matters*), and Ruth Newton (*The Attachment Connection*) taught me much of what I know about brain development.

Magda Gerber (*Your Self-Confident Baby*), Edward Hallowell (*The Childhood Roots of Adult Happiness*), and Mihály Csíkszentmihályi (*Flow*) inspired me to think more deeply about mastery.

I first understood the power of play from Virginia Axline (*Dibs in Search of Self*). Lawrence Cohen (*Playful Parenting*), Anthony T. DeBenedet (*Roughhousing*), O. Fred Donaldson (*Playing by Heart*),

Joseph Chilton Pearce (*Magical Child*), and Patty Wipfler continue to inspire me with their instinctive understanding of how play heals us.

My work would not be possible without the cross-pollination of my brilliant colleagues in the parenting field. We are part of a great wave that is transforming our society's understanding of children, beginning with the premise that children are, indeed, human beings who have much to teach us from the time they are born. There are too many people making wonderful contributions to list them all, but I must offer a shout-out to Naomi Aldort (*Raising Our Children, Raising Ourselves*), Judy Arnall (*Discipline Without Distress*), Becky Bailey (*Easy to Love, Difficult to Discipline*), Sandy Blackard (*Language of Listening*), Tina Payne Bryson, Christine Carter (*Raising Happiness*), Claudia Gold (*Keeping Your Child in Mind*), Robin Grille (*Parenting for a Peaceful World*), Lu Hanessian (*Let the Baby Drive*), Bonnie Harris (*When Your Kids Push Your Buttons*), Mary Hartzell, Jan Hunt (*The Natural Child*), Mary Sheedy Kurcinka (*Raising Your Spirited Child*), Kathryn Kvols (*Redirecting Children's Behavior*), Jane Nelsen (*Positive Discipline*), Elizabeth Pantley (*The No-Cry Sleep Solution*), and Nancy Samalin (*Love and Anger*).

My gratitude list would not be complete without mention of the loving community of parenting educators/bloggers who inspire me daily, especially Becky Eanes (Positive Parenting), Ariadne Brill (Positive Parenting Connection), Dionna Ford (CodeNameMama, Natural Parents Network), Tom Hobson (Teacher Tom), L. R. Knost (Little Hearts Books), Janet Lansbury (Elevating Childcare), Jennifer Lehr (Good Job), Scott Noelle (Daily Groove), Lori Petro (Teach Through Love), Leslie Potter (PureJoy Parenting), Kimberley Price (The Single Crunch), Laura Schuerwegen (Authentic Parenting), Genevieve Simperingham (The Way of the Peaceful Parent), Lisa Sunbury (Regarding Baby), Gill Connell (Moving Smart Now), and Lauren Wayne (HoboMama).

And then there are the groundbreakers, who deserve a special thank-you because they lit the way for all of us:

Haim Ginott (*Between Parent and Child*), whose work was popularized first by Thomas Gordon (*Parent Effectiveness Training*) and then by Adele Faber and Elaine Mazlish (*How to Talk So Kids Will Listen & Listen So Kids Will Talk*).

Theodore Dreikurs, who inspired a new approach to discipline and empowering kids, and Alfie Kohn, who brought us the research that challenges conventional discipline.

Pam Leo, who crystallized attachment as children grow into "Connection Parenting."

Peggy O'Mara, who brought us the community-coalescing force that is *Mothering* magazine.

And to Dr. William Sears, Dr. Jay Gordon, Lysa Parker and Barbara Nicholson (authors of *Attached at the Heart*), and all the folks at Attachment Parenting International, who took attachment theory and helped us develop it into practices that encourage responsive parenting and secure attachment,

Thank you for the privilege of trailing your very large footprints.

NOTES

Chapter 1. Peaceful Parents Raise Happy Kids

1. Benedict Carey, "Lotus Therapy," *New York Times*, May 27, 2008.
2. Sharon Salzberg, *Real Happiness: The Power of Meditation* (Workman, 2010), p. 107.
3. Daniel Seigel and Mary Hartzell, *Parenting from the Inside Out* (Tarcher, 2004).

Chapter 2. The Essential Ingredient for Peaceful Parents, Happy Kids

1. Sue Gerhardt, *Why Love Matters* (Routledge, 2009), p. 37.
2. Allan N. Schore, "The Neurobiology of Attachment and Early Personality Organization," *Journal of Prenatal and Perinatal Psychology and Health* 16, no. 3 (2002), p. 258.
3. L. Luby, D. M. Barch, A. Belden, M. S. Gaffrey, R. Tillman, C. Babb, T. Nishino, H. Suzuki, K. N. Botteron, "Maternal Support in Early Childhood Predicts Larger Hippocampal Volumes at School Age," *Proceedings of the National Academy of Sciences* (2012). www.pnas.org/content/early/2012/01/24/1118003109.
4. E. Z. Tronick and J. F. Cohn, "Infant-Mother Face-to-Face Interaction: Age and Gender Differences in Coordination and the Occurrence of Miscoordination," *Child Development* 60 (1989), pp. 85–92.
5. NICHD Early Child Care Research Network, "Early Child Care and Self-Control, Compliance and Problem Behavior at 24 and 36 Months," *Child Development* 69 (1998), pp. 1145–1170.
6. NICHD Early Child Care Research Network, "Chronicity of Maternal Depressive Symptoms, Maternal Sensitivity, and Child Functioning at 36 Months," *Developmental Psychology* 35 (1999), pp. 1297–1310.

Chapter 3. Raising a Child Who Can Manage Himself: Emotion Coaching

1. Daniel Goleman, *Emotional Intelligence: Why It Can Matter More Than IQ* (Bantam, 2006).

2. W. Middlemiss, D. A. Granger, W. A. Goldberg, and L. Nathans, "Asynchrony of Mother–Infant Hypothalamic–Pituitary–Adrenal Axis Activity Following Extinction of Infant Crying Responses Induced During the Transition to Sleep," *Early Human Development* 88 (2012), pp. 227–232.

3. A. N. Schore, "The Experience-Dependent Maturation of a Regulatory System in the Orbital Prefrontal Cortex and the Origin of Developmental Psychopathology," *Development and Psychopathology* 8 (1996), pp. 59–87.

4. E. Z. Tronick and J. F. Cohn, "Infant-Mother Face-to-Face Interaction: Age and Gender Differences in Coordination and the Occurrence of Miscoordination," *Child Development* 60 (1989), pp. 85–92.

5. E. M. Leerkes, A. N. Blankson, and M. O'Brien, "Differential Effects of Maternal Sensitivity to Infant Distress and Nondistress on Social-Emotional Functioning," *Child Development* 80 (2009), pp. 762–775.

6. A. Gianino and E. Z. Tronick, "The Mutual Regulation Model: The Infant's Self and Interactive Regulation Coping and Defense," in T. Field, P. McCabe, and N. Schneiderman (eds.), *Stress and Coping* (Erlbaum, 1988), pp. 47–68.

7. Joanna Maselko, "Mother's Affection at 8 Months Predicts Emotional Distress in Adulthood," *Journal of Epidemiology and Community Health* (2010), http://jech.bmj.com/content/early/2010/07/07/jech.2009.097873 .abstract.

8. Lisa J. Berlin, J. M. Ipsa, M. A. Fine, P. S. Malone, J. Brooks-Gunn, C. Bracy-Smith, C. Ayoub, and Y. Bai, "Correlates and Consequences of Spanking and Verbal Punishment for Low-Income White, African American, and Mexican American Toddlers," *Child Development* 80 (2009), pp. 1403–1420.

9. Allan Schore, *Affect Dysregulation and Disorders of the Self* (Norton, 2003).

10. Sue Gerhardt, *Why Love Matters* (Routledge, 2009), p. 37.

11. Lawrence J. Cohen and Anthony T. DeBenedet, *The Art of Roughhousing: Good Old-Fashioned Horseplay and Why Every Kid Needs It*. (Quirk, 2011).

12. Lawrence J. Cohen, *Playful Parenting* (Ballantine, 2002).

Chapter 4. Raising a Child Who Wants to Behave: Dare *Not* to Discipline

1. Ignatius J. Toner, "Punitive and Non-Punitive Discipline and Subsequent Rule-Following in Young Children," *Child Care Quarterly* 15 (1986), pp. 27–37.
2. Lisa J. Berlin, J. M. Ipsa, M. A. Fine, P. S. Malone, J. Brooks-Gunn, C. Bracy-Smith, C. Ayoub, and Y. Bai, "Correlates and Consequences of Spanking and Verbal Punishment for Low-Income White, African American, and Mexican American Toddlers," *Child Development* 80 (2009), pp. 1403–1420.
3. Alfie Kohn, *Unconditional Parenting* (Atria, 2005), p. 70.
4. Kohn, *Unconditional Parenting*.
5. Berlin et al., "Correlates and Consequences."
6. Barbara Aria, "How to Say No (Without Saying No)," *Redbook*, www .redbookmag.com/kids-family/advice/how-to-say-no.
7. H. L. Bender, J. P. Allen, K. B. McElhaney, J. Antonishak, C. M. Moore, H. O. Kelly, and S. M. Davis, "Use of Harsh Physical Discipline and Developmental Outcomes in Adolescence," *Development and Psychopathology* 19 (2007), pp. 227–231.
8. E. T. Gershoff, "Corporal Punishment by Parents and Associated Child Behaviors and Experiences: A Meta-analytic and Theoretical Review," *Psychological Bulletin* 128 (2002): 539–579.
9. J. Durrant and R. Ensom, "Physical Punishment of Children: Lessons from 20 Years of Research," *Canadian Medical Association Journal* 101314; published ahead of print February 6, 2012.

INDEX

Page numbers in **bold** indicate tables; those in *italics* indicate figures.

ABOUT THE AUTHOR

Photo by Jeremy Folmer

Dr. Laura Markham is also the author of *Peaceful Parent, Happy Siblings: How to Stop the Fighting and Raise Friends for Life*. She earned her PhD in clinical psychology at Columbia University and has worked as a parenting coach with countless families across the English-speaking world. Her books have been translated into ten languages.

A leading advocate for parents and children, Dr. Laura is frequently interviewed by the press, from *Real Simple* and the *Wall Street Journal* to Fox News. She is in constant demand as a conference keynoter and workshop leader because of her warmth in connecting with audiences and her practical, research-based interventions.

More than 100,000 moms and dads enjoy Dr. Laura's free coaching posts via e-mail. You can sign up on any page of her website, AhaParenting.com, which serves up Aha! Moments for parents of babies through teens. You can also join her community on Facebook (www.facebook.com/AhaParenting) and follow the latest research in parenting on Twitter via @DrLauraMarkham.

Dr. Laura's aspiration is to change the world, one child at a time, by supporting parents. The proud mother of two thriving young adults who were raised with her peaceful parenting approach, she lives in Brooklyn, New York.

Also by Dr. Laura Markham

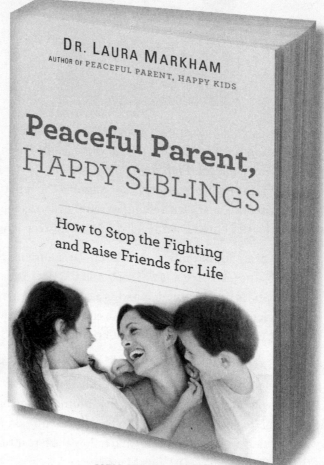

DR. LAURA MARKHAM
AUTHOR OF PEACEFUL PARENT, HAPPY KIDS

Peaceful Parent,
HAPPY SIBLINGS

How to Stop the Fighting
and Raise Friends for Life

ISBN: 978-0-399-16845-1

PERIGEE